The Seafood Cookbook

Times
BOOKS

THE SEAFOOD COOKBOOK

Classic to Contemporary

PIERRE FRANEY
& BRYAN MILLER

Illustrations by Lauren Jarrett

Library of Congress Cataloging-in-Publication Data

Franey, Pierre.
  The seafood cookbook.

  Includes index.
  1. Cookery (Seafood)   I. Miller, Bryan.   II. Title.
TX747.F68 1986   641.6'92   86-5779
ISBN 0-8129-1604-2

Manufactured in the United States of America

9   8   7   6   5   4   3   2

FIRST EDITION

Coordinating Editor: Rosalyn Badalamenti

Typography and Binding: Holly McNeely

Layout: Margaret Wagner and Holly McNeely

To Elizabeth Franey
and Anne de Ravel d'Esclapon

Contents

Introduction

The impetus for this book was twofold. In our respective dining experiences around the United States, we have noted a rising tide of interest in seafood, both in restaurants and among home cooks; second, we continue to receive an increasing volume of letters at *The New York Times* from readers who want to know how to prepare the expanding variety of fish and shellfish on the market. Home cooks have come to appreciate the important role of seafood in the diet, yet many are intimidated when it comes to preparing it. That is what this book is all about: easy to follow techniques and recipes for all varieties of seafood.

Statistics support our hunch that the image of the prototypical meat-and-potatoes American is fading. Whether out of health concerns or gastronomic curiosity, consumers are turning to seafood in growing numbers. According to the National Marine Fisheries Service, per capita fish consumption in the United States rose from 11.8 pounds (edible weight) in 1970 to 14.5 pounds in 1985, a rise of nearly 23 percent. (These figures do not count the substantial haul by sports fishermen.) In the same period, per capita consumption of beef dropped from about 87 pounds to 78.6 pounds. Newspapers and magazines continue to report emerging scientific information about the health benefits of seafood. It is a fact, for example, that a diet relatively high in fish increases the percentage of polyunsaturated fatty acids in the body, as opposed to saturated fats from meats and dairy products, and may help to lower the risk of atherosclerosis. Fish is also an excellent source of protein.

Studies reported by the *New England Journal of Medicine* in 1985 offer some of the latest and most compelling evidence that eating fish once or twice a week may reduce the risk of heart disease. In one study, Dutch researchers tracked 852 middle-aged men for twenty years, a fifth of whom ate no fish. Those who consumed seven ounces of fresh fish per week (about one and a half servings) had half the rate of heart disease as those who consumed very little or no fish. This pattern was true regardless of other factors, such as age, blood pressure, and initial blood cholesterol levels. Moreover, the more frequent the consumption of fish, the study found, the lower the risk of heart disease. Related studies discovered, surprisingly, that the benefits were derived regardless of whether one consumed fatty fish, such as tuna and salmon, or lean fish, such as cod and flounder. They suspect that fish oil may be the key.

Health considerations alone should not be the reason we consume fish; it should also be enjoyable. Preparing seafood is still a mysterious task to many home cooks, especially when it comes to the growing number of unfamiliar species appearing on the market (monkfish, skate, shark, tilefish, squid, and so on). For years the primary species sold in American markets were sole, flounder, bass, cod, salmon, halibut, and the most familiar shellfish and crustaceans, including lobster, crabs, shrimp, and clams. As our national appetite for seafood grows—and prices swell accordingly—merchants are introducing less-familiar but equally tasty species. The recipes that follow apply to all of these. In some cases, a particular recipe works equally well with three or four types of fish. This is noted right below the recipe title.

For purposes of the home cook, it is important to understand that seafood can be categorized as fatty, medium, and lean (see the fish profile chart on pages 280–281). The fat content of a fish dictates the best methods for cooking. Lean and delicate fish, such as lemon sole, lend themselves exceptionally well to poaching and pan sautéing; grilling over charcoal is possible, but tricky. The flesh tends to dry out quickly over a grill and fall apart. Bluefish and salmon, on the other hand, are ideal for grilling.

Keep in mind that these categories are broad generalizations at best. Within a particular species, say tuna, which is relatively fatty, the fat level can vary from fish to fish, depending on its diet and the type of water in which it lives. As recent studies have suggested, so-called fatty fish may have the same salubrious effects as lean fish.

A consumer survey commissioned by the National Marine Fisheries Service, released in 1983, revealed a great deal about attitudes among seafood eaters. Researchers tracked the buying and consumption habits of 7,500 households across the United States. The survey found that only 30 percent of the participants knew a good range of techniques for preparing fish; 42 percent said they buy only fish without small bones. Forty-three percent said they are usually satisfied with the quality of seafood available in stores, while 27 percent were dissatisfied. Thirty percent had no opinion.

Our intention in this book is to remove the cloak of mystery that surrounds buying and preparing seafood. Individual chapters are arranged around cooking techniques (baking, broiling, sautéing, etc.) rather than different fish species. This makes the most sense, we believe, since a given technique can apply to more than one species.

There has been a revolution in cooking on both sides of the Atlantic in the past decade, and that applies to seafood as well. Fresh fish is tampered with as little as possible to let its natural flavors and textures shine through; sauces are lighter, herbaceous, and come in as many colors as an island sunset. We have included many of the bright new-style recipes in this book as well as the classics from which all the others derive.

Other chapters address buying, handling, and storing fish and shellfish. And because wine has become such an integral part of cooking and dining, we have included a short guide to wines that enhance the dishes found in this book.

From the familiar to the exotic, the quick everyday meal to more elaborate fare, it is all here—so shed your inhibitions, roll up your sleeves, and enjoy.

Pierre Franey and Bryan Miller

East Hampton, Long Island
February 1986

Fish Nutrition Chart
and
Fish Varieties

FISH NUTRITION CHART

| Type of Fish | Values for edible part of foods | | | | | | | |
| | Water | Food energy | Protein | Fat | Carbohydrate | Calcium | Phosphorus |
	(C)	(D)	(E)	(F)	(G)	(H)	(I)
all figures are for 8-ounce portions	*Grams* *Percent*	*Calories*	*Grams*	*Grams*	*Grams*	*Milligrams*	*Milligrams*
Bluefish, baked or broiled with butter:	224 68.0	360	59.2	1.2	0	64	648
Cod, baked or broiled with butter:	224 64.6	384	64.8	12	0	72	624
Haddock, pan- or oven-fried:	224 66.3	376	44.8	14.4	12.8	88	560
Halibut, Atlantic or Pacific, broiled with butter or margarine:	224 66.6	384	56.8	16.0	0	40	560
Mackerel, Atlantic, broiled with butter or margarine:	224 61.6	536	49.6	36	0	16	632
Oysters, raw, eastern:	224 84.6	152	22.4	4.0	8.0	216	328
Salmon, broiled or baked with butter or margarine:	224 63.4	416	61.6	16.8	0	—	936
Scallops, bay and sea, steamed:	227 73.1	254	52.6	3.2	—	261	766.5
Shad, baked:	224 64.0	456	528	25.6	0	56	712
Shrimp, fried:	224 56.9	512	46.4	24.8	22.4	160	432
Sturgeon, steamed:	224 67.5	360	57.6	12.8	0	88	600
Tilefish, baked:	224 71.6	312	55.2	8.0	0	—	—
Clams, raw, meat only, hard or round:	227 81.7	172.5	28.6	3.7	4.55	157	368
Crab—blue, Dungeness, rock, king, cooked:	227 78.5	211	39.25	4.3	1.2	98	397
Bass, striped, oven-fried:	224 60.8	448	48.8	19.2	15.2	—	—
Flounder, baked with butter or margarine:	224 58.1	456	68	18.4	0	56	784
Lobster, northern, cooked:	227 76.8	216	43	3.4	.7	148	436
Swordfish, broiled with butter or margarine:	224 60.8	448	48.8	19.2	15.2	—	—

			Values for edible part of foods				
Iron (J)	Sodium (K)	Potassium (L)	Vitamin A value (M)	Thiamin (N)	Riboflavin (O)	Niacin (P)	Ascorbic acid (Q)
Milligrams	Milligrams	Milligrams	International units	Milligrams	Milligrams	Milligrams	Milligrams
1.6	232	—	80	.24	.24	4.0	—
2.4	248	920	400	.16	.24	7.2	—
2.4	400	792	—	.08	.16	7.2	8
1.6	304	1192	1520	.08	.16	19.2	—
2.4	—	—	(1200)	.32	.64	17.6	—
12.8	168	272	720	.32	.4	5.6	—
2.4	264	1008	400	0.4	.16	22.4	—
1.8	601	1080	—	—	—	—	—
1.6	76	856	80	.32	.56	19.2	—
3.2	424	520	—	.08	.16	6.4	—
4.8	248	536	—	—	—	—	—
—	—	—	—	—	—	—	—
13.9	272	411	225	.225	.41	2.95	22.5
1.8	—	—	4920	.365	.18	6.35	4.5
—	—	—	—	—	—	—	—
3.2	5.36	1328	—	.16	.16	5.6	8
1.8	477	408	—	.225	.16	—	—
2.4	—	—	4400	.08	.08	23.2	—

Blowfish

Black Bass

Blue Crab

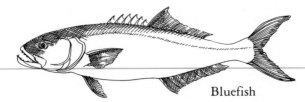

Bluefish

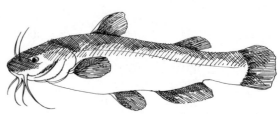

Catfish

Cod

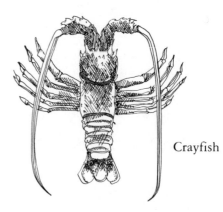

Crayfish

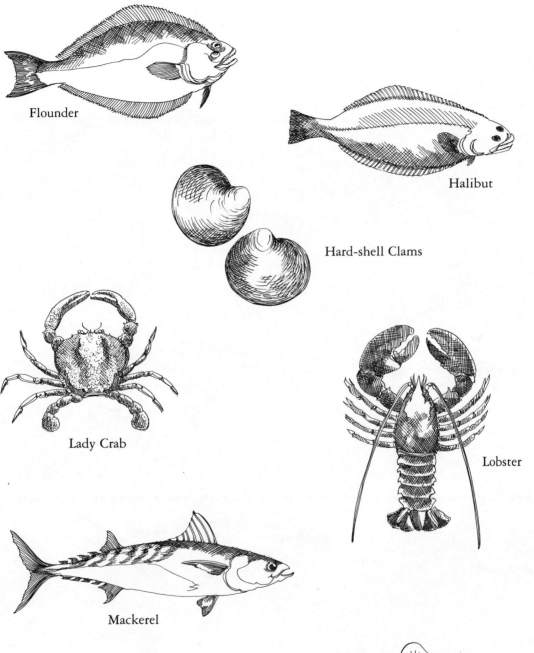

Flounder

Halibut

Hard-shell Clams

Lady Crab

Lobster

Mackerel

Monkfish

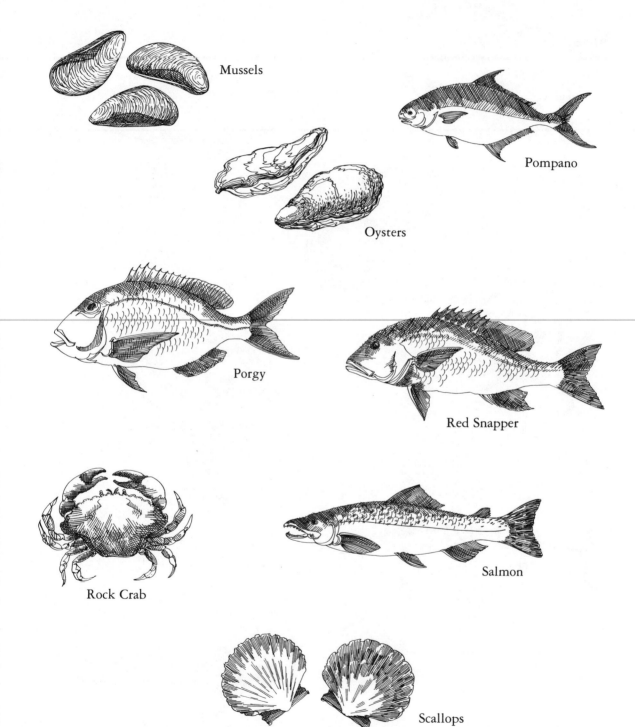

Mussels

Pompano

Oysters

Porgy

Red Snapper

Rock Crab

Salmon

Scallops

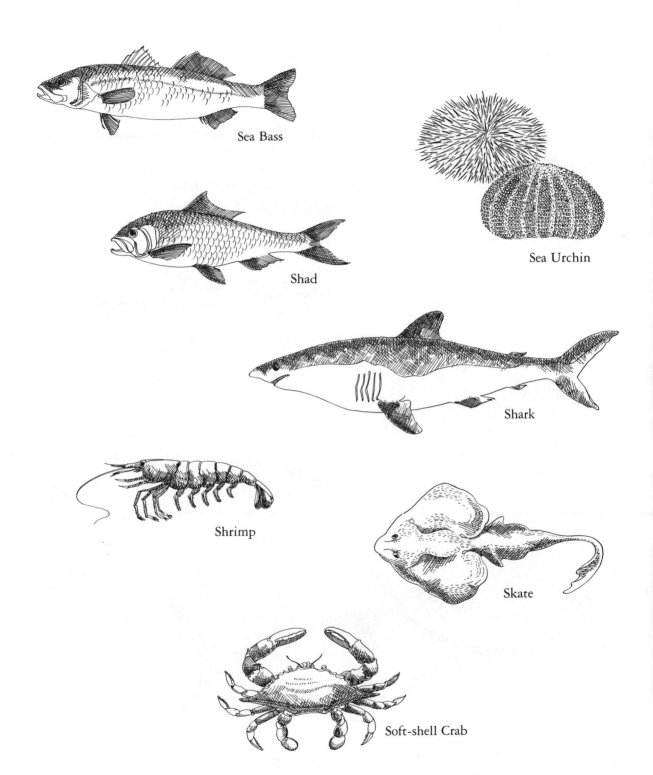

Sea Bass

Sea Urchin

Shad

Shark

Shrimp

Skate

Soft-shell Crab

Soft-shell clams

Sole

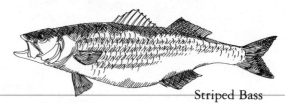

Striped Bass

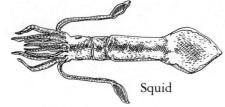

Squid

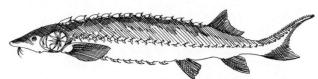

Sturgeon

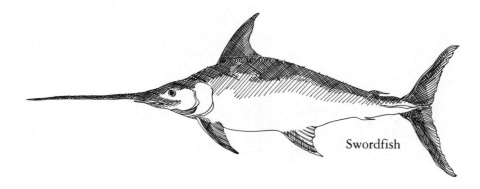

Swordfish

Tilefish

Trout

Tuna

Weakfish

Whitefish

Whiting

The Seafood Cookbook

Buying and Storing Seafood

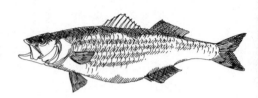

We have a friend, named Giovanni Cosulich, who grew up before the Second World War in an Italian fishing village on the tiny North Adriatic Island of Lussinpiccolo (now part of Yugoslavia, the village is called Mali Losing). His family subsisted on a diet almost exclusively of seafood, and quite naturally he grew up with a keen palate when it comes to fish. Giovanni has a three-word definition for good seafood: "Freshness, freshness, freshness." While talking of his childhood one day he told us a story that illustrates his point.

"Every morning at sunrise," he recalled, "the overnight boats returned to port and sold their catch right from the dock. Women of the village would wait for them and take the fish straight home to begin cleaning and preparing it for lunch. Families who were on a tight budget would wait until about 10 o'clock to go down to the boats. By then prices were cut in half because the fish was already considered old."

Freshness, of course, is the *sine qua non* when it comes to any kind of seafood. In recent years, as the demand for fish and shellfish has surged, impressive new markets with high standards for freshness and cleanliness have appeared in cities around the country. Unless you live by the sea and can catch your own, though, there is really no way to know exactly how fresh a fishmonger's supply is. The bafflingly complex system of food distribution that has developed in this country makes major cities like New York dependent on provender from hundreds and sometimes thousands of miles away; consumers today have access to varieties of fish and shellfish species that were unheard-of outside of their localities a decade ago. But how fresh are they? Let's count the days.

If we are speaking of North Atlantic fish that are distributed through the Fulton Fish Market in lower Manhattan, the largest such wholesale facility in the country, freshness is as hard to predict as the stock market. Under the best conditions, a day boat leaves a port, such as Point Judith, Rhode Island, at 5 A.M. The boat returns to port at 5 P.M. with its catch of flounder, sole, bass, monkfish, and squid. The fish are gutted and iced at a dockside facility that evening; then they are loaded onto trucks that make the five-hour journey to New York overnight.

If a restaurateur or fishmonger arrives at the market early the next morning, say 5 A.M., he can pick up fish that are less than a day out of the water. If a consumer buys the fish later that morning it should be in excellent condition, providing it has been kept cool the entire time.

The scenario assumes, however, that everything goes without a hitch. Many large fishing boats go to sea for up to a week. The daily catch is cleaned onboard and packed in ice. These week-old fish may be tossed into the retail system along with day-old ones. This is why it is so important to know how to judge freshness at the marketplace.

What about all of the imported seafood we see on the menus of expensive restaurants and in specialty seafood shops? It has been made possible largely by improvements in jet transportation. Every day jets take off from European airports carrying meaty Atlantic turbot, succulent tiny Mediterranean shrimp, beansprout-size Spanish eels, French oysters, and Irish salmon. Assume that a batch of turbot is caught near the mouth of the English Channel on a Monday morning and brought back to port that evening. First it is gutted and iced on board or at a dockside facility at night and then trucked to an airport and loaded on a plane the next morning. If the connections are smooth, the fish could reach a U.S. airport in a little over 24 hours from the time it is caught. It is then trucked to a wholesaler who in turn delivers it to a retailer or restaurant. From the U.S. airport to restaurant could take another day. By the time a chef prepares it for a customer might be another day or more. Fresh fish? It depends on your definition; nonetheless one must marvel at the system.

The most voracious fish eaters in the world are the Japanese, who consume more than 148 pounds per capita, compared with Americans, who consume about 35 pounds.* Japanese tuna boats may remain at sea for months at a time, particularly those scouring the tuna-rich North Atlantic. In late summer and fall, when tuna are their fattest, Japanese boats bring their fresh iced catch to eastern Long Island, where small planes race them to Kennedy airport. Within hours they are on their way to Japan in the cargo holds of commercial airliners. It takes as little as 48 hours to reduce these half-ton beauties into tekkamaki rolls in Tokyo sushi bars. Counting time at sea, this "fresh" tuna could be more than a week old. The same applies to sushi served in New York, Boston, and Washington during winter months when North Atlantic tuna are not running. Most supplies at that time of year come from southern and Pacific waters.

Fortunately fish, unlike humans, cannot camouflage their age with cosmetics. If you know what to look for, it is easy to tell whether a fish is worth buying.

WHOLE FISH

1. When buying a whole fish, look at the eyes. They should be bright, clear, and shiny. As a fish ages, its eyes become cloudy.
2. Lift one of the gills. The lungs underneath should be bright red. The whiter the gills, the older the fish. Brownish lungs indicate the fish has been frozen.
3. A fresh fish does not smell fishy. It should have virtually no odor.
4. Check the skin. Is it clear and bright? If a thin, transparent coat of slime covers it, be suspicious. Fish become slimy when they have not been properly iced in transit. Fish at the market should always be packed well on ice, not just laying in refrigerated compartments.

* These figures represent "live weight" of fish and shellfish. The 13.6 pounds per capita consumption in the U.S. in 1984 represents cleaned "edible weight."

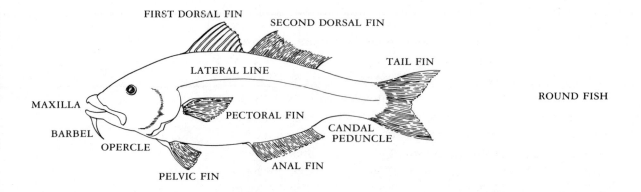

ROUND FISH

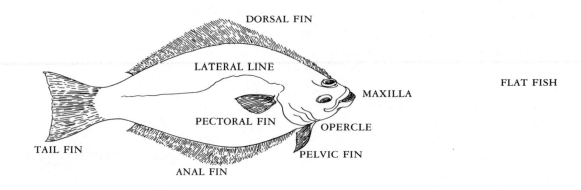

FLAT FISH

FILLETED FISH

1. The best fish markets allow you to choose a whole fish which they fillet on the spot. Fish retains freshness better on the bone. Precut fillets should be displayed on ice and not sealed in plastic wrap. Those that are wrapped in plastic (this is common in supermarkets) can develop a fetid odor because air is trapped inside.

2. Fish fillets should maintain their true colors: clear pearly white for gray sole, reddish and meaty for bluefish. Browning around the edges indicates age. Moreover, if the fillet begins to curl up around the perimeter it has been stored too long.

3. Skin or no skin? In general, fillets of fatty fish, such as bluefish, mackerel, and salmon, should be purchased with the

skin intact. That way it will hold together better during cooking. Of course, make sure it is well scaled. Lean fish, such as sole and flounder, should be skinless.

STORING FISH

1. Fresh fish, whether whole or filleted, is usually wrapped in wax paper by your fishmonger. This is adequate protection if you refrigerate it immediately. All fresh seafood should be consumed as soon as possible.
2. Freshly caught and cleaned fish may be frozen for several months if wrapped exceedingly well. It is not a good idea to freeze store-bought fish because it already has been out of the water for some time and may have been partially frozen in transit. Never refreeze fish once it has thawed.
3. The leaner species of fish tend to have a longer freezer life than fatty fish, two months versus one month respectively. After that, both will begin to dry out and lose their flavor. Cleaned whole fish lasts longer than fillets. Commercially frozen fish is a different story. They are flash frozen at very low temperatures under controlled conditions. Even so, three months at the outside is a good guideline.

LOBSTER

1. As a rule of thumb, the colder the water the tastier the lobster. That is why Maine lobsters are so highly prized. Whenever you buy lobster, first touch the shell (assuming the claws are well immobilized). It should be hard and thick. Soft shells indicate one of two things: Either the lobster has recently shed its shell and is growing into the new one, in which case the meat could be skimpy, or the lobster comes from warm waters.
2. Female lobsters are more flavorful and tender than males, especially when broiled. To perform a quick gender check, flip the lobster on its back and look at the junction of the head and the body. You will see two small spiny "feet." If the appendages feel hard to the touch, it is a male; if soft, a female.
3. Whenever possible buy lobsters as close to cooking time as possible. If you must store them in the refrigerator overnight,

place them in a double-thick paper bag or any sort of bag that "breathes" (no plastic bags) and ice them well. If you have access to seaweed, add that. Place the whole assembly in a stockpot or large roasting pan to prevent the melting ice from dripping all over the refrigerator.

4. Never buy lobster that has been killed and cut into serving pieces. When picking lobsters from a tank, choose those that are lively. Lobsters do not generally eat in captivity and over time their meat gradually begins to constrict. If a lobster is extremely listless, it could be near death from starvation.

CLAMS, OYSTERS, AND MUSSELS

1. Both clams and oysters should be firmly closed and odorless. If a clam or mussel is slightly open, pinch it closed. If it remains closed on its own, it's alive. If it remains open, discard it.

2. Fresh clams, oysters, and mussels should be consumed as soon as possible after being purchased. If you need to store them for a short time, refrigerate them in a plastic bag with small holes at the top to allow air inside.

SHRIMP

1. Almost all shrimp sold in the Northeast is frozen. Much of it comes from the Gulf states. Flash-frozen shrimp can be delicious when handled and stored properly. Its shelf life is about six months if well wrapped. Inspect the shells for signs of freezer burn. Shrimp should always be purchased in the shell and not precooked. A stale shrimp has an offensive ammonia odor.

2. At the many retail outlets shrimp are categorized according to size. A jumbo shrimp, sometimes called a prawn, generally numbers 15 or fewer per pound; 16 to 20 per pound are called extra large, while 21 to 30 are large, and 31 to 40 medium. More than that are small.

CRABS

Crabs, like lobsters, should be lively when purchased. Refrigerate them in punctured plastic bags.

C H A P T E R 2

Handling Fish

Unlike many Europeans, who prefer to purchase fish whole, Americans like their fish filleted. While this no doubt is more convenient, you pay a price in flavor. Invariably, fish on the bone is tastier and with better texture than fillets. It is often more economical, too. As a rule of thumb, three pounds of whole fish yield one pound of fillets. Cleaned and scaled whole fish can be poached, broiled, baked, and so on. You can fillet it at the table for guests or have each person do it.

The following illustrations define the features of the two major types of edible fish, flat and round.

CLEANING AND SCALING A WHOLE FISH

The technique for cleaning and scaling a whole round fish is essentially the same as that for a flat fish. If you plan to fillet the fish, it is not necessary to remove all the fins and gills. Nor is it essential to gut the fish unless you plan to store it before filleting. If you want to cook the whole fish, however, follow the instructions below for removing the intestines, fins, and gills.

SCISSORS

1. Using scissors, cut off the pelvic, pectoral, and anal fins.
2. Cut off the dorsal fins.

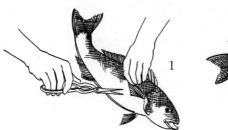 

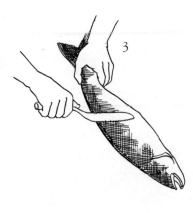

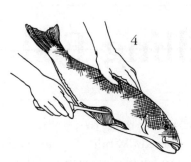

3. Hold the fish by the tail with one hand and, using a scaling knife, scrape off the scales working from the tail to the head.

SCALING KNIFE

4. With a small sharp knife, make a shallow incision from the vent (just forward of the anal fin) all the way to the gill (just under the mouth). Be careful not to sever the entrails.

5. Remove all the entrails. Scrape out any remaining tissue.

6. Lift the gill cover with one hand. Using scissors, cut out the reddish gills underneath. Repeat on the other side. Rinse the fish all over with cold running water. Pat dry with paper towels.

FILLETED FISH

1. Place a sharp fish filleting knife directly behind the gill and the pectoral fin. Cut at a shallow angle toward the head just above the center bone. Be careful not to cut through the bones.
2. At the end of the first stroke, turn the blade until it faces the fin and rests atop the center bone. Run the knife along the center bone and the ribs toward the tail.
3. Run the knife back toward the head using a series of short strokes, gently lifting the flesh as you go. Once you have separated enough flesh to grab securely with your fingers, peel back the fillet as you continue cutting. Work the knife over the center bone and continue removing the remaining fillet.
4. Sever the fillet.

FILLETING KNIFE

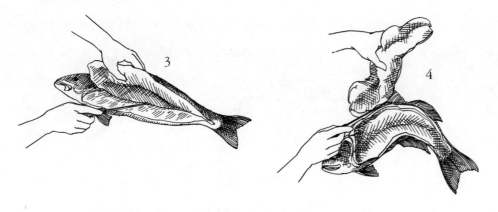

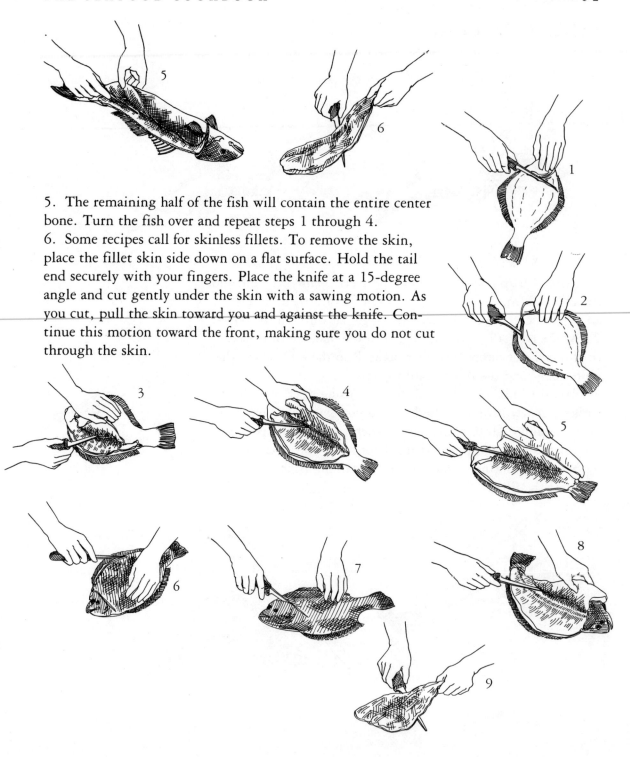

5. The remaining half of the fish will contain the entire center bone. Turn the fish over and repeat steps 1 through 4.

6. Some recipes call for skinless fillets. To remove the skin, place the fillet skin side down on a flat surface. Hold the tail end securely with your fingers. Place the knife at a 15-degree angle and cut gently under the skin with a sawing motion. As you cut, pull the skin toward you and against the knife. Continue this motion toward the front, making sure you do not cut through the skin.

SHUCKING OYSTERS

1. Protecting your hands with a heavy cloth, hold the oyster, flat side up, with the narrow hinge side facing out. Insert the tip of an oyster knife into the hinge.
2. Twist the knife to pry open the hinge.
3. Run the knife along the underside of the top shell to sever the muscle.
4. Discard the upper shell. (Note: Never sever the small muscle that connects the edible flesh to the bottom shell before eating. This will cause the oyster meat to shrivel and lose flavor quickly.)

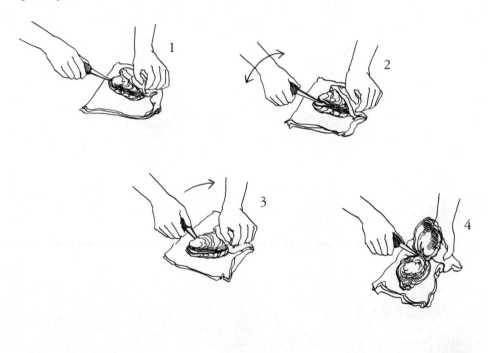

OYSTER KNIFE

OPENING LITTLENECK
AND CHERRYSTONE CLAMS

1. Hold the clam in one hand with the hinge against the joint of your thumb and palm. Position the clam knife as shown.
2. Push the knife into the small crack between the shells.
3. Twist the knife to pry open the hinge.
4. Run the knife against the upper shell all the way around.
5. Separate any edible meat clinging to the upper shell. Remove and discard the upper shell. (Note: Do not sever the muscle holding the clam meat to the bottom shell before eating.)

CLAM KNIFE

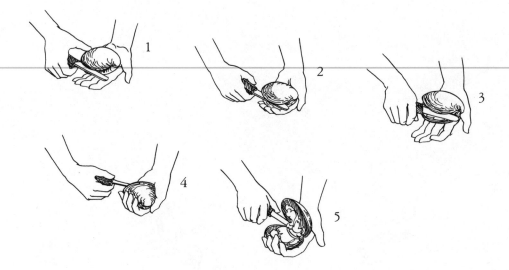

CLEANING MUSSELS

1. Using a clam knife, scrape any barnacles from the shells.
2. Remove the beard-like strands.

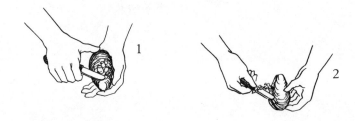

3. Place the mussels in a bucket and cover with cool fresh water by about 2 inches. Agitate the mussels with your hand in a washing machine motion. Drain and discard the water. Repeat several times until the water becomes clear. Drain again and keep the mussels cool until ready to cook.

CLEANING SHRIMP

1. Insert the tip into the top side of the head end of the shrimp.
2. Push in toward the tail.
3. As you continue pushing the tip past the tail, the thick end of the tool will separate the shell from the meat. The tool also removes the thin black vein running along the shrimp.
4. As the shell separates, gently remove it.
5. Rinse the shelled shrimp under cool running water. Drain well.

SHRIMP SHELLER AND DEVEINER

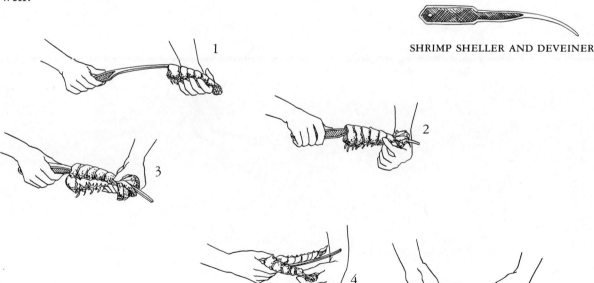

CLEANING SQUID

1. Place the squid on a flat surface. Peel off the thin spotted skin from the body section and rinse it with cold tap water.
2. Pull off the head, tentacles, and intestines.
3. Remove the translucent cartilage in the center.
4. Sever the tentacles from the head and the intestines. Discard the head and intestines.
5. Remove the small hard beak from the middle of the tentacles. Rinse the body and tentacles well with cool water. Drain.

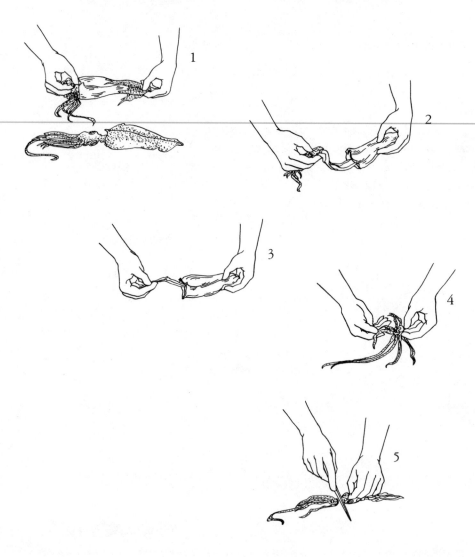

CLEANING SOFT-SHELL CRABS

1. Place the crab, top side up, on a cutting board. Cut off the protruding eyes.
2. Turn the crab onto its back. Remove the triangular-shaped apron as shown.
3. Lift the flaps on each side and remove the spongy gill tissue underneath. Rinse the crab with cool water and pat dry with paper towels.

SPLITTING A LOBSTER

1. To kill a lobster instantly, place the lobster on a cutting board and insert the tip of a large knife between the eyes.

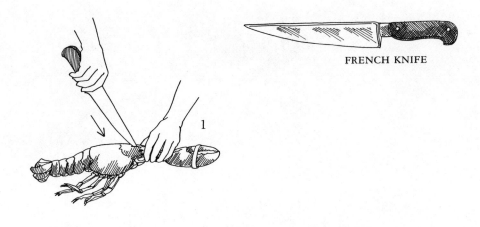

FRENCH KNIFE

2. Cut entirely through the lobster toward the tail.
3. Work the knife toward the tail end to split the body and tail in half.
4. Using a paring knife, remove the intestinal track, which resembles a thin vein running the length of the lobster.
5. Remove the sandy sac underneath the eyes.

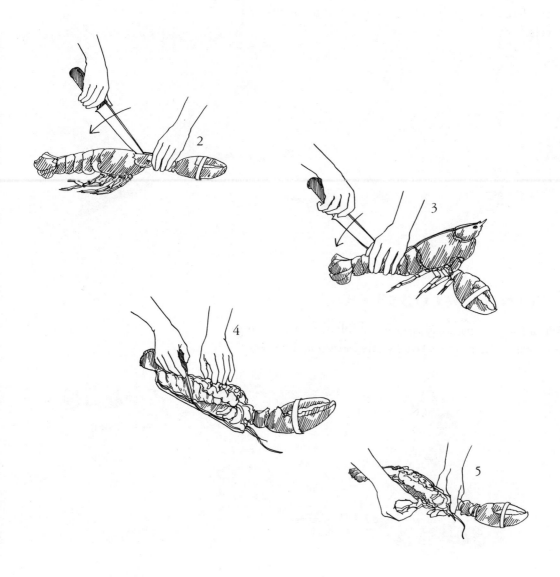

CHAPTER 3

Mousses

Sea Scallop Mousse

1½ pounds sea scallops
2 large eggs
Salt and freshly ground white pepper to taste
Pinch of cayenne pepper
⅛ teaspoon freshly grated nutmeg
2 cups heavy cream
2 tablespoons unsalted butter
Quick Tomato Sauce (page 250)

1. Preheat the oven to 375 degrees.
2. Put the scallops, eggs, salt and pepper, cayenne, and nutmeg into the bowl of a food processor. Start blending and gradually add the cream. Purée until the mixture is smooth.
3. Butter six 1½-cup soufflé dishes. Spoon equal portions of the mixture into each soufflé dish. Smooth over the tops and cover with aluminum foil.
4. Put the dishes in a high-sided metal baking pan and pour hot water halfway up the sides of the dishes. Place the pan on top of the stove and bring the water to a boil. Transfer the pan to the oven and bake for 25 minutes. Test for doneness by inserting a meat thermometer into a mousse. If the thermometer registers 140 degrees, or if the end comes out clean, the mousse is done. Unmold the mousses onto warm serving plates and serve with Quick Tomato Sauce.

YIELD: 6 SERVINGS.

To test for seasoning and texture before cooking the entire mousse, drop a teaspoonful of the mixture into a small saucepan filled with simmering water. Cook until it reaches a firm mousse-like texture and taste. If the sample is too dense, add more cream to the batch to lighten it.

Shrimp Quenelles

This recipe also works well with salmon and sole.

1½ pounds very cold raw shrimp, shelled and deveined
Salt and freshly ground white pepper to taste
⅛ teaspoon cayenne pepper
¼ teaspoon freshly grated nutmeg
2 large egg whites
2½ cups heavy cream
Sauce Américaine (page 246)

1. In the container of a food processor, combine the shrimp, salt and pepper, cayenne, and nutmeg. Blend for about 30 seconds, stopping the blender and scraping down the mixture from the wall of the container with a rubber spatula if necessary. Add the egg whites and blend for about 20 seconds. Add the cream slowly while blending. Blend for 35 to 40 seconds. Butter a shallow pan (a gratin or roasting pan will do).

2. To form the quenelles, dip a large soup spoon into a container of hot water. Spoon out a heaping portion of the mixture, enough to create the desired football shape of the quenelle (illustration 1). Each should roughly measure 2¾ inches long by 1¾ inches wide. Smooth the mixture with another spoon (illustrations 2, 3, and 4). Then, with the spoon used for shaping, scoop the mixture cleanly into the pan (illustration 5). There should be about 20 to 24 quenelles (illustration 6).

3. Cut wax or parchment paper into the shape of the pan's interior. Cut a hole in the center about an inch in diameter. Butter one side of the paper and cover the quenelles with the buttered side.

4. Bring a large quantity of lightly salted water to a boil. Gently ladle the water over the wax paper so that it will flow gradually into the dish. Continue adding water until the quenelles are covered. Bring the water back to a simmer. Lower the heat and simmer gently for 5 minutes.

5. Remove the wax paper and turn the quenelles once. Cover again and turn off the heat.

6. Remove the quenelles carefully and quickly with a slotted spoon and drain them briefly on paper towels. Serve immediately with the Sauce Américaine.

YIELD: 20 TO 24 QUENELLES; SERVES 8 TO 10 AS AN APPETIZER OR 4 AS A MAIN COURSE.

Quenelles are light and tasty dumplings made with fish or forcemeat bound with cream and eggs. They can be formed into all shapes and sizes and used as garnishes or entrées.

Salmon Mousse

This recipe also works with sole, red snapper, scallops, and flounder.
The amount of cream may vary, depending on the texture of the fish: The
leaner the fish, the more cream it needs.

1½ pounds very cold skinless salmon fillets, cut into 2-inch
*   cubes*
Salt and freshly ground white pepper to taste
⅛ teaspoon freshly grated nutmeg
1 large egg
2 cups heavy cream
2 teaspoons unsalted butter, softened
Tomato Sauce with Dill (page 251)

1. Preheat the oven to 375 degrees.

2. Put the cubed salmon into the container of a food processor. Season with salt and pepper and nutmeg. Add the egg. Blend for 10 seconds. Continue blending while adding the cream for about 30 seconds, or until the mixture has a fine texture.

3. Butter a 6-cup mold (a charlotte, ring, or fluted ring mold will do) with a pastry brush. Press the mousse mixture evenly into the mold, smoothing the top with a rubber spatula.

4. Cover the mold tightly with aluminum foil and place it in a baking pan containing enough water to come 1½ inches up the side of the mold.

5. Bring the water to a boil on top of the stove; then place the pan in the oven and bake for about 45 minutes, or until the internal temperature of the mousse is about 140 degrees.

6. Carefully invert the mold onto a serving plate. Serve the mousse with Tomato Sauce with Dill.

YIELD: 6 SERVINGS.

A mousse is a purée of fish, meat, or vegetables bound with cream and eggs and served warm or cold. Dessert mousses are often made with fruit.

Cold Seafood Mousse

A seafood mousse can be made with many kinds of fish and shellfish.

1½ pounds very cold skinless sole fillets, cut into 1-inch cubes
1 large egg
Salt and freshly ground white pepper to taste
⅛ teaspoon cayenne pepper
½ teaspoon freshly grated nutmeg
2 cups very cold heavy cream
½ pound very cold sea scallops, cut into ½-inch cubes
½ pound shrimp, shelled and deveined
¾ pound skinless salmon fillets, cut into ¾-inch cubes
3 tablespoons finely chopped shallots
2 teaspoons unsalted butter
Sauce Gribiche (page 257)

1. Preheat the oven to 375 degrees.
2. Put the sole into the container of a food processor along with the egg, salt and pepper, cayenne, and nutmeg. Process until smooth. Continue blending while adding the cream for about 40 seconds, or until a very smooth mixture is formed.
3. Scrape the purée into a mixing bowl.
4. In a second mixing bowl, combine the scallops, shrimp, salmon, shallots, and salt and pepper to taste. Blend well. Combine with the sole and blend well with a wooden spoon.
5. Butter the inside of a 9- by 5-inch loaf pan (8-cup capacity). Add the mousse mixture and smooth over the top with a spatula. Cover with aluminum foil. Place the loaf pan in a baking dish or large pan holding about 2 inches of hot water. Bring the water to a boil on top of the stove.
6. Place the pans in the oven and bake for 1 hour and 15 minutes, or until the internal temperature of the mousse reaches 140 degrees. Remove it from the oven and let cool. Serve with the sauce.

YIELD: 8 TO 10 SERVINGS.

Mousseline usually refers to mousse-type preparations that have been lightened with whipped cream.

Brandade de Morue

MOUSSE OF SALTED COD

2 pounds salted cod, preferably boneless and skinless
1 pound potatoes, peeled and cut into 2-inch cubes
2½ cups milk
1 onion pierced with 2 whole cloves
1 bay leaf
4 parsley sprigs
1 cup heavy cream
2 tablespoons minced garlic
1 cup olive oil
¼ teaspoon freshly grated nutmeg
⅛ teaspoon cayenne pepper
Sea salt and freshly ground black pepper to taste
1 truffle, minced, optional
Croutons (page 274)

1. Put the cod into a large bowl and cover it with cold water. Let it soak for 18 to 24 hours, changing the water often.

2. Put the potatoes in a pot and cover them with water. Simmer for about 20 minutes, or until the potatoes are soft. Drain.

3. Meanwhile, drain the soaked cod and transfer it to a large saucepan. Cover with cold water and add ½ cup of the milk, the onion, bay leaf, and parsley sprigs. Bring to a boil, lower the heat, and simmer for about 3 minutes, or until the fish is cooked. Drain well. Carefully remove any bones and skin if necessary.

4. In another saucepan, blend the remaining milk and the cream. Warm it over low heat.

5. Combine the potatoes and garlic in a bowl and beat at low speed. Add the cod and beat at a high speed.

6. Warm the oil in a saucepan. Alternately add the milk mixture and warm oil until all is used. Beat in the nutmeg, cayenne, and freshly ground black pepper. Add salt only if needed. Stir the truffle in at the end. Serve with the Croutons.

YIELD: 12 SERVINGS.

Salt cod is one of the great underrated foods of America. Anyone who has traveled to Spain or Portugal has been exposed to the countless wonderful stews and salads built around it. Brandade de Morue, a garlicky salt cod purée that one eats with toast triangles, is one of our favorites.

Large white sides of salted cod are available in many ethnic fish stores and groceries. It must be soaked in fresh water before cooking—the time depends on the saltiness of the dried fish.

Salads and Cold Dishes

Seafood Salad with Corn and Rice

2 pounds mussels, well scrubbed and with beards removed
2 bay leaves
2 whole cloves
¼ cup plus 2 tablespoons red wine vinegar
4 cups water
Salt to taste
1 cup converted rice
⅓ pound snow peas, trimmed and washed
½ cup plus 2 tablespoons olive oil
1 cup finely chopped red onion
1 firm sweet red pepper, cut into thin strips
1 firm sweet green pepper, diced
4 ears fresh corn, kernels removed (about 2¼ cups)
1 teaspoon ground cumin
1¼ pounds shrimp, shelled, deveined, and halved lengthwise
Freshly ground black pepper to taste
¼ teaspoon hot red pepper flakes
1 teaspoon finely minced garlic
¼ cup finely chopped fresh coriander or parsley leaves

1. Put the mussels in a pot and add the bay leaves, cloves, and 2 tablespoons of the vinegar. Cover tightly and cook for about 2 minutes, or until the mussels open. Remove from the heat.

2. Pour the 4 cups of water into a saucepan and bring it to a boil; add salt to taste. Add the rice, return to a boil, and simmer for 17 minutes, stirring occasionally. Drain and let cool. There should be about 4 cups of rice.

3. Cook the snow peas in boiling salted water for about 2 minutes. Drain.

4. When the mussels are cool enough to handle, remove their meat from the shells.

5. Heat 2 tablespoons of the olive oil in a frying pan over medium-high heat. Add the onion, red and green peppers, and corn. Sprinkle with the cumin and cook, stirring, for about 2 minutes. Add the shrimp and season with salt and black pepper; cook, stirring, for about 30 seconds. Cover and cook about 2 minutes.

6. Put the rice in a large bowl and add the cooked vegetables, shrimp, hot pepper flakes, mussels, snow peas, garlic, coriander, and salt and pepper to taste. Combine the remaining oil and vinegar. Stir it in, folding over to blend thoroughly. Serve warm or at room temperature.

YIELD: 6 TO 8 SERVINGS.

Shrimp Salad with Feta Cheese

1 bunch watercress, washed and dried
2 cups orange sections
36 cooked shrimp, shelled and deveined (page 15)
1½ cups thinly sliced red onion
3 hard-boiled eggs, quartered
¾ cup crumbled feta cheese
¼ cup fresh coriander leaves
1 tablespoon Dijon mustard
3 tablespoons fresh lemon juice
2 tablespoons red wine vinegar
1 tablespoon finely chopped garlic
6 tablespoons olive oil
Tabasco sauce to taste
Salt and freshly ground black pepper to taste

1. Distribute the watercress evenly over the center of 6 plates. Arrange equal amounts of orange sections in a fan pattern around each dish. Place 6 shrimp on each plate between the orange sections, forming a decorative pattern. Distribute the onion slices over the plate in concentric circles. Place the quartered eggs over the onions.

2. Sprinkle the feta cheese over everything. Garnish with coriander leaves.

3. Combine the remaining ingredients in a jar and shake well. Pour the dressing over the salads and serve. (The dressing can be mixed with a whisk, but I find a jar more effective.)

YIELD: 6 SERVINGS.

Crab Meat and Red Pepper Salad

1 sweet red pepper
½ cup olive oil
⅓ cup red wine vinegar
1¼ pounds crab meat, shell and cartilage removed
½ cup chopped red onion
1 tablespoon candied ginger
Salt and freshly ground black pepper to taste
2 ripe avocados, peeled and sliced (3 cups) (Coat with a
*   tablespoon or so of lime juice to prevent discoloring.)*
4 tablespoons chopped fresh coriander or dill leaves

1. Cut the red pepper in half and remove the seeds. Blanch it in boiling water for 2 minutes. When the pepper is cool, slice it crosswise into thin strips.

2. Heat the olive oil and vinegar in a frying pan. Add the crab meat, onion, ginger, and salt and pepper. Cook the mixture for 1 minute, stirring. Add the avocado and red pepper strips. Mix the ingredients well and transfer the salad to individual plates. Sprinkle with the coriander and serve immediately.

YIELD: 6 SERVINGS.

Lobster and Vegetable Salad with Basil

½ pound fresh string beans, trimmed and cut into 1½-inch lengths
4 carrots, about ¾ pound, trimmed, scraped, and cut into ¼-inch cubes
4 stalks celery heart, cut into ¼-inch cubes
Salt and freshly ground black pepper to taste
1 yellow squash, cut into ¼-inch cubes
1 zucchini, about ½ pound, cut into ¼-inch cubes
Meat from 4 steamed lobsters (see page 182 for steaming lobsters), coral and liver reserved
½ cup chopped fresh basil leaves
1 tablespoon Dijon mustard
1 tablespoon white wine vinegar
1 tablespoon fresh lemon juice
⅓ cup vegetable oil
Red leaf lettuce or Boston lettuce (one or two heads, depending on the size), rinsed and dried
1 cup Mayonnaise (page 259)

1. Put the string beans, carrots, and celery in a large kettle. Cover with cold water and add salt to taste. Bring the water to a boil and simmer for 5 minutes. Add the yellow squash and zucchini and cook 2 more minutes. Drain immediately.

2. Meanwhile, cut the lobster meat into bite-size pieces. You should have about 4 cups. Finely chop the liver and coral.

3. Put the cooked vegetables in a mixing bowl along with the basil, liver, and coral. Set aside.

4. Combine the mustard, vinegar, and lemon juice in a small bowl and start beating with a wire whisk while slowly adding the oil until it is well blended. Season with salt and pepper. Combine this sauce with the vegetables and toss well.

5. Arrange the lettuce leaves on a cold serving platter. Spoon

the vegetable salad onto the center and scatter the lobster meat all over. Serve the Mayonnaise on the side.

YIELD: 6 SERVINGS.

Spicy Lobster Salad

This salad can also be made with lump crab meat.

1 cup Mayonnaise with Fresh Herbs (page 260)
½ cup drained capers
½ cup finely chopped celery
¼ cup finely chopped shallots
½ cup finely chopped scallions
1 teaspoon Worcestershire sauce
1 tablespoon Dijon mustard
3 drops of Tabasco sauce
1 pound steamed lobster meat
Salt and freshly ground black pepper to taste
3 tablespoons chopped fresh parsley or coriander leaves

1. Put the mayonnaise into a mixing bowl and add the capers, celery, shallots, scallions, Worcestershire sauce, mustard, Tabasco sauce, and salt and pepper. Blend well.

2. Add the lobster meat and carefully fold it in, leaving the lumps as large as possible. Sprinkle with the parsley before serving.

YIELD: 6 SERVINGS.

Scallop Salad with Cumin Dressing

6 tablespoons olive oil
1½ tablespoons sherry or red wine vinegar
2 teaspoons freshly ground cumin seeds
Salt and freshly ground black pepper to taste
1 jalapeño pepper, seeded and minced
4 scallions, trimmed (leaving 1 inch of green section) and
*   chopped*
1 large ripe tomato, peeled, seeded, and chopped
3 cups water
1 cup dry white wine
1 tablespoon thyme (dried or fresh)
1 bay leaf
6 whole black peppercorns
1 pound bay scallops
1 head Bibb lettuce or radicchio

1. Prepare the scallop sauce by combining the olive oil, vinegar, cumin, salt and pepper, and jalapeño pepper in a small bowl. Mix well and set aside.

2. In a serving bowl, combine the scallions and tomato.

3. In a deep pot combine the water, wine, thyme, bay leaf, and peppercorns. Season generously with salt. Bring to a boil and add the scallops. Poach the scallops for 2 minutes. Drain them in a colander and let them cool.

4. When the scallops are well drained and cool, add them to the tomato and scallions. Add the sauce and toss well. Taste for seasoning. Serve the scallops on beds of lettuce on individual serving plates.

YIELD: 4 TO 6 SERVINGS.

Italian Squid Salad

---

3 pounds fresh squid, cleaned and washed (see page 16)
4 cups water
2 tablespoons red wine vinegar
1 onion pierced with 4 whole cloves
1 celery stalk
¼ teaspoon hot red pepper flakes
1 teaspoon dried oregano
2 parsley sprigs
2 lemon slices
Salt and freshly ground black pepper to taste
½ cup finely chopped onion
½ cup finely chopped celery
1 tablespoon finely chopped garlic
½ cup finely chopped fresh parsley leaves
¼ cup red wine vinegar
¼ cup fresh lemon juice
10 tablespoons olive oil

1. Cut the squid into bite-size pieces, making rings out of the body.

2. Bring the water to a boil in a saucepan. Add the squid rings and tentacles, vinegar, onion, celery, hot pepper flakes, oregano, parsley, lemon slices, and salt and pepper. Simmer for 25 to 30 minutes, or until the squid is tender. Remove the saucepan from the heat and cool to room temperature.

3. Remove the squid from the cooking liquid, drain well, and place in a salad bowl. Add the remaining ingredients and toss well. Serve at room temperature.

YIELD: 6 SERVINGS.

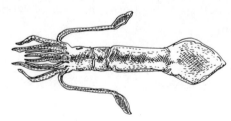

Salted Cod and Chick-pea Salad

---

2 pounds boneless dried salted cod
1 pound dried chick-peas
8 cups water
1 medium-size onion pierced with 2 whole cloves
2 bay leaves
Salt and freshly ground black pepper to taste
½ cup milk
½ teaspoon dried thyme
4 ripe tomatoes, peeled and chopped
2 cups diced red onion
1 tablespoon minced garlic
¾ cup chopped fresh fennel (half white stalk, half green tops)
3 tablespoons chopped fresh parsley leaves
¾ cup olive oil
½ cup red wine vinegar
¼ teaspoon hot red pepper flakes

1. Soak the cod in cold water for 24 hours, changing the water four or five times.

2. Sort and rinse the chick-peas. When the cod is ready for cooking, put the chick-peas into a soup pot with the water, onion pierced with a clove, and 1 bay leaf. Add a tablespoon of salt and simmer, covered, for 3½ hours, or until the chick-peas are tender. Remove the pot from the heat and set it aside.

3. Put the cod in a deep skillet and cover it with water (add enough to submerge it by about 4 inches). Add the milk, thyme, and remaining bay leaf.

4. Bring the liquid to a boil; lower the heat to a simmer and cook for 5 minutes.

5. When the cod is done, drain the chick-peas and put them into a large serving bowl. Remove the cod from the liquid and drain it; shred it roughly with your fingers and add it to the chick-peas. Add the tomatoes, red onion, garlic, fennel, and parsley. Pour in the olive oil and vinegar and sprinkle the hot

pepper flakes over all. Toss well, season with salt and pepper, and serve. This dish may be served lukewarm or cold.

YIELD: 10 TO 12 SERVINGS.

Warm Salmon Salad with Ginger

4 endives
½ pound (about one head) red lettuce, torn into large pieces
  (or an equal amount of radicchio)
⅓ pound arugula, torn into 4-inch pieces
1½ pounds skinless salmon fillets
6 tablespoons olive oil
Freshly ground black pepper
½ cup chopped scallions
2 tablespoons chopped shallots
2 tablespoons finely chopped gingerroot
⅓ cup red wine vinegar
2 tablespoons soy sauce
2 tablespoons dry white wine
6 tablespoons chopped fresh dill leaves

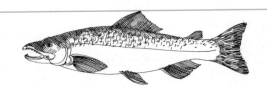

1. Trim the hard bottoms from the endives and remove the leaves. Arrange 8 leaves on each of 6 plates with the bottoms at the center and the tops forming a fan pattern. Leave room between each leaf.

2. Distribute the red leaf lettuce over each of the plates between the endive leaves. Place a clump of arugula at the center of the fan pattern.

3. Cut each salmon fillet into thirds lengthwise. Then cut each strip on the bias into 2-inch-long pieces.

4. Heat the oil in a nonstick frying pan over medium-high heat. Put the salmon into the pan and sprinkle with pepper. Add the scallions, shallots, and ginger. Sauté the salmon on both

sides for a total of 2 minutes. Add the vinegar and soy sauce and then the white wine. Blend well. Remove from the heat.

5. Place the salmon strips over the salad. Evenly distribute the sauce over the salmon and the greens. Garnish each plate with a tablespoon of chopped dill. Serve immediately.

YIELD: 6 SERVINGS.

Herring Salad with Dill Sauce

If you want to use fresh herring in this recipe, see the method for Pickling Herring on page 36.

1 pound small red skin potatoes
Salt
1 pound herring in wine sauce, cut into small pieces
1½ cups diced beets
2 apples, peeled, cored, and cut into ½-inch cubes
3 hard-boiled eggs, cut into ½-inch cubes
1 pound boiled ham, cut into ½-inch cubes
¾ cup chopped sour pickle

THE SAUCE

4 tablespoons white wine vinegar
1 teaspoon sugar
2 tablespoons mild mustard
1 cup sour cream
¼ cup chopped fresh dill leaves
Salt and freshly ground black pepper to taste

1. Place the potatoes in a saucepan and cover with water. Add salt to taste. Bring to a boil and simmer for 20 minutes. Drain and cool the potatoes. Leaving the skins on, cut them into ½-inch cubes.

2. Combine the potatoes with the herring, beets, apples, eggs, ham, and pickle in a salad bowl. Toss to blend.

3. To make the sauce, combine the vinegar, sugar, and mus-

tard in a small saucepan. Bring to a boil; then cool and blend with the sour cream. Add the dill and salt and pepper, if necessary, and pour the sauce over the salad. Blend well and serve cold.

YIELD: 6 TO 10 SERVINGS.

Pickled Mackerel or Herring

2 pounds fresh mackerel or herring fillets with skin
2 cups water
1 cup dry white wine
¾ cup white wine vinegar
2 tablespoons sugar
1 teaspoon coriander seeds
1 teaspoon yellow mustard seeds
2 whole cloves
6 whole allspice
2 bay leaves
¼ teaspoon hot red pepper flakes
1 teaspoon whole black peppercorns
1 large onion, coarsely chopped
2 parsley sprigs
1 tablespoon salt, or more if needed

1. Cut the fillets widthwise into 2-inch pieces. Put the pieces into a bowl, cover with plastic wrap, and refrigerate.

2. Combine all the remaining ingredients in a saucepan and bring to a boil. Simmer for 5 minutes. Remove the pan from the heat and let the pickling mixture cool at room temperature.

3. Pour the pickling mixture over the fish fillets, cover, and refrigerate for 2 or 3 days. (You can also put the combination in a large mason jar or crock.) Serve as an appetizer.

YIELD: 8 SERVINGS.

Herring is believed to have been a staple in the diet of Northern Europeans in Neolithic times. It remains exceedingly popular there to this day. The flesh is relatively high in fat, about 6 percent, which makes it suitable for grilling.

The term "red herring" comes from an English recipe in which the fish is salted and then smoked. Its colloquial meaning derives from hunters who used to lay the red herring across the fox's trail, to make the hunt more challenging by throwing the hounds off course.

Kidney Beans and Tuna Salad

This is an excellent way to use leftover fresh tuna. Canned tuna may also be substituted.

THE BEANS

1 pound dried white kidney beans
1 onion pierced with 2 whole cloves
1 bay leaf
2 carrots, scraped and cleaned
1 celery stalk
2 parsley sprigs
2 thyme sprigs, or ½ teaspoon dried thyme
Salt and freshly ground black pepper to taste

THE VINAIGRETTE

5 tablespoons red wine vinegar
¾ cup olive oil
¾ cup finely chopped onion
¾ cup finely chopped fresh parsley leaves
1 tablespoon finely chopped garlic
¼ teaspoon hot red pepper flakes
¼ cup drained capers
Salt and freshly ground black pepper to taste

14 ounces cooked tuna, cut into small pieces
Lemon wedges

1. The night before, place the beans in a bowl and cover with 6 cups of cold water. Let them stand overnight.

2. Drain the beans and put them into a saucepan. Cover with 8 cups of cold water and add the onion, bay leaf, carrots, celery, parsley, thyme sprigs, and salt and pepper. Bring to a boil, lower the heat, cover, and simmer for about 1 hour, or until tender. Let the beans cool in their cooking liquid.

3. When cool, drain the beans and cut the carrots into ¼-inch cubes. Discard the celery and parsley.

4. Put the beans and carrots into a salad bowl. Combine all the ingredients for the sauce in a mixing bowl and blend. Pour the sauce over the beans. Add the tuna fish and toss well. Serve with lemon wedges.

YIELD: 6 SERVINGS.

Crab Meat and Avocado Salad

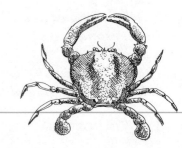

½ cup Mayonnaise (page 259)
½ cup sour cream
¼ cup finely chopped celery
¼ cup finely chopped scallions
¼ cup finely chopped fresh coriander leaves
¼ teaspoon cayenne pepper
Salt and freshly ground black pepper to taste
1 pound lump crab meat, shell and cartilage removed
2 tablespoons Cognac
3 unblemished ripe avocados, halved and seeded
Chopped coriander leaves or whole coriander leaves for
   garnish

1. In a mixing bowl, combine the mayonnaise, sour cream, celery, scallions, coriander, cayenne pepper, and salt and pepper.
2. Fold in the crab meat and Cognac, mixing as little as possible so as not to break up the lumps. Fill the avocado halves with the mixture. Sprinkle with the coriander.

YIELD: 6 SERVINGS.

Cold Mackerel in White Wine

1 tablespoon vegetable oil
1½ cups thinly sliced white onions
½ cup thinly sliced carrots
1 teaspoon minced garlic
½ cup dry white wine
½ cup white wine vinegar
1 bay leaf
3 thyme sprigs, or 1 teaspoon dried thyme
4 whole cloves
⅛ teaspoon hot red pepper flakes
4 parsley sprigs
10 whole black peppercorns
Salt and freshly ground black pepper to taste
2 pounds mackerel fillets, cut into 8 to 10 pieces
10 lemon slices

1. Heat the oil in a saucepan; then add the onions, carrots, and garlic. Cook and stir for 2 to 3 minutes, or until the ingredients are wilted. Add the wine, vinegar, bay leaf, thyme, cloves, hot pepper flakes, parsley, peppercorns, and salt to taste. Bring to a boil, lower the heat, and simmer for 10 minutes.

2. In a metal pan large enough to hold the fish pieces in one layer, arrange the fish skin side down and sprinkle with salt and pepper. Pour the hot mixture over the mackerel and cover closely with aluminum foil. Bring to a boil, lower the heat, and simmer for 5 minutes. Cool in the liquid. Serve cold garnished with lemon slices.

YIELD: 8 TO 10 SERVINGS.

Raw Sea Bass with Coriander and Basil

This dish is one of the most popular appetizers at the four-star seafood restaurant, Le Bernardin, in Manhattan. The recipe comes from chef and co-owner Gilbert Le Coze. It also works well with salmon and tuna.

2 tablespoons virgin olive oil
1 tablespoon fresh lemon juice
1 teaspoon fine julienne strips fresh basil leaves
1 teaspoon chopped fresh coriander leaves
5 boneless sea bass fillets (4 ounces each)
Salt and freshly ground white pepper to taste

1. Make the dressing by combining the olive oil, lemon juice, basil, and coriander in a bowl.

2. Slice one of the fillets in half lengthwise with a sharp knife. Cut each half on the bias crosswise into thin strips (they should be about the thickness of quarters). Overlap the pieces on a chilled serving plate, starting from the rim and working toward the center in concentric circles. When all the slices are in place, lay a strip of plastic wrap over the plate and press gently with your hands to form a smooth surface and fill in any gaps where the plate shows through. As you press, the slices should adhere to each other. Repeat this process with the remaining bass. Keep all finished plates well chilled until served.

3. Season all the fish well with salt and pepper. Drizzle the dressing over each evenly and serve.

YIELD: 4 SERVINGS.

Marinated Salmon with Ginger and Coriander

---

2 pounds skinless salmon fillets
½ cup fresh lime juice
1 cup very thinly sliced Bermuda onion
2 tablespoons white wine vinegar
2 tablespoons olive oil
1 tablespoon freshly grated gingerroot
¼ teaspoon hot red pepper flakes
Salt and freshly ground black pepper to taste

Cut the salmon fillets into ¾-inch cubes and put them into a mixing bowl. Add the remaining ingredients, stir gently, and cover with plastic wrap. Refregerate for 6 hours before serving.

YIELD: 6 SERVINGS.

Gravlax

---

2 bunches fresh dill
1 4-pound fresh salmon fillet, preferably cut from the center
  of the fish
¼ cup kosher or any coarse salt
¼ cup sugar
1 teaspoon coarsely ground black pepper
2 tablespoons Cognac
Mustard–Dill Sauce (page 256)

1. Cut off and discard the tough stems from the dill. Rinse the dill and pat it dry.
2. Cut the fillet widthwise into two pieces of roughly equal

size. Remove any small white bones from the flesh. Pat the fish dry with paper towels.

3. Combine the salt, sugar, and pepper. Rub this mixture into the pink flesh of the salmon.

4. Spread one third of the dill over the bottom of a flat dish. Put 1 of the fillets, skin side down, over the dill. Sprinkle Cognac over it. Cover this with another third of the dill. Place the other piece of salmon, skin side up, on top of the dill. Cover with the remaining dill and place a plate on top. Weight the top plate down with a heavy object and refrigerate the fish for 48 hours. Turn it every 12 hours, always covering again with the plate and weighting it down.

5. When the gravlax is ready, slice it thinly on the bias (without removing the skin), as you would smoked salmon. Serve with Mustard–Dill Sauce.

YIELD: 12 TO 20 SERVINGS.

Salmon Seviche

This recipe also works well with red snapper, black fish, sea bass, and bay or sea scallops.

1½ pounds salmon fillets, cut into ½-inch cubes
½ cup fresh lime juice
½ cup thinly sliced red onion
1 tablespoon finely chopped garlic
¼ teaspoon minced jalapeño pepper
1 or 2 teaspoons freshly ground black pepper, or to taste
1 cup peeled and seeded ripe tomatoes
Salt to taste
1 teaspoon ground coriander
½ teaspoon ground cumin
4 tablespoons olive oil
½ cup chopped fresh coriander or parsley leaves
6 romaine lettuce leaves

1. Put all the ingredients, *except* the lettuce, in a bowl and blend well. Cover with plastic wrap and refrigerate for at least 4 hours.

2. When ready to serve, scoop the fish mixture onto crisp romaine lettuce leaves.

YIELD: 6 SERVINGS.

Carpaccio of Fresh Tuna with Ginger–Lime Dressing

This light and summery dish is one of the most popular appetizers at the four-star seafood restaurant, Le Bernardin, in Manhattan. The recipe comes from the chef and co-owner Gilbert Le Coze. This technique also works well with salmon. The fish must be impeccably fresh and well chilled. The plates should also be well chilled.

4 tablespoons virgin olive oil plus oil to coat the plastic wrap
4 skinless trimmed tuna steaks, ⅜ inch thick (each about 4½ ounces)
1 large egg yolk
1 tablespoon fresh lime juice
2 tablespoons heavy cream
1 teaspoon grated fresh gingerroot
⅛ teaspoon minced garlic
½ teaspoon grated lime rind
1½ teaspoons finely chopped fresh chervil leaves
1½ teaspoons finely chopped fresh basil leaves
Salt and freshly ground white pepper to taste

1. Brush two 10-inch-square sheets of plastic wrap with olive oil. Place one of the tuna steaks between the sheets of plastic wrap and place on a hard flat surface. Using a meat pounder or any flat-bottomed heavy implement, gently pound the tuna evenly into about a ⅛-inch-thick circle. Use a sharp knife or

scissors to trim the ragged edges of the flattened fillet into a neat circle. Reserve the trimmings in the refrigerator.

2. Remove the top layer of plastic and lift the fillet onto an 8- to 10-inch-diameter chilled serving plate. Remove the top layer of plastic. Repeat this process with the remaining tuna steaks, placing one each on a chilled plate. Refrigerate the finished plates.

3. Make the dressing by putting the egg yolk in a bowl and whisking vigorously. Add the lime juice as you whisk. Continue whisking and pour in a thin stream of oil. When the combination has thickened to mayonnaise consistency, gradually whip in the cream, ginger, garlic, lime rind, 1 teaspoon of the chervil, 1 teaspoon of the basil, and the salt and pepper.

4. Season the fillets with the pepper. Coat them with a thin layer of the sauce. Remove the tuna trimmings from the refrigerator. Make decorative garnishes in the center of each plate by arranging the trimmings roughly into the shape of a rose (or any form desired). Sprinkle the remaining chervil and basil over each serving. Serve immediately.

YIELD: 4 SERVINGS.

Tartare of Tuna, Salmon, and Snapper

This is another popular recipe from Le Bernardin. This technique also works well with red snapper, tilefish, bass, fluke, sole, and halibut. Because salmon is such a fatty fish, omit the mayonnaise.

1 *pound* each *tuna, salmon, and red snapper fillets (The fillets should be trimmed, boneless, skinless, free of all sinew and very cold.)*
3 *tablespoons fresh lemon juice*
3 *tablespoons finely chopped cornichons or gherkins*
3 *tablespoons drained capers, minced*
3 *tablespoons finely chopped shallots*
3 *tablespoons minced fresh chives*

3 tablespoons virgin olive oil
2 tablespoons mayonnaise
Salt and freshly ground white pepper to taste
Chervil sprigs for garnish

1. Cut the tuna into ½-inch cubes. Put them in the bowl of a food processor and pulse the machine carefully to chop the fish to a very fine consistency without puréeing (it should resemble raw hamburger). This can also be done with a very sharp chef's knife. Transfer the tuna to a bowl. Repeat the process with the other two fish, putting each in a separate bowl.

2. Combine each fish with 1 tablespoon of the next 7 ingredients (do not add mayonnaise to the salmon). Season with salt and pepper and mix well with a rubber spatula. Cover and refrigerate until ready to serve.

3. Place three oval-shaped scoops of the tartare on each chilled serving plate (an oval ice cream scoop works well for this). Garnish with a sprig of chervil.

YIELD: 6 SERVINGS.

Tuna Carpaccio with Lime

As in any dish calling for raw or uncooked marinated fish, freshness is critical.

1¼ pounds center-cut tuna in one piece with all dark meat
   removed
4 tablespoons fresh lime juice
4 tablespoons virgin olive oil
½ cup finely chopped fresh coriander leaves
1 jalapeño pepper, finely chopped
Salt and freshly ground black pepper to taste
3 limes, cut into very thin slices

1. Chill 6 serving plates.
2. Slice the tuna very thin. Place the slices on the plates. Do not allow the tuna slices to overlap.

3. In a bowl, blend the lime juice, olive oil, coriander, jalapeño pepper, and salt and pepper.

4. Spoon equal amounts of the sauce over each serving plate. Arrange the lime slices around the edges of the plates.

5. Cover the plates with plastic wrap and refrigerate for at least 30 minutes.

YIELD: 6 SERVINGS.

Smoked Trout with Watercress Sauce

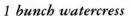
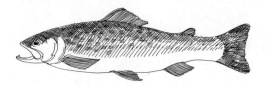

1 *bunch watercress*
1 *cup sour cream*
1 *tablespoon fresh lemon juice*
2 *dashes of Tabasco sauce*
Salt and freshly ground black pepper to taste
3 *smoked trout, skinned and filleted into 6 pieces*
6 *lemon wedges*
6 *watercress sprigs*

1. Wash and trim the watercress. Pat it dry and chop it (you should have about 1½ cups).

2. Put the watercress in the bowl of an electric blender with the sour cream, lemon juice, Tabasco sauce, and salt and pepper. Turn the blender on high for several seconds, or until the mixture is very smooth.

3. Serve the sauce over the trout. Garnish each serving with a lemon wedge and a sprig of watercress.

YIELD: 6 SERVINGS.

Cold Poached Salmon

This recipe, which is ideal for summer entertaining, also works well with striped bass, fresh tuna, sea trout, and red snapper.

1 cup ⅛-inch-thick strips julienned carrots
¾ cup ⅛-inch-thick strips julienned turnips
1 cup ⅛-inch-thick strips julienned zucchini
2 salmon fillets, about 2 pounds each, with skin (Reserve head and bones.)
6 cups Fish Broth (page 241) or bottled clam juice
4 tablespoons Mayonnaise, preferably homemade (page 259)
2 tablespoons chopped fresh dill leaves
Salt and freshly ground white pepper to taste
Red Pepper Mayonnaise (page 261), Mayonnaise with Fresh Herbs (page 260), or Cucumber and Dill Mayonnaise (page 259)

1. Cook the carrots in a large pot of lightly salted boiling water for about 3 minutes. Add the turnips and cook for 1 minute; then add the zucchini and cook for 1 minute; drain.

2. Place the fillets side by side in a deep roasting pan or fish poacher, skin side up. Pour the fish broth over them to cover. Cover the pan with foil and bring the liquid to a boil on top of the stove. Lower the heat to a simmer and cook for about 8 minutes. Remove the foil and let the fish cool in the broth.

3. While the fish is cooling, combine the mayonnaise, dill, and seasonings. Add the julienne strips of turnips, carrots, and zucchini. Taste and adjust the seasoning if necessary. Chill.

4. When fish is cool, gently remove it from the liquid (you might need two large spatulas to prevent the fish from falling apart) and place it on a serving platter. Remove any excess liquid with paper towels. Gently remove the skin by scraping it off with a small knife.

5. Arrange the vegetable-mayonnaise salad down the middle of each fillet. Serve with one of the mayonnaises.

YIELD: 10 TO 12 SERVINGS.

Hamburgers and hot dogs may be the popular picnic fare of twentieth-century Americans; however, celebrants in late eighteenth-century New England had slightly loftier ideas. Simmered fresh salmon with an onion cream sauce, boiled potatoes, and new peas were the focus of many Fourth of July get-togethers.

Taramasalata

GREEK APPETIZER MADE WITH CARP ROE

Serve this sprightly saline spread cold over buttered toast as an appetizer.

1 cup ½-inch-square white bread cubes, crust removed
2 tablespoons water
5 tablespoons carp roe
Juice of 1 lemon
1 tablespoon finely chopped garlic
1 tablespoon grated onion
1 cup olive oil
2 tablespoons chopped fresh parsley leaves
Buttered toast

1. Put the bread into a small bowl and sprinkle with the water. Blend well to dampen the cubes.

2. Put the carp roe into the bowl of an electric blender. Add the bread cubes, lemon juice, garlic, and onion. Blend well on high speed, gradually adding the oil in a thin stream, until all the oil is used. Garnish with parsley and serve over the toast.

YIELD: 6 SERVINGS.

CHAPTER 5

Broiling and Grilling

Broiling, which refers to overhead heat in an electric or gas oven, and grilling, which involves a heat source below (it can be electric, charcoal, wood, or gas), are interchangeable as far as these recipes are concerned. A recipe that calls for broiling can be applied to grilling of any sort.

Broiled Shrimp with Fresh Herbs

3 small zucchini (about ¾ pound total weight)
30 medium-size shrimp, shelled and deveined (about 1¾
pounds total weight before shelling)
Salt and freshly ground black pepper to taste
2 teaspoons finely chopped garlic
3 tablespoons each chopped fresh parsley, coriander, and basil
leaves
4 tablespoons olive oil
2 bay leaves, crumbled
4 tablespoons fresh lemon juice
½ teaspoon chopped fresh thyme leaves, or ¼ teaspoon dried
thyme

1. Preheat the broiler to high (500 degrees).
2. Trim the zucchini and cut them lengthwise into 30 disks of equal size.

3. Shortly before cooking (no more than 15 minutes), place the shrimp in a mixing bowl and add the zucchini, salt and pepper, garlic, parsley, coriander, basil, olive oil, bay leaves, lemon juice, and thyme. Blend well.

4. Place alternating pieces of zucchini and shrimp on 6 skewers. Brush them with the marinade remaining in the bowl.

5. Arrange the skewers on a baking pan and place it under the broiler about 4 inches from the heat source. Broil for about 3 minutes; then turn the skewers and broil for another 3 minutes, or until done.

YIELD: 6 SERVINGS.

Barbecued Shrimp with Pernod–Butter Sauce

24 jumbo shrimp (about 2 pounds), shelled and deveined
¼ teaspoon hot red pepper flakes
Salt and freshly ground black pepper to taste
4 tablespoons spicy mustard
2 tablespoons mayonnaise
2 tablespoons olive oil
Beurre Blanc with Herbs and Pernod (page 244)
  or Anchovy Butter (page 265), optional

1. Preheat a charcoal or gas grill or oven broiler to high.

2. In a mixing bowl, combine all the ingredients, *except* the olive oil and butter sauce. Blend well.

3. Arrange 6 shrimp neatly on each of 4 skewers so that they lie flat. Brush both sides with oil.

4. Place the shrimp on the grill or under the broiler about 4 inches from the heat source. Cook for about 2 minutes and turn. Continue grilling for about 2 minutes more. Serve with the sauce or the butter.

YIELD: 4 TO 6 SERVINGS.

Crab Meat au Gratin

3 tablespoons unsalted butter
3 tablespoons all-purpose flour
2 cups milk
Pinch of cayenne pepper
⅛ teaspoon freshly grated nutmeg
Salt and freshly ground white pepper to taste
¾ cup heavy cream
½ cup dry sherry
1 large egg yolk
3 tablespoons finely chopped shallots
1½ pounds crab meat, preferably lump style, shell and
  cartilage removed
6 hard-boiled eggs, quartered
6 tablespoons freshly grated Gruyère or Parmesan cheese

1. Preheat the broiler to high (500 degrees).

2. Melt 2 tablespoons of the butter in a saucepan over medium heat. Add the flour and stir to combine. Whisk in the milk and cook until well blended and smooth. Season with cayenne pepper, nutmeg, and salt and pepper.

3. Add the cream, bring to a boil, and simmer briefly, about 4 to 5 minutes. Stir in half of the sherry. Beat in the egg yolk and remove from the heat.

4. Melt the remaining butter in a nonstick skillet over medium-high heat. Add the shallots and cook them briefly. Stir in the crab meat and cook just to heat it through. Sprinkle with the remaining sherry.

5. Spoon the crab meat into a baking dish and smooth over the top with a spatula. Arrange the egg quarters on top, cut side down. Cover with the hot sauce and smooth over with a rubber spatula. Sprinkle with the cheese.

6. Place the dish under the broiler and cook just until golden brown and bubbling hot.

YIELD: 6 SERVINGS.

Broiled Lobster
with Tarragon Stuffing

4 lobsters (about 1½ pounds each)
¼ cup vegetable oil
Salt and freshly ground black pepper
1 cup fine fresh bread crumbs
8 tablespoons unsalted butter at room temperature
4 tablespoons finely chopped fresh tarragon, or 2 tablespoons
*   dried tarragon*
1 teaspoon paprika
4 tablespoons unsalted butter, melted
4 lemon wedges

1. Preheat the broiler to high (500 degrees).

2. Kill the lobsters by inserting the tip of a large knife between the eyes (see page 17). Turn each lobster on its back and split it lengthwise. Remove and discard the small sac near the eyes.

3. Remove the grayish liver and the dark green coral from the lobsters and put them in a mixing bowl. Discard the blackish intestine that runs along the tail.

4. Arrange the lobster halves, split side up, in a baking pan and brush them with some oil. Sprinkle with salt and pepper.

5. Add to the coral and liver the bread crumbs, softened butter tarragon, paprika, and salt and pepper to taste. Blend well.

6. Spoon equal portions of the filling into the cavities of each lobster half. Brush the tops with the remaining oil.

7. Place the lobsters under the broiler about 5 to 6 inches from the heat source. It may be necessary to use two pans to hold the lobsters. If so, place one pan under the broiler and the other on the rack below. Alternate the pans as they cook.

8. After 5 minutes turn off the broiler and bake at 450 degrees for 10 minutes or longer if necessary. Serve with melted butter and lemon wedges.

YIELD: 4 TO 8 SERVINGS.

Broiled Stuffed Lobster
with Ginger Butter

3 2¼- to 2½-pound lobsters
¾ cup bread crumbs
½ tablespoon chopped fresh tarragon leaves
12 tablespoons unsalted butter
Salt and freshly ground black pepper
2 tablespoons vegetable oil
2 large shallots, finely diced (about ¼ cup)
2 tablespoons white wine vinegar
2 teaspoons grated fresh gingerroot
2 tablespoons heavy cream

1. Preheat the broiler to high (500 degrees).

2. Kill the lobsters by inserting the tip of a large knife between the eyes (see page 17). Halve the lobsters lengthwise. Discard the sac near the head of each half lobster. Also remove the long dark strip of the intestines. Remove the lobster coral and reserve it.

3. In a large bowl, combine the bread crumbs, tarragon, 6 tablespoons of the butter, the lobster coral, salt, and a generous amount of pepper. Fill the lobster cavities with the mixture.

4. Brush the meat of the lobsters with the vegetable oil and place them in a baking pan about 6 inches from the broiler coil. If you need to use two baking pans, place one under the heat and the other on the rack below. Alternate the pans as you cook. Broil for 5 minutes; then bake at 450 degrees for 10 minutes.

5. Meanwhile, sauté the shallots in 1 tablespoon of the butter in a saucepan over medium-high heat for 2 minutes. Add the vinegar and ginger. When the vinegar has reduced, in about 2 minutes, add the heavy cream and stir well. Bring to a boil, reduce by half and then stir in the remaining butter. When all the butter has melted, remove from the heat and keep warm.

6. To serve pour the sauce over each lobster half.

YIELD: 6 SERVINGS.

Marinated Seafood Brochettes with Anchovy Butter

12 sea scallops
12 jumbo shrimp, shelled and deveined
1½ pounds boneless monkfish fillets, cut into 24 1½-inch
    cubes
3 tablespoons olive oil
1 tablespoon dried rosemary
2 tablespoons fresh lemon juice
1 teaspoon dried coriander
4 tablespoons chopped fresh parsley leaves
Salt and freshly ground black pepper to taste
Anchovy Butter (page 265)

1. Blend all the ingredients, except the Anchovy Butter, together in a large bowl. Cover with plastic wrap and marinate for 15 minutes at room temperature.

2. Heat the grill or oven broiler to high.

3. On each of 6 skewers, arrange alternately 2 shrimp, 2 scallops, and 4 pieces of monkfish. Brush with the marinade.

4. Place the skewers on the grill or under the broiler and cook for about 4 minutes; turn the skewers and cook for 4 minutes on the other side. (An oven broiler should take less time.) Serve with the Anchovy Butter.

YIELD: 6 SERVINGS.

Prawns, which are often confused with large shrimp, are, in fact, completely different in appearance; they resemble tiny lobsters with long, thin claws. More than 100 species are found around the world. The French call them langoustines. Like lobsters, most of the prawn meat is in the tail.

Broiled Scallops and Shrimp on Skewers

---

24 medium-size sea scallops
24 medium-size shrimp, shelled and deveined
Salt and freshly ground black pepper to taste
⅛ teaspoon hot red pepper flakes
½ teaspoon paprika
3 tablespoons olive oil
1 tablespoon chopped fresh tarragon leaves, or 1 teaspoon dried tarragon
2 tablespoons fresh lemon juice
4 tablespoons chopped scallions
¾ cup fine fresh bread crumbs
4 tablespoons unsalted butter, melted
Lemon wedges

1. Put the scallops and shrimp into a mixing bowl with all the remaining ingredients, *except* the bread crumbs, melted butter, and lemon wedges. Blend well and refrigerate, covered, for 1 hour.

2. Arrange the scallops and shrimp alternately on 6 skewers. On a flat surface, roll the skewered ingredients in the bread crumbs to coat them lightly. Place the skewers on a baking sheet 6 or more inches from the heat source. Broil about 5 minutes and turn, cooking about another 5 minutes. Brush frequently with the melted butter. Serve hot with lemon wedges.

YIELD: 6 SERVINGS.

Broiled Scallops with Sweet Peppers and Capers

2 pounds sea or bay scallops
Salt and freshly ground black pepper
2 tablespoons olive oil
4 tablespoons unsalted butter
¾ cup finely chopped sweet green pepper
¾ cup finely chopped sweet red pepper
1 teaspoon finely chopped garlic
¼ cup drained capers
½ cup fresh bread crumbs
¼ cup dry white wine

1. Preheat the broiler to high (500 degrees).
2. Sprinkle the scallops with salt and pepper.
3. Heat the olive oil in a large skillet and sauté the scallops over high heat, stirring, for 2 minutes if they are bay scallops or 3 minutes if they are sea scallops. Transfer the scallops to a baking dish large enough to hold them in one layer. Set aside.
4. In the same skillet, melt 2 tablespoons of the butter. Add the green and red peppers, garlic, and salt and pepper to taste and cook, stirring, for 2 minutes, or until the peppers are wilted.
5. Stir in the capers, bread crumbs, and wine. Cook and stir until the bread crumbs are lightly browned. Spoon the mixture over the scallops.
6. Dot the scallops with the remaining butter and place the dish under the broiler. Broil for about 4 minutes.

YIELD: 6 SERVINGS.

Stuffed Flounder with Crab Meat

This recipe also works well with small gray sole.

1½ cups lump crab meat, shell and cartilage removed
1 large egg
½ cup finely chopped scallions
2 tablespoons Dijon mustard
4 tablespoons fine fresh bread crumbs
4 tablespoons chopped fresh parsley leaves
Salt and freshly ground black pepper
12 flounder fillets, each roughly the same size (about 2 pounds
  total weight)
6 tablespoons unsalted butter
2 tablespoons chopped shallots
¾ cup dry white wine

1. Preheat the broiler to high (500 degrees).
2. In a mixing bowl, combine the crab, egg, scallions, mustard, bread crumbs, parsley, and salt and pepper to taste. Blend well. Place equal amounts of the stuffing on six of the fillets, directly in the center. Smooth the filling over each fillet, leaving a small margin all around. Season the other six fillets with salt and pepper. Arrange them, skin side down, over the filling. Press lightly.
3. Use 3 tablespoons of the butter to coat the bottom of a baking dish large enough to hold the fillets in one layer. Arrange the stuffed fillets in it. Sprinkle the chopped shallots around the fish.
4. Melt the remaining butter in a small saucepan and brush it over the fillets. Pour the wine around the fillets.
5. Place the baking dish on the top of the stove and bring the wine to a boil; let it simmer for 15 seconds. Place the dish under the hot broiler about 7 to 8 inches from the heat source. Broil for 8 to 10 minutes. Remove the fish to serving plates and pour over them the melted butter accumulated in the baking dish.

YIELD: 6 SERVINGS.

Quick-Broiled Sole Fillets

This recipe also works well with flounder, small fillets of fluke, porgy, red snapper, and mackerel.

6 tablespoons unsalted butter, melted
1 teaspoon paprika
1 tablespoon fresh lemon juice
1 tablespoon vegetable oil
6 lemon sole fillets (up to ½ pound each)
Salt and freshly ground black pepper
¾ cup fresh bread crumbs
Lemon wedges

1. Preheat the broiler to high (500 degrees).
2. In a small mixing bowl, blend the butter, paprika, and lemon juice.
3. Select a baking dish just large enough to hold the fish fillets in one layer. Oil the bottom of the dish. Arrange the fillets, skin side down, in it. Sprinkle with salt and pepper and brush the butter mixture over the fillets. Sprinkle the bread crumbs over them evenly. Place the pan about 3 to 4 inches from the heat source and broil until the fillets are golden brown. Cooking time may vary, from 5 to 10 minutes, depending on the thickness of the fish. Serve with lemon wedges and a sauce of your choice, Maître d'Hôtel Butter (page 265), for example.

YIELD: 6 SERVINGS.

Broiled Cod with Grapefruit

This recipe also works well with red snapper, tilefish, sea trout, and striped bass.

3 skinless cod fillets (about 3 pounds total weight)
2 teaspoons dried coriander
¾ cup fresh grapefruit juice
Salt and freshly ground black pepper to taste
3 grapefruits
3 tablespoons olive oil
8 tablespoons Maître d'Hôtel Butter (page 265)

1. Cut the fillets crosswise into 6 portions. Arrange the pieces close together in a baking dish.
2. Blend the coriander, grapefruit juice, and salt and pepper in a bowl. Pour this mixture over the fish and marinate for 30 minutes.
3. Peel the grapefruits, cutting away all the fibrous sections under the skin. Cut the grapefruit flesh into neat sections, slicing between the fibrous white skin. Set aside.
4. Preheat the broiler to high (500 degrees).
5. Drain the fillets; then rub some olive oil on both sides of the fillets and arrange them in a baking dish. Sprinkle with salt and pepper and place under the broiler, about 3 inches from the heat source. Leave the door slightly ajar and broil for 5 minutes, or until the fish is done. Transfer the fish to warm serving plates and arrange the grapefruit sections around the fillets. Slice the rolled Maître d'Hôtel Butter into 6 disks about ¼ inch thick. Place a disk of butter over each fillet and serve immediately.

YIELD: 6 SERVINGS.

Cod played a major economic and culinary role in the early days of New England. The English explorer and adventurer Bartholomew Gosnold, who sailed south from Nova Scotia along the coast in 1602, was so impressed by the abundance of cod that he named the curved arm of land off the latter-day Boston coast "Cape Cod."

Some of the earliest fortunes accumulated in Massachusetts derived from a thriving fishing industry based on cod, hence the term "codfish aristocracy." In recognition of the fish's immeasurable importance to the economy of the new state of Massachusetts, the House of Representatives voted in 1784 to hang a wooden carving of a cod in its grand assembly room. It remains there today.

Grilled Salmon with Fennel Butter

This recipe also works well with mako shark, tilefish, and red snapper.

2½ pounds salmon fillets, cut into 6 pieces
Salt and freshly ground black pepper
2 tablespoons olive oil
1 head fennel (about ¾ pound)
⅓ cup water
8 tablespoons unsalted butter at room temperature
Dash of Tabasco sauce
⅛ teaspoon freshly grated nutmeg

1. Preheat the broiler to high (500 degrees).

2. Sprinkle the fillets with salt and pepper and rub them with the olive oil. Set aside.

3. Trim the fennel, leaving only the white bulb at the bottom. Cut the bulb into ¼-inch cubes. There should be about 1½ cups. Put the fennel pieces into a saucepan, cover with the water, and add 1 tablespoon of the butter. Bring to a boil and cook for 5 minutes.

4. Pour the fennel mixture into a blender or a food processor. Add the remaining butter and blend to a very fine purée. You should have about 1¼ cups. Pour the mixture into a saucepan and bring to a boil. Season with salt, pepper, Tabasco sauce, and nutmeg. Simmer for 3 minutes.

5. Meanwhile, arrange the fish fillets on a flat tray and place it under the broiler about 4 inches from the heat source. Cook for about 3 minutes; then turn the fillets and cook for another 3 minutes.

6. Transfer the fish to warm plates and spoon some hot fennel butter over each. Serve immediately.

YIELD: 6 SERVINGS.

Mako sharks are among the most popular game fish on the Atlantic Coast, along with blue sharks. The mako's flesh is deep pink and its flavor comparable to swordfish: Many contend it is actually superior. Cook it as you would swordfish. Grilled or barbecued, mako shark with a ginger vinaigrette is a particular favorite. The flesh is very lean, so even a minute's overcooking will dry it out.

Broiled Bluefish with Capers and Onions

This recipe also works well with small fillets of mackerel.

6 boneless bluefish fillets with skin (about ⅓ pound each)
Salt and freshly ground black pepper
5 tablespoons olive oil
2 teaspoons chopped fresh rosemary leaves
2 cups onion cut into ¼-inch cubes
1 teaspoon finely chopped garlic
½ cup drained capers
2 tablespoons white vinegar
4 tablespoons chopped fresh parsley leaves

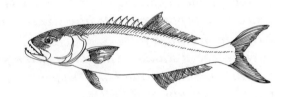

1. Preheat the broiler to high (500 degrees).
2. Put the bluefish fillets on a flat dish and sprinkle them with salt and pepper, 3 tablespoons of the olive oil, and the rosemary. Set aside.
3. Heat the remaining oil in a saucepan over high heat and sauté the onion until it is wilted. Add the garlic and salt and pepper and cook, stirring occasionally, until the onion is soft and golden. Stir in the capers and cook for 2 minutes. Sprinkle the vinegar over the onion, stir well, and remove the pan from the heat.
4. Put the bluefish fillets skin side up under the broiler and cook for about 3 minutes. Carefully flip the fillets and cook for another 4 minutes, or until the fish is cooked through.
5. Transfer the fillets to warm serving plates and spoon equal portions of the onion—caper sauce over them. Sprinkle with parsley and serve immediately.

YIELD: 6 SERVINGS.

The largest bluefish ever caught with a rod and reel weighed 31 pounds, 2 ounces. It was snagged in the Hatteras (S.C.) Inlet on January 30, 1972, by James M. Hussey.

Grilled Monkfish Brochettes with Orange–Butter Sauce

This recipe also works well with large shrimp or sea scallops. Adjust the cooking time accordingly.

2¼ *pounds skinless monkfish fillets, cut into 1- by 2-inch pieces (about 3 dozen)*
1 sweet yellow pepper, cut into bite-size squares
1 sweet red pepper, cut into bite-size squares
2 cups fresh orange juice
½ *cup chopped scallions (including green part)*
Salt and freshly ground black pepper
6 tablespoons unsalted butter
2 small ripe tomatoes, peeled, seeded, and diced (about ¾ *cup)*
2 tablespoons vegetable oil
2 tablespoons chopped fresh coriander leaves

1. Place 6 pieces of monkfish on each skewer, alternating with pieces of red and yellow peppers. Continue until all the fish and peppers are used. Set aside.

2. In a saucepan, combine the orange juice, scallions, and salt and pepper to taste. Reduce by half over the grill or on the top of the stove. Add the butter, tomatoes, and salt and pepper to taste. Mix well. When the butter has melted, set the sauce aside in a warm spot while you cook the brochettes.

3. Brush the brochettes with the oil and place them over the grill. Cook until done, about 15 minutes, turning occasionally. Place the brochettes on serving plates. Pour the sauce over them and garnish with the coriander.

YIELD: 6 SERVINGS.

The so-called Canadian Fish Rule, an all-inclusive guideline for determining cooking times for fish, is, in our opinion, a good starting point but not necessarily a fool-proof rule. It calls for measuring a whole fish (or fillet) at the thickest point and that it be cooked, no matter how, for precisely 10 minutes per inch.

We have found that this can lead to slight overcooking in some cases. We believe it is safer to calculate 8 to 9 minutes per inch and then check for doneness. You can always put the fish back for further cooking. If you are sautéing, broiling, or grilling, watch for little moisture drops coming to the surface. That is an indication it is sufficiently cooked. If poaching fillets, remove them from the water when the flesh flakes when pricked with a fork.

Whole fish is the easiest to check. Pull on the dorsal fin bone (see

Broiled Swordfish with Ginger Sauce

*illustration on page 6).
If it comes out easily, the
fish is done; if not, it
needs more cooking.*

This recipe also works with mako shark, fresh tuna, halibut, or any kind of thick, meaty fillets.

1 swordfish steak, about 1 inch thick (1½ to 2 pounds)
Salt and freshly ground black pepper
2 tablespoons unsalted butter, melted
1 tablespoon Dijon mustard
1 tablespoon crushed yellow mustard seeds
2 tablespoons mayonnaise
Lemon wedges
Monique Picot's Ginger Sauce (page 248)

1. Preheat the broiler to high (500 degrees).
2. Sprinkle the swordfish with salt and pepper on both sides and then brush with the melted butter. Combine the mustard, mustard seeds, and mayonnaise in a small bowl. Blend well. Brush the steak on both sides with the mustard mixture.
3. Place the swordfish on a broiler tray about 4 to 5 inches from the heat source. Broil for about 3 to 4 minutes, or until browned. Gently turn the fish. Broil on the other for about 4 to 5 minutes, or until done. Do not overcook. Serve with lemon wedges and the ginger sauce.

YIELD: 4 TO 6 SERVINGS.

The feisty swordfish, which can grow to well over 1,500 pounds, is found in temperate and tropical seas throughout the world. It is usually harpooned or snagged in large tuna nets by commercial fishermen. The price of this meaty delicacy has soared in recent years to more than $8 a pound, prompting consumers to turn to a similar-tasting species called mako shark.

Broiled Swordfish Steak
with Thyme

This recipe also works well with mako shark and salmon steak.

2 swordfish steaks, each about 1½ inches thick (about 2½
pounds total weight)
Salt and freshly ground black pepper
2 tablespoons corn or vegetable oil
Juice of 1 lemon
3 thyme sprigs, chopped, or ½ teaspoon dried thyme
Melted lemon butter or Fresh Ginger Vinaigrette (page 255)

1. One hour before cooking, sprinkle the swordfish steaks on all sides with salt and pepper and brush with a mixture of the oil, lemon juice, and thyme. Cover with plastic wrap and refrigerate.

2. When ready to cook, preheat the broiler to high (500 degrees).

3. Brush a broiler rack with oil and place the swordfish steaks on it. Put the rack under the broiler about 2 to 3 inches from the heat source. Leave the door partly open. Broil the fish for 5 to 7 minutes; carefully turn it on the other side and continue broiling for about 3 minutes, or until done. Transfer to a warm plate and serve with melted butter flavored with some fresh lemon juice or Fresh Ginger Vinaigrette.

YIELD: 6 SERVINGS.

The largest swordfish ever caught with a rod and reel weighed 1,182 pounds. L. Marron reeled it in near Iquique, Chile, on May 7, 1953.

Broiled Tuna Provençal Style

This recipe works equally well with salmon.

4 tuna or salmon steaks, each about 1 inch thick, a total of
  about 2 pounds
Salt to taste if desired
Freshly ground black pepper
1 tablespoon grated fresh ginger root
1 tablespoon fresh lemon juice
1 tablespoon olive oil
Sauce Provençale (page 263)

1. Preheat broiler to high, or preheat an outdoor grill.
2. Put the tuna on a plate and sprinkle both sides with salt and pepper. Rub ginger on both sides and sprinkle evenly with lemon juice and oil. Cover closely with aluminum foil and let stand until ready to broil.
3. If broiling, arrange the steaks on a rack and place under the broiler about 6 inches from the heat source. Broil 5 minutes with the door partly open. Turn the steaks. Continue broiling, leaving the door open, about 5 minutes.
4. If grilling, put the steaks on the hot grill and cover. Let cook 5 minutes. Turn the fish, cover the grill, and continue cooking about 5 minutes. Serve with Sauce Provençale on the side.

YIELD: 4 SERVINGS.

Baking

Baked Shrimp with Herb Stuffing

1¾ pounds medium-size shrimp, shelled and deveined (about
   24)
1¼ cups coarse fresh bread crumbs
4 tablespoons unsalted butter
1 cup finely chopped scallions
2 teaspoons finely chopped garlic
½ cup chopped sweet green pepper
½ cup chopped celery
2 hard-boiled eggs, coarsely chopped
1 teaspoon paprika
1 teaspoon chopped fresh thyme leaves, or ½ teaspoon dried
   thyme
4 tablespoons chopped fresh parsley or basil leaves
Salt and freshly ground black pepper to taste
3 tablespoons olive oil

   1. Preheat the oven to 500 degrees.
   2. Butterfly the shrimp by splitting them lengthwise partly
through the middle.
   3. Spread the bread crumbs over the bottom of a flat pan and
place the pan in the oven until the crumbs turn golden brown.
Stir occasionally. Set aside.
   4. Melt the butter in a saucepan and add the scallions, garlic,
green pepper, and celery. Cook, stirring, until the vegetables are

wilted but still firm. Add the chopped eggs, bread crumbs, paprika, thyme, parsley, and salt and pepper. Blend.

5. Lay the shrimp on a flat surface, split side up. Spoon an equal amount of the stuffing into the crevice of each. Press the stuffing down and smooth it over.

6. Lightly oil a baking sheet or pan large enough to hold the shrimp in one layer. Arrange the shrimp in the pan. Brush the tops lightly with the olive oil. Bake for 6 to 8 minutes.

YIELD: 4 SERVINGS.

James Nassikas' Shrimp with Hot Chili

2 pounds medium-size shrimp, shelled and deveined
1 lemon
12 tablespoons unsalted butter
¼ cup Worcestershire sauce
Salt and freshly ground black pepper to taste
1½ teaspoons dried rosemary
1 teaspoon hot chili paste (available at Oriental markets)
2 tablespoons fresh lemon juice
½ teaspoon Tabasco sauce
2 tablespoons chopped fresh parsley leaves

1. Preheat the oven to 450 degrees.
2. Arrange the shrimp in one layer in a baking dish.
3. Remove and discard the peel of the lemon and cut the pulp into ⅛-inch-thick slices. Remove and discard the seeds. Arrange the lemon slices around the shrimp.
4. Melt the butter in a saucepan and add the Worcestershire sauce, salt and pepper, rosemary, chili paste, lemon juice, and Tabasco sauce. Mix well.
5. Pour the mixture evenly over the shrimp and bake for about 10 minutes. Garnish with the parsley and serve.

YIELD: 6 SERVINGS.

Shrimp and Noodles Gratinéed

This recipe also works well with sea scallops and crab meat.

3 tablespoons unsalted butter
3 tablespoons all-purpose flour
1 cup Shrimp Broth (page 243) or bottled clam juice
½ cup milk
½ cup light cream
1 large egg yolk
Salt and freshly ground black pepper to taste
⅛ teaspoon freshly grated nutmeg
½ pound medium egg noodles
1 cup drained chopped Italian canned tomatoes
1¾ pounds shrimp, cooked, shelled, and deveined (page 15)
4 tablespoons freshly grated Gruyère or Parmesan cheese

1. Melt 2 tablespoons of the butter in a saucepan and add the flour. Stir with a wire whisk until blended and smooth. Add the shrimp broth, stirring; then stir in the milk. Simmer, stirring occasionally, for about 5 minutes. Add the cream, egg yolk, salt and pepper, and nutmeg. Whisk well. Remove from the heat.

2. Cook the noodles in lightly salted boiling water for about 7 minutes, or until *al dente*. Preheat the broiler to high (500 degrees).

3. Put the tomatoes and the remaining butter in a saucepan and cook briefly to warm thoroughly. When the noodles are done, drain well and put them into a baking dish measuring about 13 by 8 by 2 inches. Spoon the warm tomato mixture over the noodles.

4. Scatter the shrimp over the tomatoes. Spoon the sauce over everything and sprinkle with the cheese. Run under the broiler to brown the top.

YIELD: 4 TO 6 SERVINGS.

Seafood Quiche

PASTRY

1½ cups sifted all-purpose flour
Pinch of salt
8 tablespoons unsalted butter
1 large egg yolk
2 or 3 tablespoons ice water

FILLING

4 tablespoons finely chopped shallots
2 tablespoons unsalted butter
2 tablespoons cream sherry
2 tablespoons finely chopped fresh dill or parsley leaves
1½ cups cooked shrimp, lobster, crab meat, or mussels or any
   combination
3 large eggs
1 cup heavy cream
½ cup milk
Freshly grated nutmeg to taste
Salt and freshly ground white pepper to taste
½ cup grated Swiss or Gruyère cheese

1. Put all the ingredients for the pastry, *except* the water, in the bowl of a food processor and blend for 5 seconds (or mix by hand with a large whisk). Add the water and blend just until the pastry pulls away from the sides of the bowl and begins to form a ball.

2. Flour a flat surface. Using a rolling pin, roll out the dough into a circle about 13 inches in diameter and ¼ inch thick. Pick up the dough by rolling it onto the pin and then unroll it over a tart or quiche pan (preferably made of black steel). Work the dough into the pan with your fingers, crimping it against the walls to make the sides of the quiche thicker than the bottom. Refrigerate the pastry-lined pan for 10 to 15 minutes to relax the dough.

3. Preheat the oven to 375 degrees.

4. Line the shell with wax paper and weight it down with aluminum pellets or dried beans. Bake for 10 minutes. Remove the paper and beans and bake again for about 5 minutes. Remove the shell from the oven and let it cool on a wire rack.

5. Meanwhile, make the filling. Sauté the chopped shallots in the butter over medium-high heat. Cook briefly, do not allow them to brown; then add the sherry, dill, and seafood. Cook, stirring, for about 2 minutes. Remove from the heat.

6. In a mixing bowl, beat together the eggs, cream, milk, nutmeg, salt and pepper, and ¼ cup of the grated cheese. Combine this with the fish mixture.

7. Pour the mixture into the partially baked pastry shell and sprinkle with the remaining cheese. Bake for about 35 minutes, or until golden brown and firm.

YIELD: 6 TO 8 SERVINGS.

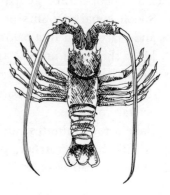

Curried Maryland Crab Meat

8 tablespoons unsalted butter at room temperature
1 teaspoon finely chopped garlic
½ cup chopped scallions
1 teaspoon Oriental Curry Powder (page 266)
1 tablespoon Dijon mustard
1 teaspoon Worcestershire sauce
¼ cup dry sherry
1 cup heavy cream
4 tablespoons chopped fresh parsley leaves
4 hard-boiled eggs, finely chopped
1 pound lump crab meat, shell and cartilage removed
Salt and freshly ground black pepper
¾ cup fresh bread crumbs
4 tablespoons freshly grated Parmesan cheese

1. Preheat the oven to 425 degrees.
2. Melt 2 tablespoons of the butter in a saucepan over medium-low heat. Add the garlic, scallions, and curry powder. Cook and stir over low heat for 2 minutes.
3. Pour the warm curry powder mixture into a bowl and add the mustard, 4 tablespoons of the butter, and Worcestershire sauce; blend well. Add the sherry and cream. Blend well with a whisk. Fold in the parsley, chopped eggs, and crab meat. Add the salt and pepper. Stir gently so as not to break up the crab.
4. Spoon equal amounts of the crab mixture into 6 scallop shells and place them in a baking dish.
5. Melt the remaining 2 tablespoons of butter in another saucepan and add the bread crumbs and Parmesan cheese. Stir until the crumbs are well coated. Sprinkle this mixture evenly over the crab mixture.
6. Bake for 15 minutes, or until the surface is bubbling and browned. To brown further, place the scallop shells under the broiler for about 30 seconds.

YIELD: 6 SERVINGS.

Crab Meat Impérial

4 tablespoons unsalted butter
4 tablespoons finely chopped shallots or scallions
¼ cup finely chopped sweet green pepper
2 tablespoons all-purpose flour
Salt and freshly ground white pepper to taste
1 cup milk or half-and-half
4 tablespoons dry sherry
Dash of Tabasco sauce
1 large egg
¼ cup heavy cream
1 pound lump crab meat, shell and cartilage removed
2 tablespoons finely chopped fresh parsley leaves
½ cup finely chopped sweet red pepper or pimientos
½ teaspoon grated orange rind
1 cup fresh bread crumbs
½ teaspoon paprika
2 tablespoons unsalted butter, melted

1. Preheat the oven to 425 degrees.

2. Melt the 4 tablespoons of butter in a saucepan over medium heat and add the shallots and green pepper. Cook briefly, stirring. Add the flour and stir; then add the salt and pepper and milk. Whisk well while bringing to a boil. Simmer for about 5 minutes. Remove from the heat and stir in the sherry and Tabasco sauce.

3. Beat the egg in a mixing bowl and gradually add the cream. Add this to the shallot and pepper mix. Then fold in the crab meat, parsley, red pepper, and orange rind. Do not overmix.

4. Spoon this combination into 6 well-buttered ramekins or scallop shells. Smooth the top; then sprinkle with the bread crumbs, paprika, and the 2 tablespoons of melted butter. Bake for 15 to 20 minutes, or until the bread crumbs are slightly browned.

YIELD: 6 SERVINGS.

Baked Lobster with Basil Stuffing

4 live lobsters (about 1½ pounds each)
1½ cups fine fresh bread crumbs
¼ cup finely chopped shallots
¼ cup finely chopped onion
½ teaspoon minced garlic
7 tablespoons unsalted butter
*¼ cup finely chopped fresh basil leaves, or 2 tablespoons dried
    basil*
Salt and freshly ground black pepper to taste
2 tablespoons corn or vegetable oil
*Beurre Blanc with Herbs and Pernod (page 244) or melted
    butter*

1. Preheat the oven to 450 degrees.

2. To kill the lobsters, insert the tip of a large knife between the eyes (see page 17). Twist off the claws and set them aside. Split the lobster in half lengthwise. Discard the small, tough sac near the eyes of each lobster. Remove the coral and livers and place them in a mixing bowl.

3. Arrange the lobster halves, split side up, in one layer in a large baking dish. Arrange the claws in another baking dish.

4. In a bowl, mix the bread crumbs with the coral and livers. Stir in the shallots, onion, and garlic. Add 6 tablespoons of the butter, basil, and salt and pepper. Blend the mixture thoroughly with your fingers.

5. Stuff the cavities of each lobster with equal portions of the mixture.

6. Drizzle oil over the exposed meat surfaces as well as the crumbs in the cavities.

7. Place the lobsters on the center shelf of the oven. Put the pan with the claws underneath and bake for about 15 minutes. Serve with the white butter sauce or just melted butter.

YIELD: 4 SERVINGS.

Scallops with Leeks and Herbs in Foil Pouches

8 tablespoons unsalted butter at room temperature
1 tablespoon chopped fresh thyme leaves, or 1½ tablespoons dried thyme
Salt and freshly ground black pepper
2 leeks, cleaned and cut into julienne strips about 1 inch long
2 carrots, peeled and cut into julienne strips about 1 inch long
1 pound bay scallops
3 tablespoons chopped fresh basil leaves
1 lemon, cut into quarters

1. Preheat the oven to 450 degrees.

2. Cut the butter into six pats and place them in a mixing bowl. Add the thyme and salt and pepper and mash the butter until the seasonings are well combined. Set aside.

3. In a pot of boiling salted water, blanch the leeks for about 3 minutes, or until they are cooked but not too soft. Remove from the water with a slotted spoon, drain well, and set aside. Blanch the carrot strips in the same water until they reach the same consistency. Drain and set aside.

4. Place a strip of aluminum foil about 12 inches long on a counter. Lay equal amounts of carrots and leeks in the center. Place a fourth of the scallops over them. Sprinkle some basil over the scallops; then sprinkle generously with salt and pepper. Squeeze some lemon juice over each mound. Place a few more strands of leeks and carrots over the scallops. Repeat to make four portions. Put about ¾ tablespoon of the herb butter on top of each.

5. Fold up the edges of the aluminum foil so they meet at the center lengthwise. Make an airtight seam along the length of the foil; then fold the edges several times to create a seal. Leave some space inside the foil for air expansion.

6. Place the packages on a baking sheet and bake for 15

minutes. Present each diner with a packet, along with rice or buttered noodles.

YIELD: 4 SERVINGS.

Oysters Casino

5 slices bacon
2 cups or more of kosher salt or rock salt
¾ cup unsalted butter, softened
½ cup finely chopped shallots
⅓ cup finely chopped sweet green pepper
2 tablespoons finely chopped sweet red pepper
⅓ cup finely chopped fresh parsley leaves
2 tablespoons fine fresh bread crumbs
2 tablespoons fresh lemon juice
Salt and freshly ground black pepper to taste
24 oysters on the half shell

1. Preheat the oven to 450 degrees.
2. Cut the bacon into 24 equal-size pieces. Put the bacon pieces in a frying pan and cook briefly on both sides over medium-high heat. They should be only partially cooked. Drain them on paper towels.
3. Place a layer of salt on the bottom of a baking dish that is large enough to hold all the oysters. The salt should be deep enough so that the oysters are stable when placed upon it.
4. Combine and blend well the butter, shallots, green and red peppers, parsley, bread crumbs, lemon juice, and salt and pepper. Spoon equal portions of the mixture over the oysters and top each one with a bacon square. Bake until the oysters are heated through and the bacon is browned, about 6 minutes. Serve as an appetizer.

YIELD: 4 TO 6 SERVINGS.

Baked Oysters with Leeks

10 *tablespoons unsalted butter*
3 *leeks, cleaned, trimmed, and cut very finely (You should*
   have about 2½ cups.)
Salt and freshly ground black pepper to taste
¾ *cup heavy cream*
⅓ *cup finely chopped shallots*
¼ *cup white wine vinegar*
24 *oysters in the shell*
Parsley sprigs for garnish

1. Preheat the oven to 500 degrees.
2. Melt 2 tablespoons of the butter in a saucepan over medium heat. Add the leeks and salt and pepper, and simmer while
stirring for about 5 minutes. Add ½ cup of the cream and
simmer for 5 minutes more, stirring occasionally. Set aside.
3. In another saucepan, combine the shallots, vinegar, and 2
tablespoons of the butter. Cook over high heat until most of the
liquid has evaporated. Add the remaining cream and bring to a
boil. Stir with a wire whisk. Add the remaining butter and stir
vigorously with the whisk. Season with salt and pepper and
remove from the heat.
4. Place the oysters on a baking dish and bake them for 5 to
7 minutes. (This is done to heat them gently and to make them
easier to open.)
5. Remove the oysters from the oven and use an oyster knife
to loosen the top shells. Open each oyster and discard the top
shell.
6. Cut away the oyster meat, reserving the liquor in the
shells, and put the meat in a bowl. Spoon an equal amount of
the leek mixture into each of the reserved shells. Top each serving
with an oyster. Spoon some butter sauce over the oysters and
serve immediately garnished with the parsley.

YIELD: 4 TO 6 SERVINGS.

Baked Oysters with
Macadamia Nut Butter

36 oysters on the half shell
1 cup unsalted butter, softened
2 tablespoons finely chopped garlic
2 tablespoons finely chopped shallots
½ cup finely chopped macadamia nuts
2 tablespoons fine fresh bread crumbs
Salt and freshly ground black pepper to taste

1. Preheat the oven to 450 degrees.
2. Place the oysters in a shallow pan.
3. In a blender or food processor (or by hand in a bowl), combine the butter, garlic, shallots, macadamia nuts, bread crumbs, and salt and pepper and blend well.
4. Spoon equal amounts of the butter mixture over the oysters and place them in the oven. Bake for about 6 minutes, or until the tops are lightly browned. Serve very hot.

YIELD: 6 SERVINGS.

Oysters on the Half Shell
with Spinach and Pernod

1 10-ounce package fresh spinach, or 1 pound loose fresh
spinach, cleaned
36 oysters
½ cup dry white wine
4 tablespoons finely chopped shallots
1 cup heavy cream
¼ teaspoon freshly grated nutmeg
Pinch of cayenne pepper

2 tablespoons Pernod or Ricard
Salt and freshly ground white pepper to taste

1. Boil lightly salted water in a pot and add the spinach. Cook while stirring for about 1 minute. Drain and cool. Squeeze the spinach to extract any excess moisture. Chop the spinach coarsely with a knife.

2. Preheat the oven to 450 degrees.

3. Open the oysters and discard the empty upper shell. Be careful not to spill the liquid in the bottom shell.

4. Arrange the oysters close together in a large baking dish. Sprinkle with equal amounts of white wine. Place in the oven and bake for 5 minutes, no longer; they should barely be heated through.

5. Meanwhile, put the shallots in a saucepan.

6. Remove the oysters from the oven and carefully pour all the liquid in the shells over the shallots. Place the oysters in the turned-off oven to keep them warm. Cook the shallots with the oyster liquid for about 30 seconds over high heat and then add the cream. Reduce the liquid to ¾ cup while stirring.

7. Add the spinach, nutmeg, cayenne, Pernod, and salt and pepper to the saucepan. Bring to a boil, lower the heat to a simmer, and cook, stirring, for about 1 minute. Spoon the mixture over the warm oysters and serve immediately.

YIELD: 6 SERVINGS.

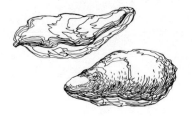

Baked Clams with Pine Nut Butter

36 *cherrystone or littleneck clams*
½ *pound unsalted butter at room temperature*
4 *tablespoons finely chopped shallots*
1 *tablespoon finely chopped garlic*
½ *cup finely chopped fresh parsley leaves*
½ *cup pine nuts, toasted*
1½ *cups fresh bread crumbs*
Salt to taste
½ *teaspoon freshly ground black pepper*
½ *cup freshly grated Gruyère or Parmesan cheese*

1. Preheat the oven to 450 degrees.
2. Open the clams and remove the meat, reserving ½ cup of the liquid. Put aside the bottom shell of each clam for stuffing. Chop the clam meat coarsely.
3. In a mixing bowl, combine the clams and the reserved liquid with the butter, shallots, garlic, parsley, pine nuts, bread crumbs, and salt and pepper. Blend well.
4. Stuff the reserved clam shells with the mixture. Smooth over the tops with a spatula and sprinkle with the grated cheese. Arrange the clams in a shallow baking dish. Bake for 15 minutes, or until lightly browned.

YIELD: 6 SERVINGS.

The major varieties of clams available in American markets are the SOFT SHELL, *which has a black spout or neck protruding from one end; the* LITTLENECK, *which, oddly, does not have a visible neck: It is smaller and more rounded; the* CHERRYSTONE, *which is similar in shape to the littleneck and suitable for eating raw on the half shell; and the* RAZOR CLAM, *which looks somewhat like an old-fashioned straight razor. In New England, the term "quahog" refers to oversized littlenecks that are used in chowders.*

Baked Cherrystone Clams with Spicy Butter

36 cherrystone clams
¼ cup chopped shallots
1 tablespoon chopped garlic
½ pound unsalted butter at room temperature
4 drops of Tabasco sauce
1 tablespoon Worcestershire sauce
1 tablespoon Dijon mustard
2 tablespoons chopped fresh parsley leaves
2 tablespoons chopped fresh basil leaves
Salt and freshly ground black pepper to taste

1. Preheat the broiler to high (500 degrees).
2. Open the clams and arrange them on the half shells neatly on a baking sheet.
3. In a mixing bowl, combine the remaining ingredients. Spoon the mixture over the clams evenly. Place them under the broiler for about a minute. Serve immediately with French bread.

YIELD: 6 TO 8 SERVINGS.

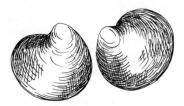

Baked Littleneck Clams
with Garlic Butter

This recipe would also work well with fresh scallops baked in their shells.

36 littleneck clams
2 tablespoons coarsely chopped garlic
3 tablespoons coarsely chopped shallots
½ cup pecan halves
½ cup coarsely chopped fresh parsley leaves
¼ cup dry white wine
½ pound unsalted butter at room temperature
¼ cup fresh bread crumbs
Salt and freshly ground black pepper to taste
4 tablespoons freshly grated Parmesan cheese

1. Preheat the oven to 500 degrees.

2. Rinse and drain the clams to remove any sand. Open them and discard the empty top shell.

3. In the bowl of a food processor or blender, combine the garlic, shallots, pecans, parsley, white wine, butter, bread crumbs, salt and pepper, and half of the Parmesan cheese. Blend for about 45 seconds, or until smooth.

4. Spoon about a teaspoon of this mixture on top of each clam and arrange them on a baking dish. Sprinkle with the remaining Parmesan cheese and bake for about 6 minutes, or until the clams are thoroughly hot but not overcooked. Serve piping hot.

YIELD: 4 TO 6 SERVINGS.

Baked Clams with Spaghetti

1½ cups Tomato and Anchovy Sauce (page 250)
Salt to taste
36 medium-size littleneck clams
1 pound spaghetti
Freshly grated Parmesan cheese, optional

1. Prepare the tomato sauce 30 minutes before the clams are to be cooked.

2. Preheat the oven to 500 degrees. Bring a large, deep pot of salted water to a rolling boil.

3. Meanwhile, open the clams with a clam knife and reserve the liquid. There should be about 1 cup of liquid and about ¾ cup of clams. Chop the clams coarsely.

4. Drop the spaghetti into the boiling water and cook for exactly 5 minutes. Drain immediately.

5. Transfer the spaghetti to a large baking dish and add the simmering sauce and the clam juice. Sprinkle the chopped clams on top. Cover the dish with aluminum foil and seal tightly. Bake for 10 minutes.

6. Remove the foil and transfer the contents of the dish to a hot platter or soup bowls and serve. Serve with grated Parmesan cheese, if desired.

YIELD: 6 SERVINGS.

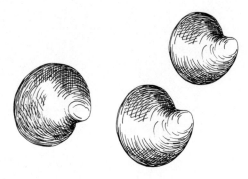

Stuffed Mussels

This recipe also works well with littleneck and cherrystone clams.

2 pounds medium-to-large mussels, well scrubbed and cleaned
½ pound unsalted butter at room temperature
½ cup fine fresh bread crumbs
2 tablespoons finely chopped garlic
¼ cup finely chopped fresh parsley leaves
½ cup grated Gruyère cheese
¼ teaspoon freshly ground black pepper
Salt to taste

1. Preheat the oven to 450 degrees.
2. Open the mussels with a paring knife and discard the empty top shells. (Another way to open them is by steaming them for about a minute, or just until the shells separate; do not let them cook.) Place the halves containing the meat in a baking dish.
3. Combine all the remaining ingredients in a mixing bowl and blend well. Put about 1 teaspoon of stuffing over each mussel (see Note) and bake for 6 to 8 minutes, or until lightly browned.

YIELD: 4 SERVINGS.

Note: The stuffed mussels may be kept in the refrigerator for an hour or two before baking.

Baked Sea Bass with Eggplant and Ginger

This recipe also works well with red snapper, fluke, and sole.

6 sea bass fillets with skin (about 6 ounces each)
Salt and freshly ground black pepper to taste
1 medium-size eggplant (about 1 pound)
5 tablespoons olive oil
1½ cups thinly sliced onion
2 teaspoons chopped garlic
1 cup peeled, seeded, and cubed tomatoes
1 tablespoon grated fresh gingerroot
¾ cup dry white wine
¼ cup coarsely chopped fresh coriander or parsley leaves
4 tablespoons fresh lime juice

1. Preheat the oven to 450 degrees.
2. Sprinkle the fillets with salt and pepper and set them aside.
3. Peel the eggplant and cut it into ¼-inch cubes.
4. Heat 4 tablespoons of the olive oil in a saucepan over medium-high heat. Add the onion and garlic and cook, stirring, until the onion is wilted but not brown.
5. Add the eggplant and stir. Add the tomatoes and cook, stirring, for about 2 minutes. Add the ginger and stir. Add the wine and salt and black pepper to taste. Stir in the coriander and bring everything to a boil. Simmer for 10 minutes.
6. Pour the remaining tablespoon of oil into a baking dish large enough to hold the fillets in one layer. Arrange the fillets in the dish, skin side down. Spoon some sauce over them, sprinkle with lime juice, and bake for about 10 minutes.

YIELD: 6 SERVINGS.

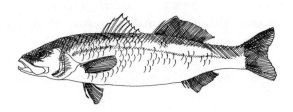

Sea Bass Baked with Wine and Herbs

This recipe also works with red snapper and sea trout.

1 whole, or 2 medium-size, sea bass (about 4 to 5 pounds
total weight), cleaned and scaled, head and tail left on
12 tablespoons (1½ sticks) unsalted butter
Salt and freshly ground black pepper to taste
¼ pound white mushrooms, coarsely chopped
4 tablespoons coarsely chopped shallots
½ teaspoon coarsely chopped garlic
3 thyme sprigs, or ½ teaspoon dried thyme
1 bay leaf
2 parsley sprigs
1 cup dry white wine
½ cup Fish Broth (page 241) or bottled clam juice
Juice of 1 lemon

1. Preheat the oven to 425 degrees.
2. Rinse the bass in cold water; then pat dry with paper towels.
3. Rub a baking dish large enough to hold the fish with 2 tablespoons of the butter. Place the fish in the center. Sprinkle it generously with salt and pepper; then add the mushrooms, shallots, garlic, thyme, bay leaf, parsley sprigs, white wine, fish broth, and lemon juice. Place four slices of butter on top and cover the dish loosely with aluminum foil.
4. Bake for 45 minutes to 1 hour, depending on the size of the fish. The fish is done when the dorsal fin (in the middle of the backbone) comes out easily and cleanly when tugged.
5. Transfer the fish to a warm serving platter. Pour the liquid from the baking dish into a small saucepan. Bring to a boil and swirl in the remaining butter but do not let it boil. Remove the thyme and parsley sprigs and bay leaf.
6. Gently remove the skin from the top of the fish (use a sharp

The term "bass" is a broad umbrella that covers many unrelated fish. Striped bass and sea bass are the most common in restaurants and fish markets: Both have thick and mild-flavored white flesh. French menus often refer to bass as loup, *which is a particular species found in European waters. Rarely will you get real* loup *in the United States, but rather domestic bass of one sort or another.*

paring knife and your fingers to do this); then ladle the sauce over the bass.

YIELD: 6 SERVINGS.

Bluefish Escabeche

6 small skinless bluefish fillets (about 2½ pounds total
   weight)
Salt and freshly ground black pepper
⅓ cup olive oil
2 cups thinly sliced onion
1 cup thinly sliced sweet green pepper
1 cup thinly sliced sweet red pepper
1 cup thinly sliced yellow pepper, optional
1 tablespoon finely chopped garlic
2 cups diced ripe tomatoes
½ cup white wine vinegar
½ cup dry white wine
1 bay leaf
1 teaspoon dried thyme, or 4 thyme sprigs
¼ teaspoon hot red pepper flakes
½ cup chopped fresh basil or parsley leaves

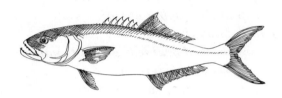

1. Preheat the oven to 425 degrees.

2. Arrange the fillets in one layer in a baking dish and season well with salt and pepper.

3. Heat the oil in a saucepan over medium-high heat and add the onion; cook briefly without browning. Add the peppers and garlic. Cook over high heat, stirring, for about 5 minutes. Add all the remaining ingredients and adjust the seasonings if necessary. Cook over high heat for about 10 minutes, stirring occasionally.

4. Pour the mixture over the fish fillets. Bake for 15 minutes. Let cool. Cover with plastic wrap and refrigerate. Serve cold, garnished with additional chopped fresh basil or parsley leaves.

YIELD: 6 SERVINGS.

Bluefish are among the sea world's most aggressive predators. They eat just about anything that moves. Their digestive enzymes are extremely potent, and they will spoil a landed bluefish within hours unless it is gutted and iced. For this reason inspect bluefish in the market closely; choose only the very freshest and cook the fish the same day you purchase it.

Baked Fresh Cod Greek Style

This recipe also works well with halibut, red snapper, and sea trout.

4 tablespoons olive oil
2 skinless cod fillets (about 2½ pounds total weight)
Salt and freshly ground black pepper
3 sweet green peppers, cored, seeded, and cut into thin strips
    (about 4 cups)
24 pitted Greek-style black olives
¾ cup finely chopped onion
1 tablespoon chopped garlic
2 cups chopped drained canned tomatoes
1 teaspoon dried oregano
½ cup Fish Broth (page 241) or bottled clam juice
¼ teaspoon hot red pepper flakes
1 bay leaf
½ pound feta cheese, crumbled

1. Preheat the oven to 450 degrees.
2. Coat the bottom of a baking pan with 1 tablespoon of the olive oil. Arrange the fish fillets close together in the pan. Sprinkle the fish with salt and pepper.
3. Heat the remaining 3 tablespoons of oil in a frying pan and add the green peppers, olives, onion, and garlic and cook over high heat until wilted. Add the tomatoes, oregano, fish broth, hot pepper flakes, and bay leaf. Stir and cook for about 5 minutes.
4. Spoon the sauce over the fillets. Sprinkle the feta cheese over the sauce and bake for about 15 minutes.

YIELD: 6 SERVINGS.

SCROD: *This ubiquitous and much confused term means a young cod.*

Fresh Cod with Noodles and Mornay Sauce

2 pounds skinless cod fillets
½ cup milk
1 small onion, sliced
1 celery stalk
4 parsley sprigs
3 whole cloves
⅛ teaspoon cayenne pepper
Salt to taste
6 whole black peppercorns
⅓ pound fine noodles
2 tablespoons unsalted butter
Freshly ground white pepper to taste
3 cups Mornay Sauce (page 247)
1 cup canned Italian crushed tomatoes
6 tablespoons freshly grated Parmesan or Gruyère cheese

1. Preheat the oven to 500 degrees.

2. Put the cod fillets in a saucepan in one layer and add water to cover. Add the milk, onion, celery, parsley sprigs, cloves, cayenne pepper, salt, and black peppercorns. Bring to a boil and simmer for 1 minute. Remove from the heat and drain.

3. Cook the noodles until *al dente*. Drain and add the butter. Toss until coated with butter and sprinkle with salt and white pepper.

4. In a saucepan, blend the Mornay Sauce with the tomatoes. Bring to a boil while stirring.

5. Pour the noodles into a baking or gratin dish and arrange the fish on top. Spoon the cheese sauce over the fish and sprinkle with the cheese. Bake for 20 minutes, or until the fish is browned on top.

YIELD: 6 SERVINGS.

Salted Codfish à la Valenciana

2 pounds boneless and skinless salted cod
4 tablespoons olive oil
3 cups thinly sliced onions (about 1 pound)
2 tablespoons finely chopped garlic
2 cups seeded and chopped sweet green pepper
2 cups seeded and chopped sweet red pepper
1 teaspoon saffron threads
1 bay leaf
1 teaspoon dried thyme
Salt and freshly ground black pepper, optional
¼ teaspoon hot red pepper flakes
3 cups canned whole Italian tomatoes, drained and crushed
3 potatoes (about 1½ pounds), peeled and cut into ¼-inch-thick slices
½ cup chopped fresh parsley leaves

1. Cut the fish fillets into 3-inch squares. Place the pieces in a bowl and add cold water to cover. Let them stand for at least 24 hours, changing the water frequently.

2. Drain and arrange the cod pieces in a saucepan large enough to hold the cod in one layer. Add cold water to cover and bring to a boil. Simmer for about 2 minutes; then remove the pan from the heat and set it aside.

3. Drain the cod, reserving 1 cup of the liquid. Preheat the oven to 375 degrees.

4. In a heavy saucepan, heat the oil over medium-high heat. Add the onions, garlic, green and red peppers, saffron, bay leaf, thyme, salt and black pepper, and hot pepper flakes. Simmer, stirring, for about 5 minutes. Add the crushed tomatoes and simmer for 5 minutes more.

5. In a large, deep baking dish, arrange the cod pieces in one layer. Lay the potato slices over the cod. Spoon the sauce over everything and cover with aluminum foil. Bake for 1 hour. Serve very hot, garnished with the chopped parsley.

YIELD: 8 TO 10 SERVINGS.

Fillets of Flounder with Parsley and Mustard Sauce

This recipe involves a special technique for cooking fish fillets. The fish is first doused with white wine, seasoned, and placed in a very hot oven. This causes it to steam and bake at the same time while absorbing the seasonings and wine. It works with virtually all fish fillets, but the cooking time will vary according to the thickness of the fillets.

1 tablespoon unsalted butter
Salt and freshly ground black pepper
1½ pounds skinless flounder fillets
⅓ cup plus 1 tablespoon dry white wine
2 cups loosely packed parsley leaves
2 tablespoons finely chopped shallots
⅓ cup heavy cream
2 teaspoons Dijon mustard

1. Preheat the oven to high (500 degrees).

2. Grease a flat baking sheet with the butter. Place all the fillets on the sheet. Dust them with salt and pepper. Brush the fillets with the 1 tablespoon of white wine.

3. Bring lightly salted water to a boil in a saucepan (enough to cover the parsley). Add the parsley and blanch for 1 minute, no longer. Drain thoroughly and cool it off under cold running water. Place the parsley in a clean piece of cheesecloth and squeeze well to extract the excess liquid.

4. Bake the fish for about 5 minutes or less, or until it is cooked. Meanwhile, place the remaining wine in a saucepan and add the shallots. Cook, stirring, until the wine has nearly evaporated. Add the parsley, cream, and mustard, as well as any liquid that may have accumulated on the baking sheet. Season with salt and pepper to taste, bring to a boil, and transfer the sauce to a blender. Blend well.

5. Reheat the sauce if necessary. Transfer the fish to warm serving plates and pour some sauce over each.

YIELD: 4 SERVINGS.

Monkfish Fillets with Mustard Sauce

This recipe also works well with fillets of tilefish and large fluke.

3 tablespoons olive oil
6 skinless monkfish fillets (about 2¼ pounds total weight)
Salt and freshly ground black pepper
4 tablespoons Dijon mustard
⅓ cup finely chopped shallots
1 tablespoon minced garlic
¾ pound small fresh mushrooms
2 teaspoons dry white wine
4 tablespoons unsalted butter
4 tablespoons chopped fresh parsley leaves

1. Preheat the oven to 450 degrees.

2. Select a steel baking pan large enough to hold the monkfish fillets in one layer without crowding. Pour the olive oil over the bottom. Turn the fillets in the oil to coat them well. Sprinkle the fillets with salt and pepper and brush them with mustard. Scatter the shallots, garlic, and mushrooms around the fillets.

3. Place the baking pan over the stovetop burners and heat until the oil begins to sizzle. Add the wine and bring to a simmer.

4. Transfer the pan to the oven and bake for 15 minutes. After 15 minutes, baste the fillets and return them to the oven. Continue baking about 5 minutes more. Remove the fish to warm serving dishes; swirl the butter into the baking pan until it melts. Pour this over the fillets. Sprinkle with parsley and serve immediately.

YIELD: 6 SERVINGS.

Pompano Fillets
in Red Wine Sauce

This recipe also works well with red snapper, salmon, and striped bass.

8 tablespoons unsalted butter
3 tablespoons finely chopped shallots
6 pompano fillets (about 2 pounds total weight)
Salt and freshly ground black pepper
1 cup dry red wine (A young Côtes du Rhone or a lighter style
  California cabernet sauvignon would be appropriate.)
½ cup Fish Broth (page 241) or bottled clam juice
1 tablespoon arrowroot

1. Preheat the oven to 425 degrees.

2. Rub the bottom of a baking pan large enough to hold the fillets in one layer with 2 tablespoons of the butter and sprinkle the shallots over it. Arrange the fillets over the bottom and dust them with salt and pepper.

3. Pour the wine and fish broth over the fish and dot with 3 tablespoons of the butter. Place the baking pan on top of the stove over high heat and bring the liquid to a boil. Transfer to the oven and bake for 5 to 7 minutes, depending on the thickness of the fillets.

4. Remove the fillets to a warm platter and keep them warm. Pour the cooking liquid and shallots into a saucepan. Reduce over high heat to about 1¼ cups.

5. Combine 1 tablespoon of the butter with the arrowroot. Blend well with your fingers. Stir this into the wine and broth mixture. Bring to a boil, stirring. Strain the liquid through a fine sieve and return to the saucepan. Swirl in the remaining butter. Taste the sauce for seasoning. Pour the sauce evenly over the fillets and serve immediately.

YIELD: 6 SERVINGS.

Baked Porgies with Lemon and Capers

This recipe also works well with red snapper and sea bass.

6 whole porgies (about 1½ pounds each), cleaned
Salt and freshly ground black pepper
18 lemon slices, each slice cut in half
¼ cup olive oil
½ cup fresh bread crumbs
½ cup finely chopped scallions
1 tablespoon chopped garlic
4 tablespoons finely chopped fresh parsley leaves
4 thyme sprigs, or 1 teaspoon dried thyme
2 bay leaves, broken in half
6 tablespoons drained capers
1 cup dry white wine
4 tablespoons unsalted butter

1. Preheat the oven to 450 degrees.
2. Place the fish on a flat surface and make 6 diagonal slits on the top of each all the way to the bone. Sprinkle the fish with salt and pepper. Insert one piece of lemon in each slit, rind side up.
3. Pour 4 tablespoons of the olive oil into a baking dish large enough to hold the fish. Sprinkle the oil with salt and pepper. Arrange the fish in the pan, lemon slice up.
4. Combine the bread crumbs, scallions, garlic, parsley, thyme, bay leaves, and capers. Sprinkle this mixture evenly around and over the fish. Pour the wine around the fish. Dot the fish with small pieces of the butter. Bake for 25 to 30 minutes. Remove the bay leaves and serve immediately.

YIELD: 6 SERVINGS.

Salmon with Fresh Dill en Papillote

This recipe also works well with striped bass, sea bass, and red snapper.

2 pounds skinless salmon fillets, cut into 6 equal-size pieces
5 carrots, peeled and trimmed (about 1 pound total weight)
¾ pound large mushrooms
6 tablespoons unsalted butter
Juice of 1 lemon
¾ cup scallions cut into 2-inch lengths
Salt and freshly ground black pepper
4 tablespoons chopped fresh dill leaves
6 tablespoons chopped shallots
6 tablespoons dry white wine

1. Preheat the oven to high (500 degrees).
2. Holding a knife at a 45-degree angle, cut each salmon piece into 4 thin slices.
3. Spread a large sheet of heavy duty aluminum foil or parchment paper on a flat surface. Invert a 12-inch-round cake pan on the foil and trace around the pan with a sharp knife to make a 12-inch circle. Repeat this until you have six of them.
4. Cut the carrots crosswise into 1-inch lengths. Cut each piece lengthwise into matchstick strips.
5. Cut off and discard the stem of each mushroom and cut the cap crosswise into thin slices.
6. Heat 2 tablespoons of the butter in a frying pan over medium-high heat. Add the mushrooms and lemon juice. Cook, shaking the pan and stirring, for 1 minute. Add the carrots, scallions, and salt; then cover and cook for 7 to 8 minutes. Sprinkle the dill on top and stir well. Cover and set aside.
7. Melt the remaining butter in a small saucepan. Place the foil rounds on a flat surface and brush them with the melted butter. Spoon equal portions of the carrot mixture on each disk

The United States Food and Drug Administration defines caviar as the eggs of sturgeon. Most of the top-grade caviar imported to the United States comes from the Soviet Union. (The supply of Iranian caviar has been sharply curtailed in recent years for political and other reasons.)

Caviar is named for the three major types of sturgeon that produce it. Those from the beluga sturgeon are the most prized, and expensive; the eggs are relatively large and grayish. Osietr (spellings vary in different countries) eggs are slightly smaller than beluga and are golden-brown in color; sevruga eggs, nearly black, are the smallest.

The term "lumpfish caviar" refers to the tiny black eggs of a North Atlantic fish that clings to rocks, resembling a "lump." Golden or red caviar comes from American salmon.

slightly below the center, leaving a margin large enough to fold over.

8. Lay a slice of salmon over each mound of vegetables. Sprinkle each serving with a tablespoon of shallots, a tablespoon of wine, and salt and pepper.

9. Fold the foil to completely enclose the contents, while leaving some room for expansion. Crimp the seal as tightly as possible. Arrange the packages on a baking sheet and bake for 8 minutes.

YIELD: 6 SERVINGS.

Leeks Stuffed with Salmon Mousse

4 large leeks
1½ pounds skinless salmon fillets
Salt and freshly ground white pepper
1 large egg
1 cup heavy cream
2 tablespoons unsalted butter plus butter for greasing the pan
6 tablespoons Fish Broth (page 241) or bottled clam juice
Beurre Blanc (page 243)
6 teaspoons salmon or whitefish caviar, optional

1. Preheat the oven to 400 degrees.

2. Remove the leaves from the leeks one at a time without breaking them (illustration 1). To do this you may need to make a shallow incision across the base of each leaf. Be careful not to cut the leaves below. You should have between 14 and 20. Rinse well.

3. Bring water to a boil in a large kettle. Salt the water lightly and add the leaves. Blanch for 2 minutes. Drain and plunge the leaves into cold water. Drain again and pat dry with paper towels. Set aside.

4. Cut the salmon fillets into 1-inch cubes. Place them in the bowl of a food processor or blender. Add the salt and pepper and egg. Turn on the machine and add the cream gradually.

5. Lay each leek leaf on a flat surface and trim the ends, retaining as much of the white as possible (illustration 2). Each strip should be about 9 inches long. Place about 3 tablespoons of the salmon mousse on each leek (on the white end). Roll each strip to enclose the mousse (illustration 3). Secure with a toothpick (illustration 4).

6. Butter a metal or flameproof baking dish measuring about 14 by 8 inches. Arrange the leek rolls in the bottom. Pour the fish broth over them. Dab the remaining butter over the rolls.

7. Place the baking dish on top of the stove and bring the broth to a boil. Cover tightly with aluminum foil. Bake for 15 minutes. Serve with Beurre Blanc. Garnish each serving with 1 teaspoon of salmon or whitefish caviar.

YIELD: 6 SERVINGS.

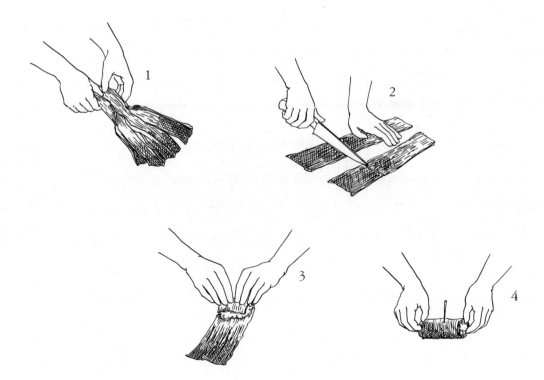

Baked Red Snapper with Goat Cheese and Ouzo

This recipe also works well with sea scallops and shrimp.

6 tablespoons olive oil
1/2 cup chopped onion
1 tablespoon finely chopped garlic
1/2 cup dry white wine
3 cups canned crushed tomatoes
4 tablespoons drained capers
1/2 teaspoon dried rosemary
1/2 teaspoon dried oregano
1/4 teaspoon hot red pepper flakes
Salt and freshly ground black pepper to taste
1/2 cup chopped fresh parsley leaves
3 red snapper fillets with skin (about 1 pound each), cut into
*   6 portions*
2 tablespoons ouzo or other anise-flavored liqueur, such as
*   Pernod or Ricard*
1/3 pound goat cheese, preferably a mild goat cheese, such as
*   Montrachet, crumbled*

1. Heat 3 tablespoons of the olive oil in a saucepan. Add the onion and garlic and cook briefly while stirring. Do not let the garlic brown. Add the wine, tomatoes, capers, rosemary, oregano, hot pepper flakes, salt and pepper, and parsley. Bring to a boil; then lower the heat and simmer for about 10 minutes. Preheat the oven to 450 degrees.

2. Pour the remaining olive oil into a baking dish large enough to hold the fish in one layer. Arrange the fish skin side down. Sprinkle liberally with salt and pepper. Pour the tomato sauce over them.

3. Bake for about 15 minutes. Sprinkle the ouzo over them and then the crumbled goat cheese. Bake for 5 minutes longer.

YIELD: 6 SERVINGS.

Lemon Sole Stuffed with Shrimp and Coriander

This recipe also works well with fluke, flounder, and gray sole.

1/3 pound fresh shrimp, shelled and deveined
4 tablespoons unsalted butter
1/3 cup chopped onion
1/2 cup diced celery
1 teaspoon chopped garlic
Salt and freshly ground black pepper to taste
2 tablespoons finely grated fresh gingerroot
1/2 cup fresh fine bread crumbs
1/2 cup finely chopped fresh coriander leaves
8 skinless sole fillets (about 1 1/2 pounds total weight)
1/2 cup dry white wine
1/4 cup heavy cream

1. Preheat the oven to 425 degrees.

2. Chop the shrimp finely with a knife. There should be about 3/4 cup.

3. In a saucepan, melt 2 tablespoons of the butter. Add the onion, celery, and garlic and cook briefly. Add the salt and pepper and then stir in the ginger. Remove the pan from the heat. Scrape the mixture into a bowl; add the shrimp, bread crumbs, half the coriander, and salt and pepper. Blend well.

4. Rub a tablespoon of butter over a metal baking pan large enough to hold four fillets. Sprinkle the dish with salt and pepper; then arrange over it four fillets, skin side down. Spoon equal amounts of the filling all along the center of each fillet.

5. Cover each portion with another fillet, skin side down. Sprinkle with salt and pepper. Brush the top of fillets with the remaining butter; then pour the wine over them.

6. Bake for 15 minutes. Pour the cream over the fish and return them to the oven for 10 minutes. Baste occasionally.

YIELD: 4 SERVINGS.

Baked Fillet of Sole with Mustard

This recipe also works well with flounder and fluke.

6 tablespoons unsalted butter
Salt and freshly ground black pepper to taste
4 tablespoons finely chopped shallots
6 sole fillets (about 2 pounds total weight)
¾ cup dry white wine
1 tablespoon Dijon mustard
6 tablespoons bread crumbs
¼ cup finely chopped fresh parsley leaves
Lemon wedges

1. Preheat the oven to high (500 degrees).

2. Spread 2 tablespoons of the butter over a baking dish large enough to hold the fish in one layer. Sprinkle the dish with the salt and pepper and the shallots.

3. Arrange the fish pieces over the shallots and sprinkle them with ½ cup of the wine. Blend the remaining wine with the mustard and brush the fillets with the mixture. Sprinkle the bread crumbs evenly over the fillets and dot with the remaining butter. Bake for 5 minutes.

4. Turn the broiler to high and run the fillets under it until they are lightly browned. Sprinkle the parsley over the fish and serve immediately with the lemon wedges.

YIELD: 6 SERVINGS.

Many North Atlantic flatfish are called sole even though they may belong to the flounder or dab family. Sole continues to be among the most popular American fish, and for the home cook it is important to know the difference between the three major varieties of fish sold under this name.

LEMON SOLE: *Actually a flounder, these North Atlantic fish usually weigh more than 3 pounds when caught. The fillets are off-white in color.*

GRAY SOLE: *The slightly smaller fillets of "gray sole" that command such a premium price because of their clear white color and delicate texture are in reality witch flounders.*

DOVER SOLE: *This is the only authentic sole commonly sold in the U.S. The name derives from the English port of Dover, a major landing point for them. These thick, meaty fish used to be sold here frozen, but*

Fillets of Sole Stuffed with Clams

improved jet transportation now makes them available fresh in restaurants and markets, though at a premium price.

This recipe also works well with fillets of flounder and small fluke.

8 tablespoons unsalted butter
½ cup finely diced shallots or scallions
½ cup finely chopped sweet green pepper
½ cup finely chopped celery
½ cup dry white wine
½ cup chopped drained shucked clams
1¾ cups coarse fresh bread crumbs
1 large egg, lightly beaten
⅓ cup finely chopped fresh parsley leaves
½ teaspoon chopped fresh thyme leaves, or ¼ teaspoon dried thyme
12 skinless lemon sole fillets, roughly equal in size (about 2¼ pounds total weight)
Salt and freshly ground black pepper to taste
Juice of 1 lemon
½ teaspoon paprika

1. Preheat the oven to 450 degrees.

2. In a small skillet over medium heat, melt 2 tablespoons of the butter. Add the shallots, green pepper, and celery. Cook, stirring, just to wilt them and evaporate the liquid. Add the wine and cook for 2 minutes. Add the clams. Remove from the heat and add the bread crumbs, egg, parsley, thyme, and salt and pepper. Blend well.

3. Place each sole fillet, skin side down, on a flat surface. Spoon an equal portion of the stuffing onto each and smooth it over neatly. Cover each fillet with a second fillet, skin side up (illustration 1).

4. Spread 2 tablespoons of the butter over a baking dish and sprinkle it with salt and pepper. Place the fillets in the baking dish. Melt the remaining butter in a small saucepan and add the

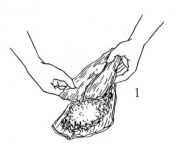

1

lemon juice. Spoon the lemon butter over the fillets. Dust them with paprika. Brush the fillets again with the butter in the pan to blend the paprika evenly. Bake for about 10 minutes.

YIELD: 6 SERVINGS.

Baked Fillets of Sole
in Lettuce Pouches

This recipe also works well with flounder, small fillets of red snapper, and porgy fillets.

3 heads Boston lettuce
12 skinless sole or flounder fillets
Salt and freshly ground black pepper
6 tablespoons unsalted butter
3 tablespoons finely chopped shallots
¾ cup dry white wine
1 cup heavy cream
Juice of 1 lemon, optional

1. Preheat the oven to 450 degrees.
2. Remove the lettuce leaves from the core and drop them into a large kettle of lightly salted boiling water. Simmer for about 1 minute. Drain the leaves in a colander and then rinse under cold water until they are thoroughly chilled. Drain well and spread out the leaves on a flat surface.
3. Sprinkle the fillets with salt and pepper. Fold the fillets into thirds to make flat packets. Layer pairs of lettuce leaves, one on top of the other. Place each fish packet on the double-thick lettuce leaves. Cover with another lettuce leaf and fold the bottom edges up and over to enclose the fish.

4. Rub 2 tablespoons of the butter over a baking dish that is large enough to hold the fish packets in one layer. Sprinkle the bottom of the dish with shallots. Arrange the lettuce-wrapped fish in the dish and pour the wine over them. Sprinkle with more salt and pepper. Put the dish on top of the stove and bring the wine to a boil. Then bake for about 8 minutes.

5. Pour the liquid from the baking dish into a saucepan (keep the fish packets warm in the turned-off oven). Bring to a boil and reduce over high heat to about ½ cup. Add the cream and season with salt and pepper. Bring to a boil. As more liquid accumulates around the fish packages, pour it, too, into the saucepan. Cook the sauce over high heat, stirring often, until it reduces to 1¼ cups. Swirl in the remaining butter and the lemon juice. Strain the sauce and reheat it. Transfer the fish packages to warm plates and spoon the sauce over them.

YIELD: 6 SERVINGS.

Tuna and Cheese Soufflé

There is something about canned tuna packed in oil that makes the texture of this dish exceedingly good. Of course, cooked fresh tuna is appropriate as well.

4 tablespoons plus 3 tablespoons unsalted butter for greasing the soufflé dishes
4 tablespoons freshly grated Parmesan cheese
¼ cup chopped shallots
2 7-ounce cans tuna fish packed in oil, well drained and flaked
2 cups milk
¼ cup all-purpose flour
2 teaspoons cornstarch
1 tablespoon cold water
1 tablespoon Dijon mustard
½ teaspoon Worcestershire sauce
¼ teaspoon Tabasco sauce
Salt and freshly ground black pepper to taste
8 large eggs, separated
¼ pound Gruyère cheese, cut into tiny cubes

1. Preheat the oven to 425 degrees. Use 3 tablespoons of the butter to grease six 1¼-cup soufflé dishes. Sprinkle the insides with the grated Parmesan cheese.

2. Melt 1 tablespoon of the butter in a saucepan and add the shallots. Cook, stirring, until they are wilted. Add the flaked tuna to the pan and cook, stirring, until warm.

3. In a saucepan, bring the milk almost to a simmer; then remove from the heat.

4. Melt 3 tablespoons of the butter over medium heat and add the flour. Stir with a wire whisk until blended and smooth. Add the milk, stirring with the whisk. Continue stirring until thick and smooth.

5. Blend the cornstarch and water in a small bowl and add it to the saucepan. Add the mustard, Worcestershire and Tabasco sauces, and salt and pepper and stir.

6. Add the egg yolks, while beating briskly with a whisk. Cook for 5 seconds—no longer. Remove the pan from the heat while continuing to beat. Scrape the mixture into a large mixing bowl and set aside briefly to cool slightly.

7. In another bowl, beat the egg whites just until stiff. Do not overbeat.

8. Fold the cheese cubes into the sauce mixture. Add about one third of the beaten egg whites and fold rapidly with a rubber spatula until they are well distributed. Add the remaining whites and do the same.

9. Fill the soufflé dishes with the mixture and smooth the tops with a spatula. Run your thumb around the inside perimeter of the dishes, making an indentation about ¼ inch deep. Arrange the dishes on a baking sheet and bake for 12 to 15 minutes, or until the soufflés are well puffed and golden brown on top. Serve immediately.

YIELD: 6 SERVINGS.

Note: The soufflé can also be baked in a single 2-quart soufflé dish. Bake for about 25 minutes, or until well puffed and golden brown on top.

Stuffed Shad with Sauce Américaine

1 pair shad roe
2 hard-boiled eggs, coarsely chopped
⅓ cup chopped fresh parsley leaves
1 cup fresh bread crumbs
½ cup heavy cream
1 large egg
Salt and freshly ground white pepper to taste
¼ teaspoon freshly grated nutmeg
2 boneless shad fillets (about 1¾ pounds total weight)
4 tablespoons unsalted butter
4 tablespoons chopped shallots
½ cup dry white wine
1 cup Sauce Américaine (page 246)

1. Preheat the oven to 400 degrees.

2. Place the shad roe on a flat surface. Chop it coarsely and combine with the chopped hard-boiled eggs. Add the parsley and mix well.

3. Put the bread crumbs in a mixing bowl and add the cream, the egg, salt and pepper, nutmeg, and roe mixture. Blend well.

4. Lay the shad fillets on a flat surface, skin side down. Open the fillets. You will see that there are two flaps on each fillet (illustration 1). Sprinkle with salt and pepper. Spread half of the bread crumb filling over the center of the fillet. Smooth it over. Lay two pieces of roe over the filling (illustration 2).

Spread the rest of the filling over the roe. Lay the second fillet over that, skin side up (illustration 3). To make them fit better, lay the wide end of the top fillet over the narrow end of the bottom fillet. The flaps of the top fillet should overlap (illustration 4). Tie the whole assembly neatly in four places (illustration 5).

5. Spread 2 tablespoons of the butter over a baking dish large enough to hold the fillets. Sprinkle the chopped shallots over it

and place the fish in the dish (illustration 6). Dust well with salt and pepper. Dot the fish with the remaining butter and pour in the white wine. Cover with aluminum foil.

6. Bake for about 40 minutes, or until the internal temperature reaches 140 degrees on a meat thermometer.

7. Transfer the fillets to a warm serving platter. Remove the string from the fish. Using your fingers, pull off and discard the exposed skin on top. Serve with the Sauce Américaine.

YIELD: 6 TO 8 SERVINGS.

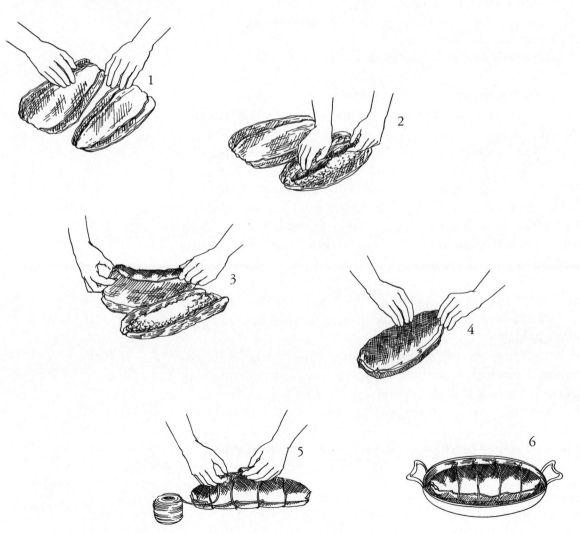

Baked Shad Roe in Caper and Dill Sauce

4 pairs shad roe (about ½ pound each)
8 tablespoons unsalted butter
4 tablespoons finely chopped shallots
4 tablespoons dry white wine
2 cups zucchini cut into 1½- by ¼-inch julienne strips
Salt and freshly ground black pepper
½ cup Fish Broth (page 241) or bottled clam juice
4 tablespoons drained capers
2 tablespoons finely chopped fresh dill leaves

1. Preheat the oven to 450 degrees.

2. Prick holes all over the shad roe with a fork or trussing needle.

3. Rub 4 tablespoons of the butter over the bottom of a baking dish large enough to hold the roe in one layer. Sprinkle the shallots over the bottom of the dish and arrange the roe over them. Sprinkle all with the wine. Distribute the zucchini in the dish and dust with salt and pepper. Pour in the fish broth. Cover the dish with aluminum foil, seal tightly, and place on the bottom rack of the oven.

4. Bake for 10 to 15 minutes, depending on the size of the roe. After 10 minutes open the foil to check for doneness. The roe should have lost its raw look. Reseal, if necessary, and continue baking.

5. Remove the roe to warm serving dishes. Pour any accumulated cooking liquid into a saucepan and add the remaining butter, capers, and dill. Stir well. Bring to a boil and pour the hot sauce over the roe. Serve immediately.

YIELD: 4 MAIN-COURSE SERVINGS OR 8 APPETIZER SERVINGS.

Shad Roe Stuffed with Shrimp

½ pound medium-size shrimp (about 15 to 20), shelled and
   deveined
Salt and freshly ground white pepper to taste
⅛ teaspoon freshly grated nutmeg
⅛ teaspoon cayenne pepper
1½ cups heavy cream
4 tablespoons finely chopped fresh coriander or parsley leaves
2 shad fillets
1 pair shad roe
4 tablespoons unsalted butter
4 tablespoons finely chopped shallots
¾ cup dry white wine
Juice of ½ lemon
White Wine Sauce (page 245)

1. Preheat the oven to 425 degrees.

2. Put the shrimp in the bowl of a food processor. Add the salt and pepper, nutmeg, cayenne, and ½ cup of the cream. Blend until smooth, about 45 seconds.

3. Spoon the shrimp mixture into a bowl and add the coriander. Blend well.

4. Lay one of the shad fillets on a flat surface skin side down. Cut open the two "flaps" on either side of the fillets where the bones were removed. Spoon half of the stuffing mixture down the center of one fillet. Place the roe on top of it. Cover the roe with the remaining shrimp mixture and bring the "flaps" of the fillet back up.

5. Open the flaps of the other fillet. Invert the fillet and place it over the top of the first fillet to enclose the mixture. Tie the fish together with twine in about four places.

6. Grease a baking dish with 2 tablespoons of the butter and dust it with salt and pepper. Arrange the fish in it and dot it with the remaining butter. Sprinkle the shallots around the fish. Season the fish with salt and pepper and add the white wine. Cover with aluminum foil. Bake for 35 minutes.

7. Take the dish from the oven and remove the foil. Pour the liquid that has accumulated in the dish into a saucepan. Keep the fish warm. Bring the liquid to a boil over high heat and reduce to one third. Add the remaining cream and simmer for 5 minutes. Add the lemon juice and taste for seasoning.

8. Remove the string from the stuffed fish, cut it crosswise into serving pieces, and serve hot with the White Wine Sauce.

YIELD: 6 SERVINGS.

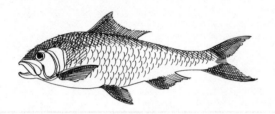

Sea Urchins in Their Own Butter

This briny and delicious appetizer comes from Gilbert Le Coze, chef of the four-star restaurant Le Bernardin in Manhattan.

20 fresh sea urchins
½ pound unsalted butter, softened
1 cup heavy cream
1 cup Fish Broth (page 241) or bottled clam juice
1 tablespoon fresh lemon juice
⅛ teaspoon cayenne pepper
Salt and freshly ground white pepper to taste

1. Preheat the oven to 450 degrees.
2. Cut a lid out of the top of each sea urchin with sharp pointed scissors by inserting the tip of the scissors into the mouth cavity of the urchin and cutting a circle in the top as if you were carving a pumpkin.
3. Discard all the liquid inside. Use a demitasse spoon to remove the dark membrane clinging to the inside and the bottom while leaving the orange coral intact. Rinse the cleaned urchins by placing them in a bowl of cold, lightly salted water. Rotate the urchins and then drain them well.
4. Remove the coral from 12 of the sea urchins and place the coral in a fine-mesh sieve. Press it through into a bowl to make a purée. Combine this with the butter, whipping with a wire whisk. Set aside.
5. In a saucepan over medium-high heat, combine the fish broth and the cream. Bring to a boil, lower the heat, and simmer for 2 minutes. Remove from the heat and use a wire whisk to mix in the butter mixture, one lump at a time. Add the lemon juice, cayenne pepper, and salt and pepper. Reserve the sauce, keeping it warm. (Do not return to a boil!)
6. Place the remaining 8 sea urchins with their coral intact on a baking sheet. Grind some white pepper inside each and heat

Sea urchins, those little round porcupines of the sea, were largely unheard of in this country just a few years ago—unless, that is, you happened to have stepped on one while bathing. Recently, though, they have been showing up on menus in seafood restaurants around the country. Called oursins *in France, these briny delicacies are found living in clusters along the Mediterranean coastline. Harvesters wearing thick gloves or using pincers pluck them from the water. About 500 species of sea urchins exist around the world, ranging in size from two to ten inches in diameter.*

The most common way of eating sea urchins is to cut a lid out of the top and scoop out the edible orange portion, which can be eaten raw with some lemon juice. The flavor is incredibly fresh and delightfully saline. Sea urchins can also enhance all sorts of sauces and

them in a 450-degree oven just until they are warm. Remove from the oven, place 2 on each warm serving plate, and pour the hot sauce evenly into each to about ¾ capacity. Serve immediately.

YIELD: 4 SERVINGS.

soups. In Japan, a popular fermented paste called uni-shiokara is made with them. Sea urchins are generally at the peak of flavor in cold months along the North American coastline.

CHAPTER 7

Pan-Frying and Sautéing

Sauteéd Shrimp with Sweet Peppers

This recipe also works well with bay or sea scallops.

4 tablespoons olive oil
¾ pound onions, peeled and thinly sliced (about 3 cups)
1 tablespoon finely chopped garlic
3 sweet red peppers, cored, seeded, and cut into ¼-inch-wide strips (about 3 cups)
2 sweet green peppers, cored, seeded, and cut into ¼-inch-wide strips (about 2 cups)
1 bay leaf
½ teaspoon dried thyme, or 3 fresh sprigs
Salt and freshly ground black pepper to taste
¼ teaspoon hot red pepper flakes
4 ripe plum tomatoes (about 1 pound), cut into small cubes
½ cup red wine vinegar
½ cup dry white wine
2 pounds large shrimp, shelled and deveined
½ cup chopped fresh basil or parsley leaves
Rice Pilaf (page 270)

1. Heat the oil in a heavy frying pan and add the onions and garlic. Cook, stirring, until the onions are wilted. Add the red and green pepper strips, bay leaf, thyme, salt and pepper, hot pepper flakes and stir; cook about 2 minutes, stirring; then add the tomatoes. Cook for 2 minutes; add the vinegar and the wine. Cover and cook for 5 minutes more.

2. Add the shrimp and stir. Cover and cook over high heat for 2 minutes, no longer. Stir in the basil and serve over Rice Pilaf.

YIELD: 6 SERVINGS.

Shrimp with Avocado and Tequila "Margarita"

1½ pounds shrimp, shelled and deveined
4 tablespoons fresh lime juice
Salt and freshly ground white pepper to taste
2 small ripe avocados
2 tablespoons unsalted butter
2 tablespoons finely chopped shallots
⅓ cup tequila
1 cup heavy cream
¼ teaspoon hot red pepper flakes
¼ cup chopped fresh coriander leaves
Rice Pilaf (page 270) or Rice Creole (page 272)

1. In a mixing bowl, combine the shrimp, 3 tablespoons of the lime juice, and salt and pepper. Let them stand for 30 minutes or longer.

2. Peel the avocados and remove the pits. Cut the flesh into ½-inch-thick slices and put them in a small bowl; add the remaining tablespoon of lime juice and mix gently to coat so the flesh does not discolor.

3. Melt the butter in a large frying pan. Add the shrimp and

the marinade and cook over high heat, stirring, for about 1 minute. Sprinkle the shallots over the shrimp and cook, stirring for about 10 seconds. Add the tequila, cream, salt and pepper, and hot pepper flakes. Mix briefly and add the avocado slices. Cook for about 1 minute.

4. Using a slotted spoon, transfer the shrimp and the avocado to hot serving plates. Bring the sauce to a full rolling boil for about 45 seconds; then add the coriander. Spoon the sauce over the shrimp and avocado. Serve with the rice.

YIELD: 6 SERVINGS.

Shrimp with Sweet Vermouth

This recipe also works well with sea scallops.

4 tablespoons unsalted butter
1½ pounds medium-size shrimp, shelled and deveined
Salt and freshly ground black pepper to taste
⅓ cup sweet vermouth (or dry vermouth, if desired)
½ cup chopped scallions
3 tablespoons red wine vinegar
⅓ cup heavy cream
2 tablespoons chopped fresh parsley leaves

1. Melt 2 tablespoons of the butter over high heat in a large frying pan. Add the shrimp and salt and pepper and cook, stirring, for 1 minute or less. The shrimp should lose their raw look. Add the vermouth and cook for 15 seconds. Drain the shrimp and reserve the cooking liquid.

2. Combine the scallions and vinegar in a separate saucepan. Add the cooking liquid from the shrimp and bring to a boil. Reduce over high heat to ¼ cup. Add the cream, return to a boil, and swirl in the remaining butter. Add the parsley and shrimp and serve immediately with rice or buttered noodles.

YIELD: 4 SERVINGS.

Mr. B's Shrimp and Ham

This recipe was given to us by Ralph and Cindy Brennan, well-known New Orleans restaurateurs. It also works well with sea or bay scallops.

1½ pounds medium-size shrimp, shelled and deveined
⅛ teaspoon paprika
Salt and freshly ground black pepper to taste
¼ teaspoon dried thyme
¼ teaspoon dried oregano
1 teaspoon finely minced garlic
1 tablespoon chopped scallions, whites only (Chop and reserve the green sections.)
1 tablespoon unsalted butter
⅛ pound smoked country ham or prosciutto, thinly sliced and cut into small cubes (In New Orleans, a spicy ham, called tasso, is used.)
2 tablespoons finely chopped shallots
¼ cup dry white wine
1 cup peeled, seeded, and cubed ripe tomatoes
1 tablespoon chopped fresh tarragon leaves
1 cup heavy cream
2 tablespoons Dijon mustard

1. In a mixing bowl, combine the shrimp, paprika, salt and pepper, thyme, oregano, garlic, and all the chopped white sections of the scallions. Blend well.

2. Melt the butter in a heavy frying pan over medium-high heat. Add the shrimp mixture, ham, and shallots. Cook, stirring, for about 2 minutes, or until the shrimp lose their pale appearance. Scoop the contents of the pan onto a warm dish.

3. Add the wine, tomatoes, and tarragon to the hot pan. Cook, stirring, for about 30 seconds. Add the cream. Season again with salt and pepper to taste. Bring to a boil and stir in the mustard. Cook, stirring, over high heat for about 2 minutes, or until the mixture thickens into a sauce.

4. Return the shrimp mixture to the pan and stir only until

they are coated with the sauce. Serve immediately garnished with the chopped scallion greens. This dish is good when served over croutons made from the Parmesan Cheese Bread on page 273.

YIELD: 4 TO 6 SERVINGS.

Indian-style Curried Shrimp

This recipe also works well with sea and bay scallops.

3 tablespoons unsalted butter
¼ cup finely chopped onion
⅓ cup finely chopped peeled apple
½ teaspoon finely minced garlic
2 or 3 tablespoons Oriental Curry Powder (page 266)
⅓ cup finely chopped banana
½ cup Fish Broth (page 241) or bottled clam juice
¼ cup crushed tomatoes
¼ cup sour cream
½ cup plain yogurt
Salt to taste
1½ pounds medium-size shrimp, shelled and deveined
Rice Creole (page 272)

1. Melt 1 tablespoon of the butter in a saucepan over medium-high heat. Add the onion, apple, and garlic and cook for about 3 minutes, stirring; then sprinkle in the curry powder. Stir and add the banana, fish broth, and tomatoes, stirring to blend well. Bring to a boil and simmer for 5 minutes. Add the sour cream, yogurt, and salt and simmer for 2 minutes.
2. Melt the remaining butter in a frying pan over high heat. Add the shrimp and cook for about 2 minutes, shaking the pan and stirring with a spatula. Add the sauce. Stir until the shrimp are coated. Bring to a boil and then remove from the heat. Serve with the rice.

YIELD: 6 SERVINGS.

Shrimp Sautéed with Pernod

This recipe also works well with sea scallops.

4 tablespoons unsalted butter
2 pounds medium-size shrimp, shelled and deveined
3 tablespoons chopped shallots or scallions
3 tablespoons Pernod or Ricard
1 cup heavy cream
Salt and freshly ground black pepper to taste
3 dashes of Tabasco sauce
¼ cup finely chopped fresh parsley leaves
Rice Creole (page 272)

1. Melt the butter in a frying pan over high heat. Add the shrimp and shallots and cook briefly, stirring, until the shrimp turn pink, about 2 minutes.

2. Add the Pernod and stir in quickly. Remove the shrimp from the pan with a slotted spoon to a warm serving dish.

3. Add the cream to the pan and reduce over high heat for about 2 minutes. Season with salt and pepper and Tabasco sauce. Return the shrimp to the pan just long enough to heat them. Transfer everything to a warm serving dish, sprinkle with parsley, and serve immediately with the rice.

YIELD: 6 SERVINGS.

Shrimp Bordelaise

This recipe also works well with either bay or sea scallops.

3 ripe tomatoes (about 1 pound total weight)
4 tablespoons unsalted butter
2 tablespoons olive oil
2 pounds medium-size shrimp, shelled and deveined
Salt and freshly ground black pepper to taste

Pernod and Ricard are trade names for two types of French anise-flavored liqueurs. In Southern France, they are cut with water as an apéritif. They are also used in cooking. Ricard is the sweeter of the two.

4 tablespoons finely chopped shallots
¼ cup fine fresh bread crumbs
¼ cup finely chopped fresh parsley leaves

1. Core and peel the tomatoes. Halve them crosswise, squeeze the halves gently to extract the seeds, and cut the tomatoes into ½-inch cubes.

2. In a frying pan large enough to hold the shrimp in one layer, heat the butter and the oil over high heat. When hot, add the shrimp, salt and pepper, and shallots and cook, stirring and shaking the pan, until the shrimp lose their raw look.

3. Sprinkle the bread crumbs evenly over the hot shrimp. Turn the heat to high and cook, stirring, for 1 minute. Stir in the tomatoes and cook for another minute. Sprinkle with parsley, stir well, and serve immediately.

YIELD: 6 SERVINGS.

Shrimp Creole

2 tablespoons unsalted butter
2 pounds shrimp, shelled and deveined
Salt and freshly ground black pepper to taste
3 cups Creole Sauce Base (page 249), heated
Rice Creole (page 272)
3 tablespoons chopped fresh parsley leaves

1. Melt the butter in a large frying pan over high heat. Add the shrimp and salt and pepper and cook, stirring, for 1 minute. Add the hot Creole Sauce and cook, stirring, for 2 minutes, or until the shrimp turn pink.

2. To serve, place ½ cup of Rice Creole in the center of each heated serving plate. Spoon the sauce around the rice and arrange 8 shrimp over the sauce. Sprinkle with chopped parsley.

YIELD: 6 SERVINGS.

Shrimp Newburgh

4 tablespoons unsalted butter
2 pounds shrimp, shelled and deveined
Salt and freshly ground white pepper to taste
1 tablespoon paprika
2 tablespoons finely chopped shallots
½ cup dry sherry
1½ cups heavy cream
2 large egg yolks
Pinch of cayenne pepper

1. Melt the butter in a large heavy saucepan. Add the shrimp, salt and pepper, paprika, and shallots; stir and add the sherry. Cook, stirring, for about 1 minute. Remove the shrimp to a skillet with a slotted spoon; cover and keep warm.

2. Over high heat, reduce the pan liquid by half and add 1 cup of the cream. Cook for about 5 minutes over medium heat.

3. In a small bowl, beat the egg yolks with the remaining ½ cup of cream and cayenne pepper. Add the mixture to the cream sauce, stirring with a whisk. Bring almost to a boil; then add the shrimp and stir. Do not boil the sauce. Serve with rice or thin noodles.

YIELD: 6 SERVINGS.

Jumbo Shrimp with Shallot–Butter Sauce

This recipe also works well with 1½ to 2 pounds of bay or sea scallops.

24 unshelled jumbo shrimp
6 tablespoons unsalted butter
Salt and freshly ground black pepper
⅓ cup finely chopped shallots
1 cup dry white wine
¾ cup heavy cream
2 tablespoons Dijon mustard
4 tablespoons finely chopped fresh parsley leaves

1. Using a sharp knife or kitchen shears, cut down the back of each shrimp lengthwise. Do not shell the shrimp. Rinse them under cold running water to remove the black thread-like intestinal track. Pat dry with paper towels and set the shrimp aside.

2. Melt 2 tablespoons of the butter in a large frying pan over high heat. Add the shrimp and salt and pepper and cook, stirring often, for about 3 minutes. Transfer the shrimp to a warm platter.

3. Add 1 tablespoon of the butter to the frying pan along with the shallots and the wine. Bring to a boil and cook over high heat until the liquid has reduced to about ½ cup. Add the cream and mustard and cook, stirring, for about 2 minutes.

4. Add the shrimp to the sauce and stir. Adjust the seasonings, sprinkle with parsley, and stir in the remaining butter. Serve immediately.

YIELD: 6 SERVINGS.

While they require a bit more work on the part of diners, shrimp cooked in the shell are always more flavorful than cooked shelled shrimp. When recipes call for shelled shrimp, save the shells and use them to make the Shrimp Broth on page 243 or sauté them with butter—the amount depends on the quantity of the shells. Strain the mixture and use this shrimp-flavored butter for basting broiled fish or in a sauce for seafood dishes.

Pan-barbecued Shrimp

This Southern recipe, although called "barbecue," is actually prepared in a hot cast-iron skillet.

16 tablespoons unsalted butter
1 tablespoon minced garlic
½ teaspoon fresh rosemary leaves, crushed
½ teaspoon dried oregano
1 teaspoon cayenne pepper
1 bay leaf, crushed
½ teaspoon freshly ground black pepper
3 to 5 thyme sprigs, or ½ teaspoon dried thyme
Salt to taste
2 pounds unshelled large shrimp, rinsed briefly in cold water
½ cup Shrimp Broth (page 243) or bottled clam juice
¼ cup dry white wine

In a large cast-iron skillet or frying pan melt 8 tablespoons of the butter over high heat. Add the remaining ingredients, *except* the remaining 8 tablespoons of butter, shrimp, shrimp broth, and wine. When the butter has melted, stir well and add the shrimp. Cook for about 3 minutes, stirring and shaking the pan. Add the remaining butter, shrimp broth, and wine. Cook, stirring and shaking the pan for 3 more minutes. Remove from the heat and serve immediately with the hot butter from the pan and crusty French bread or rice.

YIELD: 4 SERVINGS.

Crab Meat and Shrimp with Dry Vermouth

This recipe also works well with various combinations of lobster meat, scallops, crab, and shrimp. Cubed halibut is a less expensive alternative; you will need 2½ pounds.

2 tablespoons unsalted butter
1½ pounds medium-size shrimp, shelled and deveined
1 pound lump crab meat, shell and cartilage removed
Salt and freshly ground black pepper to taste
4 tablespoons chopped shallots
½ cup dry vermouth (Dry sherry would be appropriate, too.)
1 cup heavy cream
1 teaspoon Worcestershire sauce
12 fresh basil leaves
2 tablespoons chopped fresh parsley leaves

1. Melt the butter in a large frying pan. Add the shrimp and cook over high heat for 30 seconds, shaking the pan and stirring. Add the crab meat and salt and pepper and cook for another minute, stirring constantly. Use a slotted spoon to transfer the shrimp and crab to a warm serving dish.

2. Add the shallots and vermouth to the pan along with any liquid from the shrimp and crab. Cook over high heat until reduced by half.

3. Add the cream and Worcestershire sauce and reduce over high heat to 1 cup.

4. Return the shrimp and crab meat to the pan, stir well, and add the basil. Adjust the seasonings, garnish with parsley, and serve immediately.

YIELD: 6 SERVINGS.

All-American Crab Cakes

1 pound crab meat, lump style preferred, shell and cartilage
   removed
1 cup scallions, chopped
2 large hard-boiled eggs, chopped
½ cup chopped celery
1 cup crushed saltines
2 large eggs, beaten
2 teaspoons Worcestershire sauce
1 tablespoon Dijon mustard
½ teaspoon Tabasco sauce
Salt and freshly ground black pepper to taste
½ cup fresh bread crumbs
¼ cup oil

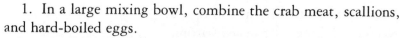

French-style Sauce Rémoulade (page 258) or Tartar Sauce
   (page 264)

1. In a large mixing bowl, combine the crab meat, scallions,
and hard-boiled eggs.

2. In another bowl, combine the celery, saltines, eggs, Worcestershire sauce, mustard, Tabasco sauce, and salt and lots of
pepper. Mix well.

3. Add the celery mixture to the crab meat and fold all the
ingredients together until well blended.

4. Divide the mixture into 12 equal parts and shape into
round cakes. Dredge them lightly in the bread crumbs.

5. Heat the oil in a 10-inch frying pan over medium-high
heat. Add the crab cakes and sauté gently for about 3 to 4
minutes on each side. Drain and serve with the Sauce Rémoulade
or Tartar Sauce.

YIELD: 6 SERVINGS.

Southern-style Crab Cakes

2 cups fine fresh bread crumbs
2 large eggs, well beaten
1 tablespoon Dijon mustard
1 teaspoon Worcestershire sauce
3 tablespoons finely chopped fresh parsley leaves
1/2 cup finely chopped scallions
1 teaspoon Old Bay Seasoning
Salt and freshly ground black pepper to taste
1 pound lump crab meat, shell and cartilage removed
4 tablespoons vegetable, peanut, or corn oil
1/2 cup Mayonnaise (page 259)
Lemon wedges

1. In a large mixing bowl, combine 1½ cups of the bread crumbs with the eggs, mustard, Worcestershire sauce, parsley, scallions, and Old Bay Seasoning. Season with salt and lots of pepper. Blend well and add the crab meat. Fold it in lightly without breaking up the lumps of crab.

2. Divide the mixture into 12 portions. Shape them in hamburger-like patties.

3. Coat each portion with the remaining bread crumbs. Refrigerate until ready to cook.

4. Heat 2 tablespoons of the oil in a nonstick frying pan over medium heat. Fry the patties, 4 or 5 at a time, for about 2 to 2½ minutes on each side, or until golden brown. Drain on paper towels and serve immediately. Use the remaining 2 tablespoons of cooking oil if necessary. Serve with the mayonnaise and lemon wedges.

YIELD: 12 CRAB CAKES; SERVES 4 TO 6.

Sautéed Soft-shell Crabs

12 cleaned soft-shell crabs (see page 17)
½ cup milk
1 cup all-purpose flour
⅛ teaspoon cayenne pepper
Salt and freshly ground black pepper to taste
4 tablespoons vegetable oil
Juice of 1 lemon
2 lemons, peeled and cut into small cubes
6 tablespoons unsalted butter
⅓ cup chopped fresh parsley leaves

1. Put the crabs in a flat dish and add the milk. Turn the crabs to coat them with the milk.

2. On a flat dish, combine the flour, cayenne pepper, and salt and black pepper. Remove each crab from the milk and dredge it in the seasoned flour. Shake to remove any excess flour.

3. Heat 2 tablespoons of the oil in a nonstick frying pan. Put 6 crabs in the pan and cook over medium heat for about 3 minutes, or until the crabs are golden brown on one side. Turn and cook until golden brown on the other side. The total cooking time is about 6 to 7 minutes depending on thickness. Transfer the crabs to a warm serving platter. Repeat the process with the other 6 crabs.

4. When all 12 have been cooked, sprinkle them with the lemon juice and lemon cubes.

5. Pour off the fat from the frying pan and wipe it clean with paper towels. Add the butter and heat it until it starts to turn brown. Pour the butter over the crabs. Serve garnished with the chopped parsley.

YIELD: 6 SERVINGS.

Lobster with Paprika–Cream Sauce

TOMATO–CREAM REDUCTION
(Make this ahead of time and set it aside until needed.)

1 large shallot, minced
1 tablespoon unsalted butter
1 cup chopped canned Italian tomatoes or fresh ripe tomatoes
  in season
½ cup heavy cream
Freshly ground white pepper to taste

LOBSTER PREPARATION

2 1½-pound lobsters
3 tablespoons unsalted butter
2 tablespoons minced shallots
1½ teaspoons paprika
1 tablespoon tomato paste
4 tablespoons Cognac
1 cup dry white wine
1½ teaspoons minced fresh tarragon leaves, or 1 tablespoon
  dried tarragon
Tomato–Cream Reduction (recipe above)
Freshly ground white pepper to taste

1. Make the Tomato–Cream Reduction: In a saucepan, sauté the shallot in the butter until the shallot is translucent. Add the tomatoes, heavy cream, and pepper. Reduce by half and set aside. Makes about ¾ cup.

2. Kill the lobsters by inserting the tip of a large knife between the eyes (see page 17). Turn the lobsters on their backs, and split lengthwise. Separate the claws so they will be easier to fit into a frying pan.

3. Melt the butter over medium-high heat in a 12- to 14-

inch high-sided frying pan. Sauté the shallots briefly and then add the paprika and tomato paste. Mix well with a wooden spoon.

4. In a small saucepan, warm the Cognac over low heat.

5. Add the lobster bodies, flesh side down, and claws to the frying pan. Cook for 1 minute; add the Cognac and ignite it with a long kitchen match. When the flames die down, add the wine and tarragon. Turn the lobsters over, baste them with the pan juices, and cover. Turn the heat to medium-low and cook for 20 minutes. Check occasionally and, if the cooking liquid evaporates, add more white wine.

6. Remove the lobsters from the pan and keep them warm. Add the Tomato–Cream Reduction to the pan, bring to a boil, and reduce the liquid by half. Add white pepper to taste; the dish should not need salt because of the salty lobster juices.

7. Pour the sauce into a blender, including any particles that cling to the bottom of the pan. Purée well at high speed. Arrange half a lobster and one claw on each serving plate. Pour the sauce over the lobster body (but not the claw).

YIELD: 4 SERVINGS.

Note: Noodles are a suitable side dish, and there should be enough sauce to pour over 4 servings.

Bay Scallops with Garlic and Fresh Tomatoes

This recipe also works well with shrimp.

1 quart bay scallops (about 1½ pounds)
Salt and freshly ground black pepper
⅓ cup virgin olive oil
⅓ cup chopped scallions
1 teaspoon finely chopped garlic
1 cup diced peeled and seeded fresh tomatoes

2 tablespoons red wine vinegar
4 tablespoons finely chopped fresh parsley leaves

1. Sprinkle the scallops with salt and pepper and set them aside.

2. Combine 2 tablespoons of the oil in a saucepan with the scallions, garlic, tomatoes, vinegar, and salt and pepper. Bring to a sizzle and simmer for 2 minutes.

3. Heat the remaining oil in another frying pan over high heat and cook the scallops, stirring, for 1 minute, or until they lose their raw look. Do not brown them. Spoon equal portions of the scallops onto warm serving plates and pour some tomato sauce over each. Sprinkle each portion with chopped parsley and serve immediately.

YIELD: 6 SERVINGS.

Sautéed Bay Scallops in Shallot Sauce

This recipe also works well with shrimp.

6 tablespoons unsalted butter
1 quart bay scallops (about 1½ pounds)
Salt and freshly ground black pepper to taste
½ cup finely chopped shallots
½ cup fine fresh bread crumbs
2 tablespoons fresh lemon juice
4 tablespoons chopped fresh parsley leaves

1. Melt 2 tablespoons of the butter in a large nonstick frying pan over high heat. Sauté the scallops, shaking the frying pan and stirring so that they cook evenly, for 3 to 4 minutes. Season with salt and pepper.

2. Meanwhile, heat the remaining butter in another frying pan over high heat. Add the shallots and bread crumbs and sauté

them, shaking the pan and stirring, until the crumbs are lightly browned.

3. When the scallops are cooked, transfer them to the pan with the bread crumbs and stir gently to blend. Add the lemon juice and parsley, cook for 30 seconds, and serve immediately.

YIELD: 6 SERVINGS.

Bay Scallops with Zucchini with Ricard

This recipe also works well with shrimp.

4 tablespoons unsalted butter
1 tablespoon olive oil
3 zucchini (about ¾ pound total weight), cut into ¾-inch cubes
Salt and freshly ground black pepper to taste
4 teaspoons finely chopped garlic
2 cups diced peeled and seeded ripe tomatoes
3 tablespoons Ricard or ouzo
2 pounds bay scallops
¼ cup chopped fresh basil or parsley leaves
Rice Creole (page 272)

1. Heat 1 tablespoon of the butter with the oil over medium high heat in a large frying pan or casserole. Add the zucchini and salt and pepper and sauté for 2 minutes. Stir in the garlic and then the tomatoes; cook for 2 minutes, stirring often. Blend in the Ricard.

2. Stir in the scallops, basil, and remaining butter. Simmer for 2 to 3 minutes. Serve immediately with the rice.

YIELD: 6 SERVINGS.

There are 400 species of scallops in the world's oceans, although fewer than 20 are harvested commercially. The principal species found in most fish markets are bay, ocean, and calico. Bay scallops, the most prized and expensive, are often misrepresented, especially in restaurants. Real bay scallops, which generally measure no more than 3 inches across the shell, must come from shallow-water bays. They are found all along the Atlantic coast and are distinguished by their buttery texture and sweet flavor.

A similar-looking, but inferior-tasting, scallop that is growing in importance is the deep-water calico. These are found in waters off the southern Atlantic coast from Florida to the Carolinas.

Sea scallops, found primarily in the chilly waters of the North Atlantic, can sometimes measure 5 inches across the shell. When freshly

Bay Scallops and Zucchini with Fresh Tomato Sauce

This recipe also works well with shrimp or sea scallops.

2 small zucchini (about ¾ pound total weight)
2 small tomatoes (about ¾ pound total weight)
2 tablespoons olive oil
Salt and freshly ground black pepper to taste
1½ pounds bay scallops
3 tablespoons unsalted butter
1 tablespoon chopped garlic
4 tablespoons finely chopped fresh Italian parsley leaves

caught and properly prepared, they are tender and delicious. In Europe, the delicate orange roe that is attached to the scallop muscle is prized. Until recently, Americans disregarded it; today, however, it can be found at certain markets and restaurants.

1. Trim the ends of the zucchini and cut them into ½-inch cubes. (You should have about 2 cups.)

2. Drop the tomatoes into boiling water for 12 seconds to loosen the skins. Remove the skins and halve the tomatoes crosswise. Squeeze the halves gently to extract the seeds. Chop the tomatoes coarsely. (You should have about 1¼ cups.)

3. Heat 1 tablespoon of the olive oil in a large frying pan and add the zucchini and salt and pepper. Cook for about 2 minutes, stirring and tossing. Remove the zucchini to a plate and keep them warm.

4. In the same skillet, heat the remaining olive oil and sauté the scallops, seasoned with salt and pepper, stirring and tossing for 2 minutes. Remove the scallops to a plate and keep them warm.

5. Add the butter and garlic to the same skillet. Cook briefly, making sure that the garlic doesn't brown. Add the tomatoes and cook briefly; add the zucchini and heat thoroughly. Transfer the mixture to a serving platter, pour the scallops over it, sprinkle with parsley, and serve immediately.

YIELD: 6 SERVINGS.

Scallops Niçoise with Green and Black Olives

This recipe also works well with shrimp.

2 tablespoons olive oil
1 tablespoon chopped garlic
4 tomatoes (about 1¼ pounds), peeled and cut into ½-inch-cubes
18 green olives, pitted and chopped
12 black olives, pitted and chopped
4 tablespoons drained capers
1 teaspoon chopped fresh thyme leaves, or ½ teaspoon dried thyme
Salt and freshly ground black pepper to taste
4 tablespoons unsalted butter
2 pounds bay scallops
4 tablespoons chopped fresh parsley leaves
Juice of 1 lemon

1. Heat the oil in a heavy frying pan over high heat. Add the garlic and cook briefly; then add the tomatoes and bring to a boil. Stir in the green and black olives, capers, thyme, and salt and pepper. Cook for 2 minutes.

2. Using two frying pans, melt 2 tablespoons of the butter in each. When the butter is hot, place an equal amount of scallops in each pan and season with salt and pepper. Cook over high heat, shaking the pans and stirring so that the scallops cook evenly and quickly. Cook the scallops for about 2 minutes or slightly longer. Be careful not to overcook them. Sprinkle the parsley and lemon juice over everything.

3. Spoon the hot tomato and olive oil sauce onto warm serving plates and distribute the scallops evenly. Serve immediately.

YIELD: 6 SERVINGS.

Scallops with Sweet Peppers and Lime

This recipe also works well with shrimp.

2 tablespoons unsalted butter
3 tablespoons olive oil
1 sweet red pepper, cored, seeded, and cut into julienne strips
about 1 inch long
4 scallions, trimmed (leaving 1 inch of the green), cut on the
diagonal into 1-inch-long pieces
Salt and freshly ground black pepper to taste
1 tablespoon dry white wine
1 pound bay scallops
2 tablespoons Pernod
2 tablespoons fresh lime juice

1. In a large frying pan, heat 1 tablespoon of the butter with 1 tablespoon of the olive oil over medium-high heat. Add the red pepper and the scallions and sauté for about 10 minutes, stirring occasionally. Season generously with salt and pepper. After 5 minutes add the wine and stir it in.

2. When the red pepper and scallions are nearly cooked, heat the remaining tablespoon of butter and the remaining 2 tablespoons of olive oil over high heat in a separate pan. Add the scallops, Pernod, lime juice, and salt and pepper. Cook for about 30 seconds, shaking the pan occasionally. Add the contents of this pan to the first pan and mix well, cooking for another minute over high heat. Serve immediately with rice or couscous.

YIELD: 4 SERVINGS.

Scallops with Endives

¾ pound bay or sea scallops
2 large endives (about ½ pound total weight)
1 tablespoon unsalted butter
3 tablespoons finely chopped shallots
Juice of ½ lemon
½ cup dry white wine
1 cup heavy cream
½ teaspoon saffron threads, optional
⅛ teaspoon hot red pepper flakes
Salt to taste, if desired
Freshly ground black pepper to taste

1. If sea scallops are used, cut them into quarters. Set them aside.

2. Trim off the ends of the endives. Cut the endives crosswise into 1-inch pieces. There should be about 4 cups loosely packed.

3. Melt the butter in a frying pan and add the shallots. Cook briefly and add the endives and lemon juice. Cook, stirring, until the endives are wilted. Add the wine and bring to a boil. Cover and simmer for 5 minutes.

4. Add ¾ cup of the cream, saffron, hot pepper flakes, and salt and pepper and cook, uncovered, over high heat, stirring often, for about 3 minutes.

5. Add the scallops and cook, stirring, for about 1 minute. Add the remaining cream and salt and pepper to taste. Cook for about 2 minutes, or until the scallops have lost their raw look. Do not overcook. Serve immediately.

YIELD: 4 SERVINGS.

During the cold months, when most fresh tomatoes on the market are pallid and cottony, certain types of canned tomatoes offer a good alternative for sauces. Italian crushed tomatoes work well in a multitude of recipes, and because they are processed at the peak of ripeness, they offer far more flavor than pale fresh winter tomatoes.

Sea Scallops Américaine

This recipe also works well with bay scallops and shrimp.

2 tablespoons olive oil
4 tablespoons finely chopped shallots
2 tablespoons finely chopped onion
1 teaspoon finely chopped garlic
1 cup dry white wine
1 cup Fish Broth (page 241) or bottled clam juice
2½ cups canned Italian tomatoes, crushed or blended
⅛ teaspoon cayenne pepper
4 tablespoons chopped fresh tarragon leaves, or 2 teaspoons
  dried tarragon
Salt and freshly ground black pepper
4 tablespoons unsalted butter
2 pounds sea scallops
3 tablespoons Cognac

1. Heat 1 tablespoon of the oil in a large saucepan over medium-high heat. Add the shallots, onion, and garlic. Cook, stirring, until the ingredients wilt. Pour in the wine and bring to a boil. Cook until the wine is reduced by half. Add the fish broth, tomatoes, cayenne pepper, half the tarragon, and salt and pepper. Bring to a boil and simmer for 10 minutes.

2. Pour the sauce through a chinoise into a clean pan. Press on the solids to extract as much of the liquid as possible from the pulp and herbs. Discard the solids. There should be about 2¼ cups of sauce.

3. In another pan, heat the remaining oil and 1 tablespoon of the butter over medium-high heat. Add the scallops and season with salt and pepper. Sauté, stirring, for about 1 minute. Pour in the Cognac. Cook about 45 seconds and add the tomato sauce. Stir to blend and bring to a boil. Stir in the remaining tarragon and butter. Adjust the seasonings. Serve over rice or fettuccine.

YIELD: 6 SERVINGS.

Sea Scallops with Watercress Sauce

This recipe also works well with shrimp.

2 pounds sea scallops
1 bunch watercress with large stems removed, washed
2 tablespoons unsalted butter
½ pound mushrooms, washed and quartered
3 tablespoons finely chopped shallots
¾ cup dry white wine
Salt and freshly ground black pepper
⅛ teaspoon hot red pepper flakes
1 cup heavy cream
2 tablespoons Ricard or Pernod

1. Halve each scallop crosswise. Set them aside.
2. Bring enough lightly salted water to a boil to cover the watercress. Add the watercress and blanch for 2 minutes, or until the watercress wilts. Drain the watercress well and rinse under cold water. Squeeze to extract the liquid and chop coarsely.
3. Melt the butter in a heavy bottomed saucepan or frying pan. Add the mushrooms and cook, stirring, over high heat for 1 minute. Stir in the shallots and cook for another minute. Add the wine and cook for 5 minutes, or until the wine has almost evaporated.
4. Add the scallops and sprinkle with salt and pepper and hot pepper flakes. Cook for 2 minutes, stirring occasionally.
5. Remove the scallops from the pan and drain them. You should have about ¾ cup.
6. Pour the cooking liquid, including the mushrooms, into a saucepan and cook over high heat for 30 seconds. Add ¾ cup of the heavy cream and cook for 1 minute. Stir in the watercress and cook for another minute.
7. Pour and scrape the mixture into a blender or food processor. Add the mushrooms. Blend until smooth.
8. Put the scallops into a saucepan. Add the mushroom–watercress sauce and the remaining cream. Bring to a simmer and cook just until the scallops are warm, no longer. Stir in the

Ricard and adjust the seasonings. Serve immediately with rice or fine noodles.

YIELD: 6 SERVINGS.

Sea Scallops and Shrimp with Parsley Sauce

2 bunches parsley with large stems removed
4 tablespoons unsalted butter
4 tablespoons finely chopped shallots
½ cup dry white wine
1 cup heavy cream
Salt and freshly ground white pepper to taste
Dash of Tabasco sauce
1 pound sea scallops, cut into ½-inch cubes
1 pound medium-size shrimp, shelled and deveined

1. Bring to a boil enough lightly salted water to cover the parsley. Add the parsley, stir, bring back to a boil, and cook for 3 to 4 minutes. The parsley must retain its color and be cooked but still firm. Drain well and chop coarsely.

2. Melt 1 tablespoon of the butter in a frying pan over medium-high heat. Add the shallots and sauté, stirring. Do not brown. Stir in the wine, bring to a boil, and cook until the wine has almost evaporated. Add the cream and cook for 2 minutes. Add the parsley and salt and pepper.

3. Pour the mixture into a blender. Add 2 tablespoons of the remaining butter and the Tabasco sauce. Purée as finely as possible.

4. Melt the remaining 1 tablespoon of butter in a large frying pan over high heat. Add the scallops, shrimp, and salt and pepper and sauté, stirring and tossing, for about 2 minutes, or until the shellfish loses its raw look. Pour in the sauce and stir to blend; cook for 1 minute. Serve with fettuccine or rice.

YIELD: 4 TO 6 SERVINGS.

Sea Scallops with Tomatoes and Garlic

This recipe also works well with shrimp.

1 ½ pounds sea scallops
¼ cup milk
Salt and freshly ground black pepper to taste
½ cup all-purpose flour
1 tablespoon olive oil
2 cups canned Italian tomatoes, drained and coarsely chopped
2 tablespoons chopped fresh basil leaves
Approximately 4 tablespoons corn or vegetable oil
4 tablespoons unsalted butter
1 tablespoon finely chopped garlic
2 tablespoons finely chopped fresh parsley leaves

1. Put the scallops in a mixing bowl and add the milk and salt and pepper. Set aside. Put the flour in a flat dish and set it aside.

2. Heat the olive oil in a heavy frying pan over medium-high heat and add the tomatoes and salt and pepper to taste. Bring to a boil and cook for 5 minutes, or until the moisture has almost evaporated. Stir in the basil and remove the pan from the heat.

3. Heat 1 tablespoon of the corn oil in a nonstick frying pan large enough to hold the scallops in one layer.

4. Meanwhile, heat the tomato sauce and spoon it into a warm serving dish.

5. Drain the scallops and dredge them in the flour. Shake off the excess flour. Add just enough scallops to the pan without crowding them and fry over medium-high heat for 3 to 5 minutes, or until they are golden brown on one side. Turn them and cook on the other side until golden. Using a slotted spoon or spatula, remove the scallops to the serving dish with the warm tomato sauce. Add more corn oil to the pan if necessary and another layer of scallops. Repeat until all the scallops are cooked.

6. When the scallops are all cooked, pour off the fat from the

pan and wipe it out with paper towels. Add the butter to the pan and cook, swirling the pan, until it starts to brown. Stir in the garlic quickly. Do not brown it. Pour this over the scallops, sprinkle with the chopped parsley, and serve.

YIELD: 4 SERVINGS.

Sea Scallops and Mushrooms in Vermouth Sauce

This recipe also works well with bay scallops and shrimp.

2 tablespoons unsalted butter
3 tablespoons finely chopped shallots
½ pound button mushrooms
1 tablespoon fresh lemon juice
1½ pounds sea scallops
Salt and freshly ground white pepper to taste
¼ cup dry vermouth
1 cup heavy cream
Pinch of freshly grated nutmeg

1. Melt the butter over high heat in a nonstick frying pan. Add the shallots and cook for 20 seconds, stirring and tossing. Do not brown them. Add the mushrooms and lemon juice and cook, stirring and tossing, for 1 minute.

2. Add the scallops to the pan with salt and pepper and sauté for 1½ minutes. Add the vermouth and cook briefly. Remove the scallops and mushrooms from the pan with a slotted spoon and keep them warm.

3. Add the cream and nutmeg to the pan juices along with any juice from the scallops and mushrooms. Reduce over high heat, stirring and scraping for 3 minutes. The sauce should reduce to 1 cup. Add the scallops to the sauce and heat just to warm. Serve immediately.

YIELD: 6 SERVINGS.

Mussels with Saffron Cream

2 tablespoons unsalted butter
4 tablespoons finely chopped shallots
4 tablespoons finely chopped onion
6 tablespoons finely chopped fresh parsley leaves
1 teaspoon saffron threads
5 pounds mussels, well scrubbed and cleaned
2 thyme sprigs, or ½ teaspoon dried thyme
1 cup dry white wine
Salt and freshly ground black pepper to taste
1 cup heavy cream
3 tablespoons Ricard

1. Melt the butter in a large, deep saucepan. Add the shallots, onion, 4 tablespoons of the parsley, and the saffron and stir over medium heat for 1 minute.

2. Add the mussels, thyme, wine, and salt and pepper. Cover, bring to a boil, and add the cream. Cover, return to a boil, and cook over high heat, shaking and tossing the mussels, for about 5 to 6 minutes, or until all the mussels have opened. Stir in the Ricard.

3. Serve in hot soup plates, sprinkled with the remaining chopped parsley.

YIELD: 6 SERVINGS.

Sea Bass Coated with Pine Nuts

This recipe also works well with sole, flounder, and red snapper.

½ cup pine nuts
1¾ pounds skinless sea bass fillets
Salt and freshly ground black pepper
4 tablespoons corn or vegetable oil
4 tablespoons plus 2 teaspoons unsalted butter
⅓ cup drained capers
1 tablespoon fresh lemon juice
2 tablespoons finely chopped fresh parsley leaves

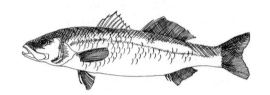

1. Grind the pine nuts finely in a food mill, food processor, or blender (or chop them extremely finely with a knife).

2. Place the ground nuts on a flat dish. Season the fillets with salt and pepper; then dredge them well on both sides in the nuts, pressing the surfaces with your hands so they adhere.

3. Heat half of the oil along with 1 teaspoon of the butter over medium-high heat in a large nonstick frying pan. Add half of the fish and sauté until golden brown on one side, about 3 minutes. Turn the fillets over and cook 2 more minutes. (If the fillets are exceptionally thick, cover and cook for another 2 minutes or so.) Repeat with the second batch, using the same amount of oil and butter.

4. Transfer the cooked fillets to warm serving plates.

5. Heat the remaining 4 tablespoons of butter in a clean frying pan over high heat. When the butter begins to turn hazelnut brown, add the capers. Shake the pan and stir for about 1 minute. Add the lemon juice and pour this mixture evenly over the fillets. Garnish with parsley and serve.

YIELD: 4 SERVINGS.

Red Snapper with Shrimp and Tomato Butter

This recipe also works well with many white fish fillets, such as sole, pompano, striped bass, and sea trout.

2 skinless red snapper fillets (about 2¼ pounds total weight), cut into six equal portions
Salt and freshly ground black pepper
3 tablespoons milk
¾ cup all-purpose flour
2 tablespoons corn oil
6 tablespoons unsalted butter
¾ pound medium-size shrimp, shelled, deveined, and halved lengthwise
4 tablespoons finely chopped shallots
1 cup diced peeled and seeded ripe tomatoes
1 tablespoon red wine vinegar
4 tablespoons finely chopped fresh parsley leaves

1. Sprinkle the fish fillets with salt and pepper. Pour the milk into a bowl and put the flour in a flat dish. Dip the fillets first into the milk and then into the flour to coat them. Shake off the excess flour.

2. Heat the oil in two nonstick frying pans over high heat. Add the fish to the pans and cook for 4 minutes, or until golden brown on one side. Turn the fillets and cook on the other side over medium-low heat for 8 to 10 minutes, depending on the thickness of the fillets. (Eight to 10 minutes is for a fairly thick fillet.) Transfer the fillets to a warm serving dish and keep them warm.

3. Melt the butter in a frying pan over medium-high heat and add the shrimp. Cook, stirring, for about 1 minute. Add the shallots, tomatoes, and vinegar and cook, stirring, for 30 seconds. Scatter the shrimp and sauce over the fish fillets. Garnish with parsley and serve immediately.

YIELD: 6 SERVINGS.

Bonito with Caper Sauce

This recipe also works well with blackfish, pompano, and red perch.

¼ cup all-purpose flour
Salt and freshly ground black pepper to taste
¼ cup milk
2 bonito fillets with skin (about 2¾ pounds total weight)
3 tablespoons vegetable oil
6 tablespoons unsalted butter
½ cup drained capers
2 tablespoons red wine vinegar
4 tablespoons chopped fresh parsley leaves

1. Combine the flour and salt and pepper in a flat dish. Pour the milk into another dish.

2. Dip the fillets first into the milk and then into the flour. Coat the fish on both sides and shake off the excess flour.

3. Heat the oil in a nonstick frying pan large enough to hold the bonito fillets in one layer. Add the fillets to the pan and cook on one side over medium heat until browned, about 7 minutes. Turn the fillets and continue cooking, turning the pieces occasionally for 7 minutes, or until done. Transfer the fish to a warm platter and keep warm.

4. Discard the fat from the pan and wipe it clean with paper towels. Add the butter and cook, shaking the pan, until it turns hazelnut brown. Add the capers and continue swirling the pan until the butter starts to turn dark. Add the vinegar and cook briefly. Pour the sauce over the fish, sprinkle with the parsley, and serve immediately.

YIELD: 6 SERVINGS.

Bonito, members of the tuna family, have dark, strongly flavored flesh. They can be found in both the Atlantic and Pacific oceans. The flesh is usually soaked before cooking. A sauce high in acid is called for to offset the rich texture of the fish.

New England Codfish Cakes

2 pounds fresh skinless cod fillets
Salt and freshly ground black pepper
2½ pounds potatoes (Russet are best.)
1 cup sliced onion
2 large eggs, well beaten
2 tablespoons Dijon mustard
1 teaspoon Worcestershire sauce
4 tablespoons finely chopped fresh parsley leaves
½ cup chopped onion
½ cup all-purpose flour
About 4 tablespoons vegetable oil

1. Season the fillets well with the salt and pepper. Place them on the rack of a steamer over boiling water. Cover and steam for 7 minutes. Remove the rack and fish from the heat and let them cool.

2. Peel the potatoes and cut them into 1½-inch cubes. Cover with cold water in a deep pot. Add the sliced onion and salt and pepper to taste, and bring to a boil. Cook for 12 to 15 minutes, or until the potatoes are tender.

3. Drain the potatoes and onion and purée them in a food mill or ricer, or mash them by hand (not in a food processor).

4. When the codfish is cool enough to handle, flake the flesh with a fork.

5. Place the potatoes in a mixing bowl. Combine with the beaten eggs, mustard, Worcestershire sauce, parsley, and chopped onion. Blend very well and add the fish, folding it in lightly, without overmixing. Place this mixture on a baking sheet (about 11½ by 15 inches), smooth over the top with a rubber spatula, cover with plastic wrap, and chill.

6. When the mixture is thoroughly cool, shape it into 20 hamburger-size patties. Put the flour on a flat dish and dredge the fish cakes in it. Shake off any excess flour.

7. Heat 2 tablespoons of the oil over medium-high heat in a large frying pan, preferably nonstick. Fry the cakes for about 2½

minutes on each side, or until golden brown. Drain on paper towels and serve immediately. Use the remaining 2 tablespoons of cooking oil if necessary.

YIELD: 20 CAKES; SERVES 6.

Note: These cakes can be served with Quick Tomato Sauce (page 250), Mayonnaise (page 259), or Tartar Sauce (page 264).

Flounder Fillets à la Française

This recipe also works well with sole, whiting, or any flatfish.

2 skinless flounder fillets (about 1½ pounds total weight)
Salt and freshly ground black pepper
1 large egg
2 tablespoons water
¼ cup all-purpose flour
3 or more tablespoons corn or vegetable oil
4 tablespoons unsalted butter
2 tablespoons fresh lemon juice
2 tablespoons finely chopped fresh parsley leaves

1. Put the fillets on a flat surface and sprinkle them with salt and pepper.
2. Break the egg into a shallow wide dish and add the water. Season with salt and pepper and beat to blend well. Spoon the flour onto a flat dish.
3. Dip the fillets in the flour. Coat well on all sides and shake off the excess. Then dip the fillets into the egg mixture to coat well on all sides. Drain off any excess.
4. Heat enough oil over high heat in a frying pan to coat the bottom lightly. Add a few pieces of fish at a time in a single layer without crowding. Cook over high heat for about 1½ minutes, or until they are golden brown on one side. Turn the pieces carefully and cook on the second side for about 1 minute, or until

golden brown. Carefully transfer the fillets to a warm platter and keep them warm.

5. Cook the remaining fish, a few pieces at a time, adding more oil as necessary.

6. When all the fillets are cooked, wipe out the pan with paper towels and add the butter. Cook over medium-high heat until it begins to brown. Add the lemon juice and pour the mixture over the fish. Sprinkle with the parsley and serve.

YIELD: 4 SERVINGS.

Flounder Fillets Coated with Macadamia Nuts

This recipe also works well with pompano, gray sole, striped bass, and red snapper.

12 small skinless flounder fillets (about 2½ pounds total weight)
Salt and freshly ground black pepper
2 large eggs
4 tablespoons water
1 cup macadamia nuts chopped finely with a knife
4 tablespoons peanut or vegetable oil
6 tablespoons unsalted butter
3 tablespoons fresh lemon juice
4 tablespoons chopped fresh parsley leaves

1. Sprinkle the fillets on both sides with salt and pepper.
2. Beat the egg and water in a bowl. Season the egg mixture with salt and pepper. Put the chopped nuts on a flat dish. Dip the fillets one at a time into the egg mixture until well coated; then dredge them in the chopped nuts. Pat them firmly so they are evenly coated.
3. Heat 1 tablespoon of the oil in a nonstick frying pan over medium-high heat and, when it is hot, add as many fillets as

The largest summer flounder ever caught with a rod and reel weighed 22 pounds, 7 ounces. Charles Nappi pulled it in off Montauk, New York, on September 15, 1975.

will fit without crowding. Sauté, turning once, for a total of about 1½ minutes, or until done. The time will vary with the thickness of the fillets. Cook only until the fillets are browned on both sides, adding a little more oil as necessary. Transfer the fillets to a warm platter and keep them warm. Then cook the remaining pieces.

4. When all the fillets are cooked, wipe the pan clean with paper towels and add the butter. Cook until the butter is foamy and starts to brown. Add the lemon juice and pour the mixture over the fish. Sprinkle with the chopped parsley and serve immediately.

YIELD: 6 SERVINGS.

Fillets of Flounder
à la Meunière with Capers

This classic method of fish preparation, which includes capers for extra flavor, works equally well with lemon sole, fluke, pompano, and small bluefish.

6 skinless flounder fillets (about 2 pounds total weight)
Salt and freshly ground black pepper to taste
¼ cup milk
½ cup all-purpose flour
4 to 5 tablespoons vegetable oil
6 tablespoons unsalted butter
⅓ cup drained capers
Juice of 1 lime
6 lime slices
4 tablespoons chopped fresh parsley leaves

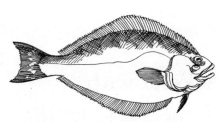

1. Sprinkle the fillets with salt and pepper.
2. Pour the milk into a shallow bowl and the flour onto a flat dish. Dip each fillet in the milk and then dredge in the flour, patting the flour to be sure it adheres.

3. Heat the oil in an oval black steel fish pan (it should be very hot to prevent sticking). If you have a nonstick frying pan, less oil will be necessary. Place in the pan as many fillets as will fit in one layer without crowding.

4. Brown the fillets thoroughly on one side; then turn the fillets with a slotted spatula and brown them on the other side. The process will take about 2 minutes on each side, depending on the thickness of the fillets. While the fish is browning on the second side, baste the top with hot oil from the pan to prevent them from drying out. Transfer the fillets to a warm platter.

5. While the pan is still warm, wipe it out with paper towels and return it to medium heat to melt the butter. Add the capers and shake the pan constantly until the butter turns hazelnut brown.

6. Squeeze the lime juice over the fillets. Pour the butter over them and garnish with the lime slices and parsley.

YIELD: 6 SERVINGS.

Mackerel with
Capers and Onions

This recipe also works well with small fillets of bluefish, red snapper, and trout.

⅓ *cup vegetable or corn oil*
4 tablespoons unsalted butter

2 cups thinly sliced small white onions
Salt and freshly ground black pepper
½ cup dry white wine
2 whole cloves
¼ cup milk
4 mackerel fillets with skin (about 1½ pounds total weight)
¼ cup all-purpose flour
⅓ cup drained capers
2 tablespoons red wine vinegar
4 tablespoons finely chopped fresh parsley leaves

1. Heat 1 tablespoon of the oil and 1 tablespoon of the butter in a saucepan over medium-high heat. Add the onions and cook, stirring occasionally, for about 10 minutes, or until they are golden brown. Sprinkle with salt and pepper. Add the wine and cloves and cover tightly. Bring to a boil, cover, turn the heat to low, and cook for about 20 minutes.

2. Pour the milk into a shallow bowl and add salt and pepper. Place the fillets in the milk and turn them to coat evenly. Let them stand until ready to use.

3. Heat the remaining oil over medium-high heat in a frying pan large enough to hold the fillets in one layer. Spread the flour over a flat dish. Remove the fillets from the milk one at a time and shake off the excess. Do not pat dry. Dip the fillets in the flour to coat them well on both sides. Shake off any excess flour.

4. When the oil is hot, add the fillets skin side up. Cook on one side for about 3 minutes, or until the fillets are lightly browned. Turn them and continue cooking for about 3 minutes. Tilt the pan and baste the fillets occasionally as they cook.

5. Arrange the fillets on a serving dish and spoon equal portions of the onions over each.

6. In another frying pan, melt the remaining butter over medium heat. Add the capers and cook them, shaking the pan, until the butter starts to brown lightly. Add the vinegar and pour the mixture over the onions and mackerel. Sprinkle with the parsley and serve immediately.

YIELD: 4 SERVINGS.

Mackerel with Tomatoes and Pepper Sauce

This dish also works well with small bluefish fillets and tuna steaks.

4 tablespoons olive oil
1 tablespoon chopped garlic
2 onions, finely minced (about 2 cups)
1 cup sliced sweet red pepper
1 cup sliced sweet green pepper
Salt and freshly ground black pepper to taste
½ teaspoon dried thyme
1 bay leaf
¼ teaspoon Tabasco sauce
3 cups cored and coarsely chopped ripe tomatoes or crushed Italian canned tomatoes
12 mackerel fillets with skin (about 2 pounds total weight)

1. Preheat the oven to 450 degrees.

2. Heat 3 tablespoons of the olive oil in a frying pan over medium-high heat and add the garlic and onions. Cook until wilted; then add the red and green peppers and continue cooking, stirring occasionally, until the onions start to brown lightly. Add the salt and pepper, thyme, bay leaf, Tabasco sauce, and tomatoes. Cook, stirring, for about 7 minutes.

3. Coat a baking dish large enough to hold all the fillets in one layer with the remaining tablespoon of olive oil. Arrange the fish side by side in the dish. Season liberally with salt and pepper. Pour the sauce over them and bake for 15 minutes. When the ingredients are cooked, place the dish under the broiler just to crisp the top. This dish can be served hot or cold.

YIELD: 6 SERVINGS.

The Atlantic mackerel is a long, thin, silvery speedster of the sea that zips along in schools, ranging from Labrador to Cape Hatteras. The flesh is rather oily and has a strong, distinct flavor. For this reason a tomato sauce that is high in acid is one of the best ways to prepare it. The smaller the fish, the milder their flavor.

Salmon Cakes

1½ pounds boneless and skinless salmon
2 large eggs, beaten
1½ cups well-crumbled saltines
1 teaspoon paprika
Salt and freshly ground black pepper to taste
½ cup finely chopped scallions
4 tablespoons finely chopped fresh parsley leaves
⅛ teaspoon freshly grated nutmeg
4 tablespoons vegetable oil

1. Put the salmon fillets on the rack of a steamer over boiling water. Cover closely and steam for 5 to 7 minutes, depending on the thickness of the fish. Remove the rack from the pot and set the salmon aside to cool.

2. When the salmon is cool enough to handle, flake the flesh with a fork.

3. In a mixing bowl, combine the eggs, 1¼ cups of the crumbled crackers, paprika, salt and pepper, scallions, parsley, and nutmeg. Blend well. Add the fish and fold it in lightly so as not to break up the flakes.

4. Shape the salmon mixture into 12 equal-size hamburger-like patties. Place the remaining crumbs on a flat dish and dredge the patties in them.

5. Heat 2 tablespoons of the oil in a large nonstick frying pan. Cook the patties for about 2½ minutes on each side, or until golden brown. Drain on paper towels and serve immediately with lemon wedges and a sauce of your choice.

YIELD: 12 CAKES; SERVES 4 TO 6.

Note: These cakes go well with any type of mayonnaise, hot or cold, as well as Mushroom–Cream Sauce (page 252) and Creole Sauce Base (page 249).

Escalopes of Salmon with Leek Sauce

1½ pounds skinless salmon fillets
2 tablespoons unsalted butter
4 tablespoons finely chopped shallots
½ pound leek whites, cleaned and finely chopped
½ cup dry white wine
1 cup heavy cream
Salt and freshly ground white pepper to taste
3 tablespoons vegetable oil

1. Put the salmon fillets on a flat surface. Slice the fillets crosswise into 12 pieces roughly ½ inch thick. Set them aside.

2. In a saucepan, combine the butter, shallots, and leeks. Cook over medium heat for 2 minutes, stirring. Add the wine and cook until most of the wine has evaporated. Add the cream and salt and pepper and bring to a boil. Lower the heat and simmer for about 5 minutes. Keep the sauce warm.

3. Heat 1½ tablespoons of the olive oil in a large nonstick frying pan. Sprinkle the salmon slices with salt and pepper. Add 6 slices of salmon to the pan and cook for 1 minute on each side. Do not overcook or the salmon will become dry. Transfer to a warm platter and keep warm. Repeat the procedure with the remaining salmon slices.

4. Distribute the sauce evenly over six warm serving dishes. Lay two slices of salmon on each plate and serve immediately.

YIELD: 6 SERVINGS.

The two principal types of salmon sold on the American market are the Pacific variety and the Atlantic variety. Atlantic salmon is recognized as the best in flavor and texture, with top honors going to those from the rivers of Ireland and Scotland; they are also the most costly. A new variety of salmon that promises to comprise an increasingly larger part of the market comes from commercial hatcheries in Norway.

Salmon Cutlets Pojarski

1½ pounds very cold skinless fresh salmon fillets
Salt and freshly ground white pepper
¼ teaspoon freshly grated nutmeg
2 dashes of Tabasco sauce
1½ cups fine fresh bread crumbs
1¼ cups very cold heavy cream
4 tablespoons vegetable oil
8 tablespoons unsalted butter

1. In a food processor or with a sharp knife, chop the salmon to a medium-coarse consistency.

2. Put the salmon in a mixing bowl and season with the salt and pepper, nutmeg, and Tabasco sauce. Blend well with a wooden spoon. Add ¾ cup of the bread crumbs and stir well. Pour in the cream, a little bit at a time, while beating vigorously. All the cream should be absorbed.

3. Divide the mixture into 12 equal-size portions and shape them into patties about ¾ inch thick. Smooth over the tops with a spatula. Dredge the cutlets lightly in the remaining bread crumbs.

4. Heat 2 tablespoons of oil in each of two nonstick 10-inch frying pans over medium heat. When the oil is hot, add the salmon cutlets. Cook on one side for about 3 minutes, or until golden brown. Turn gently and cook 3 to 4 minutes longer. Transfer to a warm platter.

5. Wipe out one of the pans with paper towels. Add the butter and cook over medium heat, shaking the pan, until the butter turns hazelnut brown. Pour the hot butter over the cutlets and serve immediately.

YIELD: 6 SERVINGS.

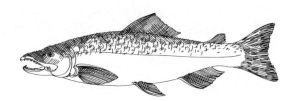

Sautéed Salmon Steaks with Orange–Butter Sauce

This recipe also works well with red snapper, pompano, sea bass, and halibut.

½ cup freshly squeezed orange juice
6 tablespoons unsalted butter at room temperature
¾ cup diced peeled and seeded tomatoes
Salt and freshly ground black pepper
2 tablespoons olive oil
4 tablespoons finely chopped shallots
6 skinless salmon steaks (about 5 ounces each)
Steamed Parsleyed Cucumbers (page 267) or Boiled Red Skin
    Potatoes with Dill (page 269)
¼ cup chopped fresh coriander or parsley leaves

1. Put the orange juice and shallots into a saucepan and reduce it by half over high heat. Add the butter and tomatoes and cook just until the combination is well blended. Season with salt and pepper to taste.

2. Heat 1 tablespoon of the olive oil in a large nonstick frying pan. Season the salmon steaks with salt and pepper. Place 3 steaks in the pan and cook over high heat until they are lightly browned, about 1½ minutes on each side. The time will vary depending on the thickness of the fish.

3. Transfer the steaks to warm plates, pour the sauce over them and garnish with the coriander. Serve with the Steamed Parsleyed Cucumbers or Boiled Red Skin Potatoes with Dill.

YIELD: 6 SERVINGS.

The main varieties of American salmon are:

CHINOOK: *Also called "king" and "spring" salmon, this is the most highly coveted by connoisseurs. It is also the biggest, weighing up to 120 pounds.*

COHO: *Sometimes referred to as "silver" salmon, this variety is becoming more popular. Its flesh is finer than that of the large Chinook, although the flavor is not quite as distinct.*

SOCKEYE: *The term "red salmon" is more appropriate for this expensive fish, for its deep rose-colored flesh sets it apart from all others. It is sometimes known as blueback salmon.*

CHUM: *Most chum salmon is sold smoked. Its coarse flesh is pale pink.*

PINK SALMON: *Found in the Pacific, this smallest of all ocean salmon has a delicate flesh and is extremely versatile. It represents about half of all canned salmon.*

English-style Breaded Sea Trout Fillets

This recipe also works well with lemon sole, flounder, red snapper, and striped bass.

2 pounds skinless sea trout fillets
1 cup all-purpose flour
2 large eggs, lightly beaten
2 tablespoons plus 1 teaspoon vegetable oil
3 tablespoons water
Salt and freshly ground white pepper
1¼ cups fresh bread crumbs
1 tablespoon unsalted butter
Lemon wedges
Mustard–Dill Sauce (page 256) or Cajun-style Sauce Rémoulade (page 258)

1. Cut the fish into 6 serving pieces.
2. Scatter the flour over the bottom of a large pan.
3. In a bowl, beat the eggs with 1 teaspoon of the oil, the water, and salt and pepper.
4. Dredge the fish pieces thoroughly in the flour. Dip them in the egg mixture and let the excess drain off; then coat them in the bread crumbs.
5. In a nonstick frying pan, heat the remaining oil and butter over medium-high heat and cook the fish pieces until golden brown on one side. Turn and cook on the other side, basting frequently with the oil in the pan. The cooking time will range from 5 to 15 minutes, depending on the thickness of the fillets. Serve with lemon wedges and either of the sauces.

YIELD: 4 TO 6 SERVINGS.

Weakfish, originally dubbed squeateague by Narraganset Indians in the Rhode Island area, is known as spotted sea trout in the South. The flesh is lean, white, and mild flavored.

Shad and Shad Roe in Cream Sauce with Capers

3 shad fillets with skin (about 3 pounds total weight)
3 pairs shad roe
Salt and freshly ground white pepper
2 tablespoons unsalted butter
4 tablespoons finely chopped shallots
1¼ cups heavy cream
½ teaspoon freshly grated nutmeg
⅓ cup drained capers
Juice of 1 lemon

1. Cut the shad fillets in half widthwise. Season the fillets and the roe with salt and pepper.

2. Put the butter and the shallots in a large frying pan over medium-high heat. When the shallots are wilted, add as much of the shad and shad roe as will fit in one layer without crowding (to save time use two pans simultaneously). Add the heavy cream, nutmeg, and capers. Bring to a boil, cover, and simmer for 6 to 8 minutes, or until everything is cooked.

3. Remove the fish with a slotted spatula to warm serving plates or a platter. Separate each roe pair lengthwise. Place a strip atop each piece of shad.

4. Bring the sauce to a boil and reduce it to about 1 cup. Add the lemon juice, stir, and pour the sauce over the shad. Serve immediately.

YIELD: 6 SERVINGS.

A staple of early American Indians along the Atlantic coast, shad is still an enormously popular game fish. In early March, the shad season is launched in New England with great hoopla as the fish enter coastal rivers en route to their spawning grounds. Every year a regional cottage industry of shad deboners provides employment for hundreds of people. Removing the dozens of tiny bones from this fish is so time consuming to the unskilled that most commercial fishermen turn the job over to local women and children, who have years of experience at it. In France, the bones are left in and the fish is braised slowly with sorrel. The acid in the sorrel dissolves the bones.

Shad season runs for about five months along the Atlantic coast, beginning in the St. Johns River in north Florida and ending in the Gulf of St. Lawrence. Shad were

Shad Roe with Beurre Blanc

3 pairs shad roe
8 tablespoons unsalted butter at room temperature, cut into cubes
¼ cup finely chopped shallots
Salt and freshly ground black pepper
⅓ cup dry white wine
2 tablespoons white wine vinegar
¼ cup heavy cream

1. Preheat the oven to 425 degrees.
2. Rinse the roe in cold water and pat dry with paper towels.
3. Melt 2 tablespoons of the butter in a skillet large enough to hold the roe in one layer. Add the shallots and the roe. Sprinkle with salt and pepper; add the wine and vinegar. Bring to a boil, cover, and simmer for 8 to 10 minutes. Remove the roe to a warm platter and keep warm.
4. Reduce the liquid to one-third its volume and then add the cream. Return to a boil, stirring constantly with a wire whisk; then add the remaining butter. Stir rapidly until the butter has melted. Season with salt and pepper to taste. Spoon the sauce over the roe and serve immediately.

YIELD: 3 TO 6 SERVINGS.

introduced to West Coast rivers in the late nineteenth century, and now can be found in rivers from northern California to Washington State.

Fanciers of this fish prefer the female shad to the male, both for its celebrated roe and meatier flesh.

Shad Roe with Sautéed Mushrooms

2 shad fillets with skin
¼ cup milk
Salt and freshly ground black pepper to taste
½ cup all-purpose flour
2 pairs shad roe
⅓ cup corn or vegetable oil
6 tablespoons unsalted butter
½ pound mushrooms, thinly sliced
Juice of 1 lemon
4 tablespoons chopped fresh parsley leaves

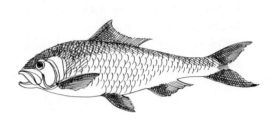

1. Cut the shad fillets in half crosswise.

2. Combine the milk and salt and pepper in a shallow dish and place the flour in another dish. Dip the fillets and the roe into the milk and then into the flour to coat them on both sides. Shake off any excess flour.

3. Heat 2 tablespoons of the oil in a nonstick frying pan over high heat. Add the fish to the pan, skin side up, and the roe. If the pan is too small cook as much as you want at once, then repeat, keeping the cooked fish and roe warm. Sauté the shad for about 2 minutes on one side, or until it is golden brown. Carefully turn the shad and the roe, turn the heat to medium-low, and sauté for another 3 to 5 minutes. Transfer the fillets and the roe to warm plates and keep warm.

4. While the fillets are sautéing, melt 2 tablespoons of the butter in another frying pan. Add the mushrooms and cook over high heat, shaking the pan and stirring occasionally, until they are golden brown.

5. Add the remaining butter and shake the pan until it is melted and bubbling. Stir in the lemon juice and spoon the sauce over the fish. Sprinkle with the parsley and serve immediately.

YIELD: 4 SERVINGS.

Sautéed Curried Shad Roe

This recipe also works well with shrimp, bluefish, and pompano fillets.

6 pairs shad roe (about ½ pound each)
¼ cup milk
3 tablespoons all-purpose flour
4 teaspoons Oriental Curry Powder (page 266)
Salt and freshly ground black pepper
2 tablespoons vegetable oil
6 tablespoons unsalted butter
6 thin lemon slices, seeded
Juice of 1 lemon
⅓ cup chopped fresh parsley leaves

1. Rinse and drain the shad roe. Put them in a flat dish and pour the milk over them.

2. Blend the flour, curry powder, and salt and pepper and spread the mixture over a flat plate. Remove the roe from the milk and dredge the pieces in the flour mixture.

3. Heat 1 tablespoon of the oil in a nonstick frying pan over medium-high heat. Add 3 pairs of roe to the pan and brown them on one side; turn and brown on the other side. When they are golden brown, cover the pan tightly and continue cooking until they are cooked through—between 5 and 8 minutes, depending on the size of the roe. To test for doneness, press the tops of the roe with your finger. If they are firm and resilient, they are done. Transfer them to a warm platter and keep warm. Repeat the procedure to cook the remaining shad roe.

4. Pour off the oil from the pan. Add the butter and cook to a hazelnut color, swirling the pan. Pour the butter over the shad roe and garnish each pair with a slice of lemon. Sprinkle with lemon juice and parsley and serve immediately. Chutney is a nice accompaniment.

YIELD: 6 SERVINGS.

Red Snapper au Poivre

This recipe also works well with red perch, blackfish, fluke, and lemon sole.

1 teaspoon sea salt or kosher salt
1 teaspoon whole white peppercorns
1 teaspoon whole black peppercorns
¼ teaspoon hot red pepper flakes
½ teaspoon dried thyme
6 red snapper fillets with skin (about 6 ounces each)
6 tablespoons unsalted butter
3 tablespoons olive oil
6 tablespoons chopped fresh coriander or Italian parsley leaves

1. Grind the salt, peppercorns, hot pepper flakes, and thyme together in a spice mill. Coat the fish thoroughly with the seasonings as if they were a breading.

2. Melt the butter in a small saucepan. Place a black cast-iron pan over high heat until it is extremely hot, virtually red hot (if you have an exhaust fan be sure it is on). Pour 1 teaspoon of the olive oil into the pan and coat it quickly (the oil will begin to smoke and burn at once). Place 2 fish fillets in the pan immediately and cook them for about 1½ minutes. Turn them and cook for another minute. (You turn the fish when the rim of the raw side begins to whiten.) Transfer the fish to a warm plate and keep warm.

3. Remove any particles of fish from the pan and repeat the cooking procedure with the remaining fillets. Before serving, brush the fillets with the melted butter and sprinkle with the coriander.

YIELD: 6 SERVINGS.

Dusan Bernic's Red Snapper Adriatic Style

This recipe was contributed by the late Dusan Bernic, the chef at The Terrace restaurant on Morningside Heights in Manhattan. It also works equally well with tuna, red snapper, swordfish, mako shark, and halibut.

4 tablespoons olive oil
4 tablespoons unsalted butter, melted
Juice of 1 lemon
1 teaspoon chopped fresh thyme leaves, or ½ teaspoon dried thyme
3 tablespoons chopped fresh basil leaves
2 tablespoons chopped fresh parsley leaves
1 tablespoon chopped garlic
3 red snapper fillets with skin (about 1 pound each), cut into 6 pieces
Salt and freshly ground black pepper to taste

1. Combine the oil, butter, lemon juice, thyme, basil, parsley, and garlic in a baking dish large enough to hold the fish in one layer.

2. Sprinkle the fish generously on all sides with salt and pepper. Put the fillets in the marinade and coat them well. Cover with plastic wrap and let stand at room temperature for 1 hour.

3. Heat two nonstick frying pans large enough to hold the fish pieces in one layer. Add the fillets to the pans skin side up and cook over high heat for about 1 minute, or until golden brown. Turn the pieces, cover tightly, lower the heat, and simmer for about 8 minutes, or until thoroughly cooked. Pour the remaining marinade over the fish and simmer for 1 minute. Serve immediately with the sauce poured over the fish.

YIELD: 6 SERVINGS.

Pay close attention to instructions about marinating fish. Fish is far more sensitive to overmarination than meat. Even half an hour too long can make a fish's texture mushy. Usually an hour or two is sufficient to impart flavor to a fillet.

Pan-fried Red Snapper with Garlic Butter

This recipe also works with flounder, striped bass, pompano, gray sole, and sea trout.

4 skinless red snapper fillets (about 1½ pounds total weight)
Salt and freshly ground black pepper to taste
4 tablespoons milk
¼ cup all-purpose flour
⅓ cup peanut or vegetable oil
6 tablespoons unsalted butter
1 tablespoon chopped garlic
Juice of 1 lemon
4 lemon slices
3 tablespoons chopped fresh parsley leaves

1. Sprinkle the fish fillets with salt and pepper.

2. Pour the milk into a shallow bowl and spread the flour over a flat dish. Dip the fillets in the milk and then dredge them in the flour, shaking to remove any excess flour.

3. In a frying pan large enough to hold the fillets in one layer without crowding them, heat the oil over medium-high heat. Add the fish and cook for 1½ minutes, or until golden brown on one side. Turn them and sauté approximately 2 minutes more, or until done. The time depends on the thickness of the fillets.

4. Transfer the fish to a warm serving platter. Pour off all the fat from the pan and wipe it clean with paper towels.

5. Melt the butter over medium-high heat, shaking the pan constantly, until the butter foams and turns hazelnut brown. Add the garlic and sauté just to heat it through. The garlic should not begin to turn golden. Sprinkle the fillets with lemon juice and pour the garlic butter over them. Garnish each piece with a lemon slice and chopped parsley.

YIELD: 4 SERVINGS.

North Atlantic blowfish, so-called because it puffs up like a balloon when threatened, is not to be confused with the Japanese fugu, which is similar in appearance. Fugu eating is sort of the Russian roulette of Japan —the flesh can be fatally toxic if it is not properly handled and cleaned. Specially trained Japanese chefs prepare the fish at special fugu restaurants—even so, as many as 100 Japanese die annually playing this most perilous of culinary games.

North Atlantic blowfish is harmless. It is delicious when dipped in milk, seasoned well, dredged in flour, and sautéed.

Breaded Sole Fillets with Fresh Tomato Sauce

This recipe also works well with fillets of flounder, pompano, fluke, and most other flatfish.

6 tablespoons unsalted butter
2 cups diced peeled and seeded ripe tomatoes
2 tablespoons finely chopped shallots
Salt and freshly ground black pepper
6 skinless lemon sole fillets (about 1½ pounds total weight)
2 large eggs, well beaten
6 tablespoons unsalted butter, melted
2½ cups fresh bread crumbs
Approximately 3 tablespoons vegetable oil
3 tablespoons red wine vinegar
4 tablespoons finely chopped fresh parsley leaves

1. Melt the 6 tablespoons of butter in a small saucepan. Add the tomatoes, shallots, and salt and pepper. Cook, stirring and shaking the pan, for 3 minutes. Add the vinegar and remove the pan from the heat. Set aside until needed.

2. Sprinkle the fillets on both sides with salt and pepper.

3. Combine the eggs and melted butter in a mixing bowl and pour the mixture into a flat dish.

4. Put the bread crumbs on another flat dish.

5. Dip the fillets in the egg mixture, one at a time, to coat them well. Then dredge them in the bread crumbs on both sides. Tap the fillets with the side of a knife to help the crumbs adhere.

6. Heat the oil in a nonstick frying pan over high heat. When the oil is hot, put 3 fillets in the pan and cook them for 1½ minutes on one side, or until golden brown. Turn them and cook for another 1½ minutes. Transfer the fish to warm plates and keep them warm. Repeat the process with the remaining fillets.

7. Spoon equal portions of the tomato sauce over the center of the fillets. Sprinkle with the parsley and serve immediately.

YIELD: 6 SERVINGS.

Sole Fillets Coated with Sesame Seeds

This recipe also works well with flounder, pompano, and red snapper.

4 tablespoons olive oil
1 tablespoon finely chopped garlic
3 ripe tomatoes (about 1 pound), cored, seeded, peeled, and
  cut into small cubes
2 tablespoons chopped fresh basil leaves
Salt and freshly ground black pepper to taste
4 tablespoons sesame seeds
1½ pounds skinless lemon or gray sole fillets
4 lemon or lime wedges

1. Heat 2 tablespoons of the olive oil in a small saucepan. Add the garlic and cook briefly. Do not brown it. Add the tomatoes, basil, and salt and pepper and cook over high heat, stirring, for 5 minutes. Remove from the heat and keep warm.

2. Spread out the sesame seeds on a large platter. Season the fillets well with salt and pepper. Lay them over the sesame seeds on one side and then the other, to coat them lightly.

3. Heat some of the remaining olive oil in a large nonstick frying pan and place in it as many fillets as will fit. Cook over medium-high heat until the fillets are golden brown on both sides. The time will vary depending on the thickness of the fillets.

4. Spoon the sauce over each serving plate. Place the fish over the sauce in the center of each plate. Garnish with lemon wedges.

YIELD: 4 SERVINGS.

Brook Trout Sautéed with Mushrooms

This recipe also works well with whole whiting, small porgy, and flounder.

6 whole trout (about ½ pound each when cleaned), or 12
    fillets with skin
¼ cup milk
Salt and freshly ground black pepper
⅓ cup all-purpose flour
3 tablespoons vegetable oil
6 tablespoons unsalted butter
6 large mushrooms, cut into thin slices
2 tablespoons fresh lime juice
4 tablespoons finely chopped fresh parsley leaves

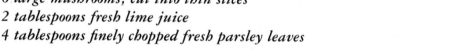

1. Put the trout in a dish, add the milk, and sprinkle with salt and pepper. Turn them several times to coat well. Set aside.

2. Spread the flour over a flat dish. Remove the trout from the milk and dredge them in the flour. Shake off any excess flour.

3. Heat half of the oil in a nonstick frying pan large enough to hold 3 trout in one layer. Cook them over medium heat for 4 minutes on one side. Turn them and cook for 6 to 8 minutes, or until brown. Transfer the trout to a warm platter and keep them warm. Repeat the process using the remaining oil and fish.

4. Meanwhile, melt 1 tablespoon of the butter in a frying pan over high heat. Add the mushroom slices and sprinkle with salt and pepper. Sauté them, stirring and shaking the pan, until the liquid has evaporated and the mushrooms are nicely browned.

5. Arrange the mushrooms over the trout and sprinkle with the lime juice.

6. Melt the remaining butter in a frying pan over high heat, shaking the pan, until the butter turns hazelnut brown. Pour it over the trout, sprinkle with the parsley, and serve immediately.

YIELD: 6 SERVINGS.

Pan-fried Trout Meunière

Virtually any fish fillet or small whole fish could be cooked in this classic method.

6 10-ounce trout, cleaned but with heads left on
½ cup milk
½ cup all-purpose flour
Salt and freshly ground black pepper
¼ cup corn or vegetable oil
8 tablespoons unsalted butter
6 lemon slices
Juice of 1 lemon
4 tablespoons finely chopped fresh parsley leaves

1. Place the trout in a large pan and pour in the milk. Turn the trout in the milk. Spread the flour over a flat dish and season it well with salt and pepper. Remove the trout from the milk and dredge them well in the flour, shaking off any excess flour.

2. Heat the oil in a heavy nonstick frying pan or black steel pan over medium-high heat and add the trout. Cook until golden brown, about 6 minutes on each side. Baste often to keep the trout moist.

3. Remove the trout to a warm platter. Pour off the fat from the frying pan and wipe it clean with paper towels. Return the pan to the heat and melt the butter, shaking the pan and stirring until it turns hazelnut brown. Do not let it burn. Place a lemon slice atop each trout. Sprinkle them with the lemon juice then pour the butter over them. Garnish with the chopped parsley and serve immediately.

YIELD: 6 SERVINGS.

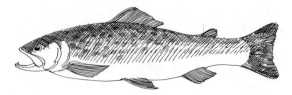

Fresh Tuna Niçoise

This recipe also works well with fresh mako shark. These fish also could be grilled on a barbecue or broiled.

THE FISH STEAKS

4 small skinless and boneless tuna steaks (about 1 inch thick and about 1½ pounds total weight)
2 tablespoons olive oil
8 sprigs fresh thyme, or ½ teaspoon dried thyme
Salt to taste if desired
Freshly ground black pepper to taste

THE SAUCE

2 tablespoons finely chopped scallions
1 tablespoon finely chopped stuffed olives
1 tablespoon finely chopped drained capers
2 tablespoons balsamic vinegar
Freshly ground black pepper to taste
1 teaspoon finely chopped anchovy fillets or anchovy paste
⅓ cup olive oil
2 tablespoons finely chopped fresh parsley leaves

The largest yellow fin tuna ever caught with a rod and reel weighed 388 pounds, 12 ounces. Curt Wiesenhutter brought it in off San Benedicto Island, Mexico, on April 1, 1977.

1. Put the tuna in a baking dish and add the oil, thyme, salt, and pepper. Turn the steaks to coat them well.

2. Heat a nonstick skillet large enough to hold the steaks in one layer. Cook the tuna for about 3 minutes on one side; then turn and cook another 3 minutes. The time will vary according to the thickness of the tuna steaks.

3. As the tuna cooks, prepare the sauce. Put the scallions, olives, and capers into a mixing bowl and stir in the vinegar and pepper. Beat in the anchovy and oil and then stir in the parsley.

4. When the steaks are done, transfer them to warm serving dishes. Spoon half of the sauce over the steaks, smoothing it over. Serve the remainder of the sauce on the side.

YIELD: 4 SERVINGS.

Whiting Fillets with Capers

This recipe also works well with other small fillets of whitefish, such as gray sole, flounder, and bluefish.

2 pounds whiting fillets (about 8 pieces)
3 tablespoons milk
Salt and freshly ground black pepper
4 tablespoons all-purpose flour
2 tablespoons vegetable oil
4 tablespoons unsalted butter
¼ cup drained capers
¼ cup chopped shallots
2 tablespoons red wine vinegar
4 tablespoons chopped fresh parsley leaves

In general, smaller bluefish—between 1 and 4 pounds—are the best for eating. The larger the bluefish the stronger the flavor.

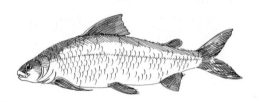

1. Put the whiting in a dish large enough to hold them in one layer. Pour the milk over the fillets and sprinkle them with salt and pepper. Turn the fillets in the milk so they are coated on both sides.

2. Scatter the flour over a large pan or dish. Lightly dredge the fish in the flour on both sides.

3. Heat the oil in a nonstick frying pan over medium-high heat. When the oil is hot, but not smoking, add the fillets. It may be necessary to do this in two batches. Sauté on one side for about 2 minutes; then turn and cook on the other side until golden brown. When the fillets are done, transfer them to a warm serving platter.

4. Wipe out the pan with a paper towel and return the pan to the heat. Melt the butter, shaking the pan frequently, until it turns light brown. Add the capers and cook briefly; add the shallots, vinegar, and parsley. Sauté briefly; then stir and pour the sauce evenly over each fillet.

YIELD: 4 SERVINGS.

Frog Legs Provençale

24 small pairs, or 12 large pairs, frog legs
2 tablespoons olive oil
3 cups peeled, seeded, and coarsely chopped ripe tomatoes or
*   drained canned tomatoes*
Salt and freshly ground black pepper to taste
1 bay leaf
½ cup milk
1 cup all-purpose flour
½ cup vegetable or corn oil
6 tablespoons unsalted butter
1 tablespoon finely chopped garlic
4 tablespoons finely chopped fresh parsley leaves

1. Cut off and discard the feet of the frog legs and place the legs in a baking dish. To keep the frog legs flat as they cook, stick the bottom of one leg through the parallel muscles at the base of the other—in effect crossing their legs at the bottom.

2. Heat the olive oil in a skillet over medium-high heat and add the tomatoes, salt and pepper, and bay leaf. Cook, stirring often, for about 1 minute. Set aside and keep warm.

3. Pour the milk over the frog legs. Place the flour in a flat dish and season the flour with salt and pepper. Drain the frog legs and dredge them one at a time in the flour; shake off any excess flour.

4. Heat the vegetable oil over medium-high heat in one or two large frying pans (nonstick if possible). Add the frog legs and sauté for about 3 to 4 minutes on each side, or until golden brown.

5. As the frog legs are removed from the pan, transfer them to a warm serving platter to keep them warm. Arrange the legs around the perimeter of the platter.

6. Remove the bay leaf from the tomato mixture and spoon the mixture onto the center of the platter.

7. Melt the butter in a skillet and briefly sauté the garlic until it is golden but not brown. Pour the butter over the frog legs

and the tomato mixture. Serve immediately with a garnish of chopped parsley.

YIELD: 4 TO 6 SERVINGS.

CHAPTER 8

Deep-Frying

Deep-fried Shrimp with Mustard–Dill Sauce

This recipe works well with all kinds of white-fleshed species as well as scallops and squid.

1¾ cups all-purpose flour
¾ cup cornstarch
2 large egg whites
2 tablespoons vegetable oil
1 tablespoon white wine vinegar
2 teaspoons baking soda
½ cup finely chopped scallions
1 cup water
Vegetable oil for frying
2 pounds medium-size raw shrimp, shelled and deveined
Mustard–Dill Sauce (page 256)
Fried Parsley (page 268)

   1. In a large mixing bowl, combine ¾ cup of the flour, cornstarch, egg whites, oil, vinegar, baking soda, and scallions. Blend well with a wire whisk. Gradually add the water, stirring constantly. The mixture should be the consistency of pancake batter.

   2. Dredge the shrimp in the remaining cup of flour.

   3. Heat the oil to 360 degrees in a deep-fryer or wok. Dip

the shrimp in the batter and quickly drop them one at a time into the hot oil. Stir and turn with a slotted spoon so the shrimp do not stick together. Cook for about 1 minute. Remove and drain well on paper towels. Serve with Mustard–Dill Sauce or a sauce of your choice. Garnish with Fried Parsley.

YIELD: 6 SERVINGS.

Deep-fried Soft-shell Crabs

6 large soft-shell crabs, or 12 small ones, cleaned
3 large eggs, well beaten
1/3 cup water
Salt and freshly ground black pepper to taste
3 cups fine fresh bread crumbs
3/4 cup all-purpose flour
6 cups vegetable oil for frying
Lemon wedges
Red Pepper Mayonnaise (page 261)

1. If the crabs are wet pat them dry with paper towels.
2. Combine the eggs, water, and salt and pepper in a shallow bowl. Place the bread crumbs in another dish and the flour in a third. Season the flour with pepper.
3. Heat the oil to 360 degrees. Dredge the crabs in the flour to coat well and shake off any excess flour. Dip them in the egg mixture and then in the bread crumbs. Fry the crabs, a few at a time, until they are crisp and well browned, about 3 minutes. Drain on paper towels. Serve with lemon wedges, Red Pepper Mayonnaise, or a sauce of your choice.

YIELD: 6 SERVINGS.

The difference between delicious and crisp deep-fried seafood and a greasy mess is literally a matter of several degrees. A good fat thermometer is a real asset. The optimal temperature of frying oil depends on the food you are cooking: Chicken, for instance, takes a lower heat, about 325 degrees, while shrimp and most other seafood should be done quickly at 360 degrees. Here are a few deep-frying hints:

- *Never salt food before frying. Salt breaks down the oil.*
- *Use a pot that holds a good amount of oil. If you have too little oil, the oil temperature will drop drastically every time a batch of food is placed in it.*
- *Dry all ingredients well before frying (or if they are battered, before dipping in the mixture).*
- *If you don't have a deep-fat thermometer, test the oil temperature by cutting cubes of white bread and dropping one or two into the oil. If*

Deep-fried Soft-shell Clams

This recipe also works well with oysters, scallops, shrimps, and frogs legs.

they turn black within seconds, the oil is too hot; conversely, if they soak up oil while cooking, it is not hot enough.

4 cups vegetable oil
1 quart soft-shell clams, shucked
1 cup buttermilk
½ teaspoon Tabasco sauce
1 teaspoon freshly ground black pepper
2 cups all-purpose flour
Salt to taste
4 lemon wedges

1. Heat the oil to 375 degrees in a deep-fryer or wok.
2. Place the clams in a mixing bowl and add the buttermilk, Tabasco sauce, and ½ teaspoon of the pepper. Blend well and set aside.
3. Place the flour and remaining pepper in a large baking dish. Blend well. Drain the clams and dredge them in the flour. Shake off any excess flour.
4. Place the clams in the preheated oil, a few at a time, without crowding them; fry, stirring, until they are crisp and lightly golden, about 1½ minutes for each batch. Remove the clams with a slotted spoon and drain on paper towels. Keep them warm while you cook the rest.
5. Sprinkle the clams with salt and serve with lemon wedges on the side. Sauce Gribiche (page 257) goes well with these.

YIELD: 4 TO 6 SERVINGS.

Deep-fried Oysters Southern Style

This recipe also works well with bay and sea scallops.

3 cups yellow cornmeal
1/2 teaspoon hot red pepper flakes
Salt to taste
2 teaspoons freshly ground black pepper
1 quart shelled oysters
6 cups vegetable or corn oil
Tartar Sauce (page 264)
Lemon wedges

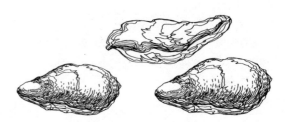

1. In a mixing bowl, combine the cornmeal, hot pepper flakes, salt, and pepper. Blend well.

2. Drain the oysters and dredge them, one at a time, in the cornmeal mixture.

3. Heat the oil to 360 degrees in a deep-fryer or wok. Add the oysters, several at a time, and fry until browned, about 1 minute. Remove to a plate lined with paper towels. Keep the cooked oysters warm. Serve with Tartar Sauce and lemon wedges.

YIELD: 6 TO 8 SERVINGS.

Deep-fried Scallops

This recipe also works well with shrimp.

1/2 cup all-purpose flour
2 pounds bay or sea scallops
2 large eggs
3 tablespoons water
Salt and freshly ground black pepper to taste
3 cups fine fresh bread crumbs

Vegetable oil for deep-frying
French-style Sauce Rémoulade (page 258)

1. Put the flour in a flat dish. Coat the scallops with flour and shake off any excess flour.

2. In a bowl, beat the eggs with the water and salt and pepper and pour the mixture into a shallow bowl. Put the bread crumbs on a flat dish.

3. Dip the scallops into the egg mixture and then roll them in the bread crumbs to coat them well. Shake off any excess.

4. Heat the oil to 360 degrees in a deep-fryer or wok. The oil should not be smoking. Fry the scallops, one batch at a time, for 1 minute (sea scallops require longer cooking). Move the scallops around in the oil with a long fork so they cook evenly and do not stick together. Scoop out the scallops and drain them on paper towels. Allow the oil to return to 360 degrees before cooking the other batch. Serve with French-style Sauce Rémoulade.

YIELD: 6 SERVINGS.

Spicy Fried Scallops

3 large eggs
2 tablespoons chopped fresh thyme leaves, or 3 tablespoons
  dried thyme
2 teaspoons hot red pepper flakes
Salt to taste
1 cup all-purpose flour
2 cups vegetable oil
1 pound sea scallops
1 bunch parsley for garnish
1 lemon, cut into quarters
Watercress Mayonnaise (page 262)

1. Put the eggs into a shallow bowl. Add the thyme, hot pepper flakes, and salt and beat well with a fork.

2. Put the flour into another bowl. In a deep pot, heat the oil to 375 degrees.

3. Dredge the scallops in the flour, about a dozen at a time, and shake them in a colander or sieve to remove any excess flour. Dip them in the egg mixture and remove them with a slotted spoon. Drop the scallops into the hot oil one at a time. Cook for about 90 seconds, or until the batter is golden brown. Drain on paper towels. Repeat for the remaining scallops. Serve with a parsley garnish, lemon wedges, and Watercress Mayonnaise.

YIELD: 4 TO 6 SERVINGS.

French-fried Squid

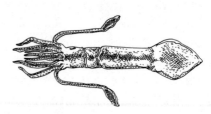

This batter recipe, which uses buttermilk to impart a rich texture, can be used with all sorts of fish and shellfish.

2 pounds squid (about 4 cups), cleaned (Your fish market can do this.)
½ cup buttermilk
2 cups all-purpose flour
1 teaspoon freshly ground black pepper
6 cups vegetable oil
Salt to taste
6 lemon wedges
Tartar Sauce (page 264), Aïoli (page 253), or Mayonnaise with Fresh Herbs (page 260)

1. Cut the squid bodies into very thin rounds, about ⅛ inch thick; slice the tentacles into bite-size pieces.

2. Put all of the pieces into a mixing bowl. Pour in the buttermilk and blend well.

3. Put the flour in 2 large flat baking dishes; add an equal amount of pepper to both and blend well. Drain the squid and distribute the pieces evenly in the two baking dishes. Mix well, shaking off any excess flour.

Squid, also known by its Italian name, calamari, is an extraordinary food source: 80 percent of this cephalopod is edible. It is very lean and versatile and is 18 percent protein.

The dark ink that it secretes as camouflage is prized as a sauce base in Spain. In Italy, it is used to flavor risotto.

4. Heat the oil to 360 degrees in a deep-fryer or wok. Drop the squid pieces into the oil, a few at a time, without crowding them. Fry and stir until crisp and lightly golden, about 1 minute for each batch. Remove the squid pieces and drain on paper towels. Keep warm. Continue cooking in batches until all the pieces are done. Serve the deep-fried squid with a sprinkling of salt, lemon wedges, and one of the sauces.

YIELD: 6 SERVINGS.

Fillets of Sole in Beer Batter

This recipe for beer batter could be used for virtually any kind of fish that is cut into bite-size pieces, or even whole fillets. Shrimp and scallops are particularly delicious cooked this way.

1 cup all-purpose flour
Salt and freshly ground white pepper to taste
2 large eggs, separated
2 cups beer at room temperature
2 tablespoons vegetable oil
2 pounds skinless sole fillets
Vegetable oil for frying
Garlic Mayonnaise (page 260) or Tartar Sauce (page 264)

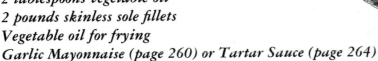

1. To make the batter, put the flour and salt and pepper in a mixing bowl and add the egg yolks. Start beating with a whisk. Stir in the beer and oil, cover, and let stand until ready to use.

2. In another mixing bowl, beat the egg whites until they form soft peaks and fold them into the batter. Let the mixture stand, covered, until ready to use.

3. Split the sole fillets in half lengthwise. There may be a small bone running down the center: Remove it. Place the fillet halves in the batter and stir to coat them.

4. Heat the vegetable oil in a deep-fryer or a wok to 360-degrees. Remove the fish fillets from the batter and let the excess batter drip off. Put them into the cooking oil. When brown on

one side (if using a wok), turn them and continue frying for about 2 to 3 minutes, or until they are crisp and brown all over. Drain the fillets on paper towels. Serve on warm plates with Garlic Mayonnaise or Tartar Sauce.

YIELD: 6 SERVINGS.

Goujonnettes of Sole
with Mustard Sauce

The French term goujonnette *refers to deep-fried strips of sole. This recipe also works with strips of fluke, flounder, and mild whitefish.*

6 cups vegetable oil
8 skinless lemon or gray sole fillets
2 large eggs
Salt and freshly ground white pepper to taste
3 tablespoons water
⅓ cup all-purpose flour
4 cups fine fresh bread crumbs
Lemon wedges
Sauce Gribiche (page 257)

1. Heat the oil to 375 degrees in a deep-fryer or wok.
2. Place the fillets on a flat surface and cut them down the center lengthwise along both sides of the little center bone. Cut each halved fillet on the diagonal into ½-inch-thick strips.
3. Combine the eggs, salt and pepper, and water in a shallow bowl and beat well with a whisk.
4. Place the flour on a flat dish and season generously with white pepper. Blend well. Place the bread crumbs on another flat dish. Dredge the fish strips thoroughly in the flour and shake off the excess.
5. Dip the coated fish in the egg mixture. Drain off the excess

and transfer the strips to the bread crumbs. Toss the pieces in the bread crumbs to coat them well.

6. Pick up each strip of fish, one at a time, and roll it between your hands or on a flat surface to make the bread crumbs adhere evenly.

7. Drop the sole strips into the preheated oil, a dozen or so at a time. Stir gently as they fry. Do not overcrowd the pieces in the oil or they will not brown evenly. Total cooking time should be about 2 minutes for each batch, or until golden. Continue cooking until all the pieces are done. Drain on paper towels and serve immediately with lemon wedges and Sauce Gribiche.

YIELD: 6 SERVINGS.

Deep-fried Whitebait

This recipe also works well with small fillets of fish, such as whiting (or whole whiting), strips of lemon or gray sole, and virtually any other white-fleshed fish fillets.

4 cups vegetable oil
2 pounds whitebait
½ cup milk
2 cups all-purpose flour
Salt to taste
Lemon wedges
Sauce Gribiche (page 257), Tartar Sauce (page 264), or
French-style Sauce Rémoulade (page 258)

1. Preheat the oil to 375 degrees in a deep-fryer or wok.
2. Rinse the fish in cool water and drain. Pat dry with paper towels.
3. Put the whitebait in a bowl and coat with the milk; mix well and drain.
4. Spread the flour on a dish. Dredge the fish in the flour to coat it well. Shake off any excess flour.
5. Place one quarter of the whitebait in the basket of a deep-

fryer or in a wok and cook, shaking the basket, for about 2 minutes, or until the fish are browned and crisp. (If you do not have a frying basket, a wire mesh strainer will do.) Drain on paper towels and season with salt to taste. Serve hot with lemon wedges and either Sauce Gribiche, Tartar Sauce, or French-style Sauce Rémoulade.

YIELD: 6 TO 8 SERVINGS.

Whiting with Fried Parsley

4 whole whiting (about ½ pound each), cleaned
¼ cup milk
3 drops of Tabasco sauce
Salt and freshly ground black pepper to taste
½ cup all-purpose flour
4 cups vegetable oil
4 lemon wedges
Fried Parsley (page 268)

1. Put the whiting in a dish and add the milk, Tabasco sauce, and salt and pepper.
2. Scatter the flour over a large pan or dish. Remove the whiting from the milk, one at a time. Do not dry them. Dredge each fish thoroughly in the flour.
3. Heat the oil to 360 degrees in a deep-fryer or a wok and add the fish two at a time. Cook for about 5 minutes, turning occasionally, until they are golden brown. Serve with lemon wedges, Fried Parsley, and a sauce of your choice.

YIELD: 4 SERVINGS.

CHAPTER 9

Poaching, Steaming, and Braising

Shrimp Poached in Beer with Dill

1 12-ounce can light beer
5 dill sprigs
3 garlic cloves, peeled and diced
1 bay leaf
¼ teaspoon dried thyme
⅛ teaspoon cayenne pepper
Salt and freshly ground black pepper
1 pound unshelled medium-size shrimp

1. In a deep pot, combine all the ingredients, *except* the shrimp, and bring to a boil. Lower the heat and simmer, covered, for 10 minutes.

2. Add the shrimp, return to a boil, and simmer for 30 seconds. Remove the shrimp from the pot, drain, and serve. This goes particularly well with Melted Dill Butter (page 264).

YIELD: 4 SERVINGS.

Beer is an excellent ingredient for cooking fish. In the poaching recipe on this page it combines well with dill to give the shrimp a dry, herby flavor. It also adds extra lightness to batters for deep-frying. A famous Belgian beef stew, called carbonnade flamande, calls for beer in the sauce.

Steamed Lobster

Water for the steamer
2 pounds seaweed, optional
6 live lobsters (about 1½ pounds each)

1. Pour about 2 inches of water into the bottom of a large steamer. Add the seaweed.

2. Place the live lobsters on steamer racks and cover the pot. Bring the water to a rapid boil over high heat and cook for about 12 minutes. Remove the lobsters from the heat and let them sit for 5 minutes over the hot water, covered.

3. Remove the lobsters, split them in half lengthwise, and crack the claws. Remove the small sac near the eyes and the intestine through the middle of the tail. Serve with a hot or a cold sauce or melted butter.

YIELD: 6 SERVINGS.

Littlenecks in Green Sauce

This recipe also works well with large mussels and soft-shell clams.

¼ cup olive oil
2 tablespoons finely chopped garlic
48 littleneck clams, rinsed and drained
¾ cup dry white wine
¼ teaspoon hot red pepper flakes
1 cup chopped scallions
1 cup chopped fresh parsley leaves
Freshly ground black pepper to taste
1 tablespoon cornstarch
2 tablespoons cold water
1 cup fresh peas, parboiled and drained, or frozen peas,
  defrosted

1. Pour the olive oil into a large saucepan or frying pan with a tight-fitting lid. Heat over medium heat and add the garlic, clams, wine, hot pepper flakes, scallions, parsley, and black pepper. Cover and cook for about 5 minutes, shaking the pan from time to time, until all the clams have opened.

2. Meanwhile, blend the cornstarch and the water in a small bowl. When the clams are cooked, pour the cornstarch mixture into the sauce and stir. Add the peas and stir again. Serve with good French bread, rice, or pasta.

YIELD: 4 TO 6 SERVINGS.

Mussels Marseillaise

¼ cup olive oil
1 tablespoon finely chopped garlic
¼ cup finely chopped well-washed leek whites
¼ cup finely chopped fennel leaves
1 cup canned crushed Italian tomatoes
¼ teaspoon saffon threads
Freshly ground black pepper to taste
⅛ teaspoon hot red pepper flakes
¾ cup dry white wine
5 pounds mussels, well scrubbed and with beards removed
¼ cup chopped fresh parsley leaves

1. Heat the oil in a pot or deep saucepan. Add the garlic and leeks and cook briefly over medium-high heat, stirring. Do not brown. Add the fennel, tomatoes, saffron, pepper, and hot pepper flakes. Simmer, stirring, for 5 minutes.

2. Add to the pot the wine and mussels, cover tightly, and cook over high heat until the mussels have opened, about 5 to 6 minutes. Sprinkle with the parsley and serve with French or Italian bread.

YIELD: 6 SERVINGS.

Steamed Mussels with Ginger and Coriander

This recipe also works well with soft-shell clams.

¼ *cup virgin olive oil*
2 *tablespoons minced garlic*
2 *tablespoons grated fresh gingerroot*
1½ *cups canned crushed and peeled tomatoes*
7 *pounds mussels, well scrubbed and with beards removed*
¼ *teaspoon hot red pepper flakes*
½ *cup chopped fresh basil leaves, or 1 tablespoon dried basil*
½ *cup chopped fresh parsley leaves*
4 *tablespoons chopped fresh coriander leaves*
1 *cup finely chopped scallions*
1½ *cups dry white wine*

Heat the oil over medium-high heat in a large, deep pan. Add the garlic and ginger and cook, stirring, for about 1 minute. Add the tomatoes and mussels and then the hot pepper flakes, basil, parsley, coriander, and scallions. Add the wine, cover, and cook over high heat, shaking the pan occasionally to redistribute the mussels. Cook for about 5 minutes, or until all the mussels have opened. Serve the mussels with some of the cooking liquid in warm soup bowls accompanied by crusty Italian or French bread.

YIELD: 6 SERVINGS.

Ed Giobbi's Steamed Mussels in White Wine and Herbs

4 tablespoons olive oil
¼ cup chopped scallions
¼ cup chopped fresh Italian parsley leaves
2 tablespoons chopped fresh basil leaves, or 1 tablespoon dried basil
1 tablespoon minced garlic
¼ cup finely chopped sweet green pepper
1 tablespoon dried oregano
½ cup dry white wine
1 tablespoon chopped fresh mint leaves, or 1 teaspoon dried mint
Salt if desired
Hot red pepper flakes to taste
5 pounds mussels, well scrubbed and with beards removed

1. Heat the oil in a pot or deep saucepan. Add all the ingredients, *except* the mussels, and cook over high heat for 3 minutes. Add the mussels, cover, and continue cooking over high heat until the mussels have opened, about 5 to 6 minutes. Shake the pan from time to time.

2. Drain the cooking liquid equally into individual serving bowls. Serve the mussels in separate bowls. As you extract the mussel meat, dip it into the hot broth before eating. Serve with French or Italian bread.

YIELD: 4 TO 6 SERVINGS.

Mussels in Tomato Sauce with Fresh Basil

4 tablespoons olive oil
¾ cup finely chopped onion
1 tablespoon finely chopped garlic
4 tablespoons red wine vinegar
3 cups chopped or crushed Italian canned tomatoes
½ teaspoon crumbled dried oregano
¼ teaspoon hot red pepper flakes
Freshly ground black pepper to taste
5 pounds mussels, well scrubbed and with beards removed
½ cup finely chopped fresh Italian parsley leaves
4 tablespoons finely chopped fresh basil leaves, or 2 teaspoons
    dried basil

1. Heat the oil in a large saucepan. Add the onion and garlic and cook until the onion is wilted. Do not let the garlic brown. Add the vinegar, tomatoes, oregano, hot pepper flakes, and pepper and bring to a boil. Cover and cook for 5 minutes.

2. Add the mussels to the pot along with the parsley and basil. Cover and bring to a boil. Cook for 4 to 5 minutes, or until all the mussels have opened. As they cook, shake the pan to distribute them evenly.

3. Serve the mussels in hot soup bowls with the liquid poured over them. Accompany the mussels with French or Italian bread.

YIELD: 4 SERVINGS.

Steamed Sea Bass Fillets with Fresh Thyme and Leek Sauce

1 tablespoon unsalted butter
2 leeks, trimmed, cleaned, and diced (about 2 cups)
⅓ cup dry white wine
1 cup heavy cream
Salt and freshly ground black pepper to taste
Pinch of freshly grated nutmeg
2 skinless sea bass fillets (about 3 pounds total weight), cut
*   into 6 equal portions*
6 thyme sprigs

1. Melt the butter in a small saucepan over medium heat. Add the leeks and cook, stirring, for 2 minutes. Add the wine and cook, stirring, until most of the moisture has evaporated. Add the cream, salt and pepper, and nutmeg. Stir, bring to a boil, and simmer for 2 minutes. Remove from the heat, cover, and set aside.

2. Pour water into the bottom of a steamer. Season the fillets with salt and pepper and place them on a steaming rack. Lay a sprig of thyme over each. Cover, bring the water to a boil, and steam for 3 to 4 minutes, or until done.

3. Transfer the fish to warm serving plates. Spoon some of the leek sauce over the fillets along each side of the thyme sprigs. Serve immediately, perhaps with Steamed Parsleyed Cucumbers (page 267).

YIELD: 6 SERVINGS.

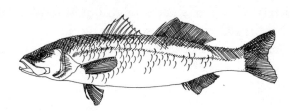

Poached Striped Bass

This recipe also works well with red snapper, salmon, and sea trout.

COURT BOUILLON

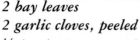

4 quarts water
1 cup dry white wine
¼ cup white vinegar
1½ cups thinly sliced onion
¾ cup thinly sliced carrots
1 cup coarsely chopped well-washed leeks
1 cup coarsely chopped celery
8 whole black peppercorns
Salt to taste
4 thyme sprigs, or 1 teaspoon dried thyme
2 bay leaves
2 garlic cloves, peeled
⅛ teaspoon cayenne pepper
6 parsley sprigs

THE FISH

1 4- to 6-pound striped bass with head and tail, cleaned and
gills removed

1. Put all the ingredients for the court bouillon in a 20-inch fish poacher, cover, bring to a boil, and boil for 15 minutes. Let it cool.

2. When the court bouillon is ready, submerge the fish entirely. (If there is not enough liquid to cover the fish by at least 1 inch, add water.) Return the liquid to a boil, lower the heat to a simmer, and poach for about 10 to 15 minutes, depending on the thickness of the fish. Let the fish stand in the cooking liquid for 10 minutes more before serving.

3. Remove the fish and carefully peel away the skin with a paring knife. Serve hot, lukewarm, or cold.

YIELD: 6 TO 10 SERVINGS.

Note: If served warm, the following sauces are excellent matches: hollandaise, sauce mousseline, mustard sauce, and any herb vinaigrette; if served cold, gribiche, tartar, herb vinaigrette, and a cucumber and dill mayonnaise. Cucumber salad is a good side dish.

Steamed Striped Bass
with Leek Sauce

Red snapper also works with this recipe.

2 skinless striped bass fillets (about 2½ pounds total weight),
*   cut into 6 equal portions*
18 thyme or dill sprigs
Salt and freshly ground black pepper to taste
1 tablespoon unsalted butter
3 cups finely chopped well-washed leeks
⅛ teaspoon freshly grated nutmeg
¼ cup dry white wine
1 tablespoon white wine vinegar
¾ cup heavy cream

1. Place the fillets, skinned side down, in the rack of a steamer. Cover each piece with 2 sprigs of thyme. Sprinkle with salt and pepper.

2. Fill the bottom of a steamer about halfway with water and add 6 sprigs of thyme. Bring to a boil.

3. Meanwhile, melt the butter in a saucepan and add the leeks, salt and pepper, and nutmeg. Sauté, stirring, for 5 minutes, or just until the leeks wilt. Add the wine and vinegar and

continue cooking, stirring occasionally, until reduced by half. Add the cream and bring to a boil; then lower the heat and simmer for 5 minutes. Keep the sauce warm.

4. Place the fish over the boiling water and cover tightly. Steam for about 5 to 6 minutes, or until the fish is tender (when pierced with a knife and has lost its raw look throughout). Serve the leek sauce over the fish.

YIELD: 6 SERVINGS.

Poached Cod Fillets
in Cream Sauce

This recipe also works well with red snapper, striped bass, halibut, and tilefish.

2 boneless and skinless fresh cod fillets, cut into 6 equal
   portions (about 2½ pounds total weight)
2½ cups milk
Salt to taste
6 whole black peppercorns
1 cup thinly sliced onion
2 thyme sprigs, or ½ teaspoon dried thyme
1 bay leaf
2 whole cloves
4 sprigs parsley
¼ teaspoon Tabasco sauce
2 tablespoons unsalted butter
3 tablespoons cornstarch
½ cup heavy cream
¼ teaspoon freshly grated nutmeg

1. Put the fish in 2 skillets large enough to hold them in one layer. Add enough water to barely cover the fish. Add the milk, salt, peppercorns, onion slices, thyme, bay leaf, cloves, parsley

sprigs, and Tabasco sauce. Bring to a simmer and cook for about 2 minutes. Set aside.

2. Melt the butter in a saucepan over medium heat and add the cornstarch, stirring with a wire whisk. Blend well. Add 2 cups of the poaching liquid. Cook over medium-high heat, stirring rapidly with a wire whisk until thickened and smooth. Add the cream and nutmeg and stir. Simmer for 5 minutes.

3. Remove the fish from the poaching liquid and drain well. Transfer to warm serving plates and pour some sauce over each. Serve with boiled potatoes and dilled cucumbers.

YIELD: 6 SERVINGS.

Poached Cod Steaks with Warm Mayonnaise

6 cod steaks, about 1½ inches thick (about ½ pound each)
¼ cup milk
1 medium-size onion, sliced
1 bay leaf
4 parsley sprigs
2 whole cloves
10 whole black peppercorns
Salt to taste
Warm Mayonnaise (page 262)

1. Put the steaks in a pan large enough to hold them in a single layer. Add water to cover. Then add the milk, onion, bay leaf, parsley sprigs, cloves, peppercorns, and salt.

2. Bring to a simmer and cover. Simmer for 3 to 4 minutes, or until the fish flakes easily. Do not overcook.

3. Drain, remove the bay leaf and parsley sprigs, and serve with Warm Mayonnaise.

YIELD: 6 SERVINGS.

Japan is the major fishing country in the world, hauling in 11.25 million tons in 1983 (latest statistics available), followed by the U.S.S.R. (9.7 million tons), China (5.2 million tons), and the United States (4.1 million tons).

Finnan Haddie with Cream Sauce

2 tablespoons unsalted butter
3 tablespoons all-purpose flour
4 cups milk
Salt and freshly ground black pepper to taste
Cayenne pepper to taste
Freshly grated nutmeg to taste
3 pounds finnan haddie, cut into 6 serving pieces
½ cup sliced onion
2 parsley sprigs
1 bay leaf
½ cup heavy cream

1. Melt the butter in a large pan. Add the flour and stir with a wire whisk. When it is well blended add 3 cups of the milk. Bring to a boil and season with salt and pepper, cayenne pepper, and nutmeg.

2. Put the fish fillets in a skillet large enough to hold them in one layer. Add the remaining cup of milk and enough water to cover the fish entirely. Add the onion, parsley sprigs, and bay leaf. Bring to a boil, lower the heat to a simmer, and cook for 2 minutes.

3. Add to the pan with the sauce ½ cup of the cooking liquid from the fish. Stir and add the cream. Check for seasonings. Transfer the fish, one piece at a time, to warm serving plates. Spoon over equal amounts of the sauce. This dish goes well with boiled potatoes.

YIELD: 6 SERVINGS.

Finnan haddie is a Scottish name for split smoked fillets of haddock. In the U.S. what is sold as finnan haddie is often smoked cod.

Steamed Halibut Fillets with Fresh Coriander and White Wine Sauce

This recipe also works with striped bass, sea trout, and red snapper.

1 cup chopped fresh coriander leaves
Salt and freshly ground black pepper to taste
2 halibut fillets (about 3 pounds total weight), cut into 6
  equal-size pieces
White Wine Sauce (page 245)

   1. Sprinkle the coriander and salt and pepper on both sides of the fillets.

   2. Put the fish fillets in one layer on a steamer rack. Steam for about 5 minutes.

   3. Transfer the halibut fillets to hot plates and spoon the hot sauce over them.

YIELD: 6 SERVINGS.

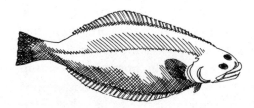

Monkfish and Potatoes in Red Wine Sauce

5 tablespoons unsalted butter
¼ cup coarsely chopped shallots
1 tablespoon chopped garlic
½ teaspoon dried thyme
4 sprigs parsley
1 bay leaf
6 tablespoons cornstarch
1 bottle dry red wine
2 cups Fish Broth (page 241) or bottled clam juice
12 small red skin potatoes, peeled
2 cups pearl onions (about 10 ounces)
¾ pound button mushrooms (about 4 cups)
1 teaspoon finely chopped garlic
4 tablespoons finely chopped shallots
Salt and freshly ground black pepper to taste
4 pounds skinless monkfish fillets, cut into 1-inch cubes
2 tablespoons Cognac
½ cup chopped fresh parsley leaves

1. Heat 3 tablespoons of the butter in a saucepan over medium heat and sauté the shallots and garlic for 3 minutes. Add the thyme, parsley, bay leaf, cornstarch, red wine, and fish broth. Bring to a boil and simmer for 20 minutes. Set aside.

2. Meanwhile, cook the potatoes in boiling salted water for about 15 minutes. Drain and set aside.

3. Melt the remaining butter in a flameproof casserole. Sauté the onions, mushrooms, garlic, and shallots over medium heat for 3 to 4 minutes. Season with salt and pepper. Add the monkfish cubes and cook for 3 minutes, stirring often. Add the Cognac. Pour the red wine sauce into the pan. Bring to a boil and simmer for 5 minutes. Add the potatoes, sprinkle with parsley, and serve immediately.

YIELD: 8 TO 10 SERVINGS.

Poached Salmon Steak with Dill

This recipe also works well with sea trout and red snapper.

4 boneless salmon steaks (about ½ pound each)
4 tablespoons white vinegar
1 cup sliced onion
4 dill sprigs
⅛ teaspoon cayenne pepper
Salt to taste
6 whole black peppercorns

1. Select a wide shallow saucepan large enough to hold the salmon steaks in one layer. Cover them with cold water and add the vinegar, onion, dill, cayenne pepper, salt, and peppercorns. Bring to a boil, lower the heat to a simmer, and poach for about 5 to 6 minutes, or until cooked. Remove the fillets and drain well.

2. Serve hot with Hollandaise–Mustard Sauce (page 254), Beurre Blanc (page 243), or Mustard–Dill Sauce (page 256). If served cold, the appropriate sauces would be Cucumber and Dill Mayonnaise (page 259) or Sauce Gribiche (page 257).

YIELD: 4 SERVINGS.

Salmon and Tilefish in Saffron Broth

4 cups *Fish Broth (page 241) or bottled clam juice*
1 cup *dry white wine*
1 1/2 cups *coarsely chopped peeled and seeded tomatoes*
18 *pearl onions, peeled*
18 *baby carrots, cleaned and scraped*
1/2 cup *coarsely chopped scallions*
1 *bay leaf*
2 teaspoons *finely chopped garlic*
1/2 teaspoon *saffron threads*
1 1/2 pounds *boneless and skinless monkfish, cut into 1 1/2-inch cubes*
Salt and freshly ground black pepper to taste
1/4 teaspoon *hot red pepper flakes*
1/4 pound *snow peas, ends trimmed*
1/2 pound *skinless salmon fillets, cut into 1 1/2-inch cubes*
1 pound *skinless tilefish fillets, cut into 1 1/2-inch cubes*
1/2 cup *finely chopped fresh coriander leaves*
Garlic Croutons (page 274)
Aïoli (page 253)

1. Put the fish broth, white wine, tomatoes, pearl onions, baby carrots, scallions, bay leaf, garlic, and saffron into a large saucepan. Bring to a boil and simmer for about 10 minutes.

2. Add the monkfish, salt and pepper, hot pepper flakes, and snow peas. Bring to a boil and simmer for 4 minutes. Add the salmon, tilefish, and coriander. Simmer for 2 minutes. Serve very hot with the Garlic Croutons and Aïoli.

YIELD: 6 SERVINGS.

Skate with Black Butter and Capers

4 *skate wings (about 3 pounds total weight)*
½ *cup white vinegar*
10 *whole black peppercorns*
2 *bay leaves*
2 *thyme sprigs, or ½ teaspoon dried thyme*
Salt to taste
10 *tablespoons unsalted butter*
½ *cup drained capers*
2 *tablespoons red wine vinegar*
4 *tablespoons chopped fresh parsley leaves*

1. Put the skate wings in a large saucepan and cover with water. Bring to a boil and simmer for 2 minutes. Drain quickly and run the skate wings under cold water until cold.

2. Remove the wings and place them on a flat surface. Use a sharp knife to gently scrape away the skin from both sides of the skate. Also scrape away any red streaks that appear across the center.

3. Transfer the skate to a wide saucepan that will hold them in one layer. Add water to cover, white vinegar, peppercorns, bay leaves, thyme, and salt. Bring to a gentle, rolling boil and turn off the heat. Let sit for 4 to 5 minutes.

4. Drain the fish and transfer them to a warm serving platter.

5. Melt the butter in a frying pan over high heat, shaking and swirling, until it is dark brown, nearly black. Add the capers and wine vinegar. Shake the skillet to blend and pour this over the skate. Sprinkle with the parsley and serve with hot boiled potatoes.

YIELD: 6 SERVINGS.

Skate, a member of the ray family, is an increasingly popular eating fish in this country. The French equivalent, called raie, *is prepared in dozens of ways. Skate are not the most comely creatures: They are flat and wide, with whip-like tails. The edible parts are the wings, which contain meat that has been compared to scallops for delicacy.*

Red Snapper with Chile Poblano Sauce

FROM JOSEFINA HOWARD, CHEF OF
ROSA MEXICANO, NEW YORK

This vibrant, mildly hot recipe also works well with any white-fleshed fillet, such as sole, flounder, and striped bass.

8 fresh chiles poblanos
1 sweet red pepper
¼ cup water
½ cup vegetable oil
2 garlic cloves, peeled and bruised
3 tablespoons chopped onion
Salt to taste
6 large red snapper fillets with skin
3 large egg yolks, or 4 small ones

1. Char the chiles poblanos and red pepper over a gas flame or in a broiler until the skins are blackened.

2. Place the charred chiles and pepper in a paper bag to "sweat" for about 5 minutes. Then peel them with your hands. Cut them open and remove the stems and most of the seeds (leave a small amount of the seeds for a mildly hot sauce, more if you like it hotter). Rinse the outsides of the peppers with cold water to eliminate all charred skin.

3. Cut the chiles into quarters and place them in a blender or food processor along with ¼ cup of water and reduce to a fine purée. Cut the red pepper into ¼-inch-wide strips and set them aside.

4. Heat the oil over medium heat in a large frying pan. Add the garlic and cook until just golden. Add the onion and cook until it is translucent. Remove and discard the garlic.

5. Add the poblano chile purée to the pan and stir for 2 minutes over medium-high heat. Season with salt to taste. Lower the heat and simmer for 3 minutes, stirring occasionally.

6. Strain the sauce into the top of a double boiler set over barely simmering water.

7. In a fish poacher filled with lightly salted water, poach the fish fillets for 5 to 7 minutes, depending on thickness.

8. While the fish is cooking, gradually stir the beaten egg yolks into the poblano sauce, constantly mixing with a wooden spoon. Do not let the eggs curdle. Taste for seasonings.

9. When the fish are cooked, drain well and arrange on warm serving plates. Pour the chile sauce over them and garnish with strips of the sweet red pepper. Rice and beans go well with this dish.

YIELD: 6 SERVINGS.

Red Snapper Fillets in Bouillabaisse Sauce

2 tablespoons olive oil
2 teaspoons finely chopped garlic
3/4 cup finely chopped onion
3/4 cup finely chopped well-washed leeks
1/2 cup finely chopped fennel leaves
1/2 cup finely chopped celery
1/2 teaspoon saffron threads
1 cup peeled and chopped ripe tomatoes
1/2 cup dry white wine
1/2 cup Fish Broth (page 241) or bottled clam juice
1 bay leaf
1/8 teaspoon cayenne pepper
1 1/2 pounds skinless red snapper fillets, cut into 4 portions
Salt and freshly ground black pepper
2 tablespoons chopped fresh parsley leaves

1. Heat the oil in a saucepan and add the garlic, onion, leeks, fennel, celery, and saffron. Cook, stirring, over medium-high heat until wilted, about 3 minutes. Add the tomatoes, wine, fish

broth, bay leaf, and cayenne pepper and cook for 10 minutes more.

2. Put the fillets in a skillet large enough to hold the pieces in one layer. Season with salt and pepper. Pour the sauce evenly over the fish. Cover and simmer for about 5 minutes, or until cooked. Sprinkle with the parsley before serving.

YIELD: 4 SERVINGS.

Stuffed Sole Fillets with Beurre Blanc

THE SCALLOP MOUSSE

¾ pound sea scallops
1 teaspoon salt
⅓ teaspoon freshly ground white pepper
½ cup heavy cream

THE BEURRE BLANC

4 tablespoons white wine vinegar
3 tablespoons dry white wine
2 tablespoons minced shallots
1½ cups (3 sticks) unsalted butter
Freshly ground white pepper to taste
Salt to taste if desired

THE FISH

8 gray sole fillets

1. Put the scallops in a food processor or blender. Add the salt and pepper and purée as you slowly pour in the cream. Stop the machine occasionally and scrape down the sides of the bowl with a spatula. Purée until the mixture is firm enough to form small balls. Place the mixture in a bowl, cover, and refrigerate.

2. Put the vinegar, wine, and shallots in a saucepan and reduce the liquid over medium-high heat by three-quarters. Turn the heat to low (or pour the sauce into the top of a double boiler over simmering water) and drop in pats of the butter, one at a time, while whisking vigorously. As soon as one pat melts, add the next. Continue until all the butter is blended. Taste for seasoning. Remove the sauce from the heat and keep it warm.

3. Lay the fillets on a flat surface, darker side up, and place a ball of scallop mousse (roughly a heaping tablespoon) on top of each. Roll the fillets around the mousse (illustration 1) and secure them with a toothpick (illustration 2).

4. Bring water to a boil in the bottom of a steamer. Place the fish rolls on the steamer rack and cover. Steam for 7 minutes.

5. Remove the fish from the poacher. Drain well before placing on warm plates, allowing 2 rolls per person. Pour the warm beurre blanc over them.

YIELD: 4 SERVINGS.

Stuffed Sole Fillets with Ginger Sauce

This recipe also works well with flounder.

12 skinless gray sole fillets (about 2½ pounds total weight)
Salt and freshly ground white pepper to taste
½ pound skinless salmon fillets, cut into 1-inch cubes
1 large egg
¼ teaspoon freshly grated nutmeg
¾ cup heavy cream
3 tablespoons chopped fresh chives or parsley leaves
1 cup Fresh Ginger Sauce with Tomatoes (page 252)

1. Arrange the sole fillets skin side up on a flat surface and pound them lightly with a flat mallet or heavy bottomed pan to flatten them. Sprinkle with salt and pepper.

2. Put the salmon cubes into the container of a food processor, add the egg, salt and pepper, and nutmeg. Blend while gradually pouring in the cream for about 30 seconds, or until smooth; add the chives and mix well.

3. Spoon an equal portion of the salmon mixture over each fillet. Fold over the ends of the fillets to enclose the mixture.

4. Pour water into the bottom of a steamer and bring to a boil. Place the fish fillets on the steamer rack. Cover closely. Steam for 5 to 6 minutes. The steaming time will vary depending on the thickness of the fillets. Serve with the sauce.

YIELD: 6 SERVINGS.

Steamed Sea Trout Fillets with Two Sauces

This recipe also works well with salmon, fluke, and halibut.

3 skinless sea trout fillets, about 1 inch thick (about 2½ to
  3 pounds total weight), cut into 6 equal portions
Salt and freshly ground white pepper to taste
6 dill sprigs
Quick Tomato Sauce (page 250)
Mushroom–Cream Sauce (page 252)

1. Put the fish fillets on the rack of a steamer and sprinkle with salt and pepper. Lay the dill sprigs over them.

2. Steam the fish, covered, for about 5 minutes, or until cooked.

3. Remove the dill sprigs and transfer the fish to warm plates. Place about 2 tablespoons each of the tomato sauce and mushroom sauce along the perimeter of each plate.

YIELD: 6 SERVINGS.

CHAPTER 10

Soups and Stews

Spicy Gazpacho with Shrimp and Crab Meat

3 cups peeled, seeded, and chopped ripe tomatoes
¾ cup chopped red onion
⅓ cup finely chopped celery
1 cup chopped sweet red pepper
2 teaspoons chopped hot peppers, or to taste
1 tablespoon finely chopped garlic
1 tablespoon dried coriander, well crumbled
½ cup chopped fresh coriander leaves
1 cup tomato juice
4 tablespoons olive oil
2 tablespoons fresh lime juice
3 tablespoons red wine vinegar
Salt and freshly ground black pepper to taste
1 pound cooked and shelled shrimp (page 15)
1 pound lump crab meat, shell and cartilage removed
Garlic Croutons (page 274)

1. Combine all the ingredients, *except* the shrimp, crab meat, and croutons, in a mixing bowl. Cover with plastic wrap and refrigerate until cold.

2. Stir in the crab meat and shrimp at the last minute. Serve in chilled bowls with the Garlic Croutons as garnish.

YIELD: 6 SERVINGS.

Fish and Shellfish Soup
with Saffron

This recipe also works well with mako shark, blackfish, and tuna.

2 pounds skinless monkfish fillets
¼ cup olive oil
1 tablespoon minced garlic
2 cups chopped onion
1½ cups chopped well-washed leeks
⅔ cup chopped celery
1 tablespoon fennel seeds
1 teaspoon saffron threads
¼ teaspoon hot red pepper flakes
3 cups Italian canned tomatoes
6 cups Fish Broth (page 241) or bottled clam juice
1 cup dry white wine
1½ pounds mussels, well scrubbed and with beards removed
1 pound medium-size shrimp, shelled and deveined
Salt and freshly ground black pepper to taste
½ cup chopped fresh parsley leaves
Garlic Croutons (page 274)

1. Cut the fish into 1½-inch cubes.
2. Heat the oil in a soup pot and sauté the garlic, onion, leeks, and celery for 1 minute. Add the fennel seeds, saffron, and hot pepper flakes and cook over high heat, stirring, for 3 minutes.
3. Add the tomatoes, fish broth, and wine and cook for 10 minutes, stirring often.
4. Add the fish and the mussels to the broth and cook for 5 minutes. Add the shrimp and cook for another 2 minutes. Season with salt and pepper and stir in the parsley. Serve immediately with the Garlic Croutons.

YIELD: 6 TO 8 SERVINGS.

Scallop Soup Provençal

1½ quarts water
Greens from 3 leeks, coarsely chopped
1 carrot, cleaned and cut into 1-inch pieces
1 celery stalk, chopped coarsely
1 onion, quartered
1 garlic clove, crushed
6 whole black peppercorns
1 bay leaf
*1 teaspoon chopped fresh thyme leaves, or 1½ teaspoons dried
    thyme*
¼ teaspoon coriander seeds, optional
3 garlic cloves, minced
3 shallots, minced
3 tablespoons olive oil
1 large ripe tomato, peeled and coarsely chopped
1 pound bay scallops
¼ teaspoon saffron threads
Salt and freshly ground black pepper to taste
Garlic Mayonnaise (page 260)
Croutons (page 274)

1. In a soup pot, combine the water, leek greens, carrot, celery, onion, crushed garlic, peppercorns, bay leaf, thyme, and coriander seeds. Bring to a boil and simmer for 30 minutes.

2. When the broth is ready, put the 3 cloves minced garlic and shallots into a deep saucepan with the olive oil and cook over medium heat for 5 minutes; do not let the garlic brown. Add the tomato and cook for 2 minutes.

3. Strain the leek and carrot broth into the saucepan and bring the liquid to a boil. Add the scallops, saffron, and salt and pepper. Cook for 2 minutes and serve immediately, stirring a spoonful of the Garlic Mayonnaise into each serving of the soup. Serve with the Croutons.

YIELD: 4 SERVINGS.

Littleneck Clam Soup

This recipe also works well with mussels.

48 littleneck clams (the smaller the better)
2 tablespoons unsalted butter
2 tablespoons finely chopped shallots
¼ cup finely chopped onion
1 teaspoon finely minced garlic
1 thyme sprig, or ½ teaspoon dried thyme
2 cups dry white wine
⅛ teaspoon hot red pepper flakes
Freshly ground white pepper
1 large egg yolk
1 cup heavy cream
1 cup milk
¼ cup chopped fresh basil or coriander leaves
Parmesan Cheese Bread (page 273)

1. Scrub and rinse the clams. Drain them well.

2. Melt the butter in a large soup pot over medium heat. Add the shallots, onion, and garlic. Cook, stirring, over medium heat until wilted. Stir in the thyme and wine.

3. Add the clams to the pot along with the hot pepper flakes and white pepper. Cover tightly, bring to a boil, and cook for 5 to 8 minutes, stirring occasionally, until all the clams have opened.

4. Combine the egg yolk, milk, and cream in a bowl and blend well. Stir this into the soup pot and bring to a simmer, stirring constantly. Remove from the heat immediately and serve in heated soup bowls. Sprinkle with the chopped basil and serve with the Parmesan Cheese Bread.

YIELD: 6 TO 8 SERVINGS.

Mussel Soup Provençal

6 tablespoons olive oil
1 tablespoon chopped garlic
½ cup finely chopped onion
¾ cup dry white wine
1½ cups imported canned tomatoes
1 tablespoon tomato paste
¼ teaspoon hot red pepper flakes
½ cup chopped fresh parsley leaves
1 bay leaf
Salt and freshly ground black pepper to taste
5 pounds mussels, well scrubbed and with beards removed
Parmesan Cheese Bread (page 273)

1. Heat the oil in a soup pot over medium-high heat and add the garlic and onion. Cook briefly, stirring well, without browning. Add the wine, tomatoes, tomato paste, hot pepper flakes, parsley, bay leaf, and salt and black pepper. Bring liquid to a boil and simmer for 5 minutes.

2. Add the mussels and cover tightly. Cook, shaking the soup pot up and down to redistribute the mussels so they cook evenly. Cook for about 5 minutes, or until all the mussels have opened. Serve with the Parmesan Cheese Bread.

YIELD: 6 SERVINGS.

Cream of Mussel Soup with Saffron

---

3 tablespoons unsalted butter
4 tablespoons chopped shallots
4 tablespoons chopped onion
1 teaspoon chopped garlic
½ teaspoon saffron threads
2 quarts mussels, well scrubbed and with beards removed
Tabasco sauce to taste
¼ cup finely chopped fresh parsley leaves
1½ cups dry white wine
2 cups heavy cream
1 cup light cream
Salt and freshly ground black pepper to taste
Parmesan Cheese Bread (page 273)

1. Melt the butter in a soup pot over medium-high heat. Add the shallots, onion, garlic, and saffron. Cook, stirring, for about 3 minutes. Add the mussels, Tabasco sauce, parsley, and wine. Cover and cook until the mussels have opened, about 5 minutes.

2. Add the creams to the cooking liquid and bring to a boil. Season with salt and pepper. If necessary, keep warm over low heat.

3. Garnish with slices of Parmesan Cheese Bread.

YIELD: 6 SERVINGS.

Soupe de Poisson
à la Marseillaise

FISH SOUP MARSEILLES STYLE

---

2 tablespoons olive oil
¾ cup minced onion
1 tablespoon minced garlic
½ cup finely chopped celery
1 teaspoon saffron threads
½ teaspoon hot red pepper flakes
½ teaspoon freshly ground black pepper
4 ripe tomatoes, peeled, seeded, and chopped
¼ cup tomato paste
¼ cup dry white wine
6 cups Fish Broth (page 241) or bottled clam juice
2 pounds monkfish fillets (or any firm whitefish)
Garlic Croutons (page 274)

1. Heat the olive oil in a soup pot and sauté the onion and garlic over medium-high heat just until the onion is wilted. Do not let the garlic brown. Add the celery, saffron, hot pepper flakes, black pepper, tomatoes, and tomato paste. Cook for 3 to 4 minutes.

2. Add the wine, bring to a boil, and add the fish broth. Bring to a boil, lower the heat, and simmer for about 15 minutes.

3. Cut the monkfish into ½-inch cubes and add them to the broth. Cook for 5 minutes, taste for seasoning, and serve with the Garlic Croutons.

YIELD: 8 SERVINGS.

Curried Fish Soup

This soup, which calls for cod, also works well with red snapper, tilefish, and monkfish. Spicy curry soups, such as this, require a sweet element to maximize flavor. Here we add some mashed banana and apple, which impart no flavor of their own but only serve to enhance the curry.

4 tablespoons unsalted butter
1 cup finely chopped onion
2 teaspoons finely chopped garlic
1 cup peeled and finely diced apple
1 banana, peeled and diced
2 tablespoons Oriental Curry Powder (page 266)
3 tablespoons all-purpose flour
6 cups Fish Broth (page 241) or bottled clam juice
½ cup orzo
Salt and freshly ground black pepper to taste
1 cup heavy cream
1½ pounds skinless cod fillets, cut into 1½-inch cubes

1. In a large saucepan, melt the butter and add the onion and garlic. Cook, stirring, until the onion is translucent. Add the apple, banana, curry powder, and flour and stir to blend. Add the fish broth and stir. Bring to a boil and simmer for 5 minutes. Add the orzo, stir well, and cook for 10 minutes more. Season with salt and pepper.

2. Add the cream, bring to a boil, and add the fish. Simmer for about 3 minutes. Serve the soup very hot.

YIELD: 6 TO 8 SERVINGS.

Cotriade

This zesty fish soup from Brittany can be made with almost any kind of meaty whitefish.

4 tablespoons unsalted butter
2 cups chopped onion
1 tablespoon finely chopped garlic
4 potatoes (about 1½ pounds total weight), peeled and cut
*   into ¾-inch cubes*
2 quarts water
1 bay leaf
4 sprigs fresh thyme, or ½ teaspoon dried thyme
¼ cup chopped fresh parsley leaves
¼ cup finely chopped fresh chives or chervil leaves
Salt and freshly ground black pepper to taste
1 pound skinless blackfish fillets, cut into 2-inch cubes
1½ pounds skinless monkfish fillets, cut into 2-inch cubes
1 pound sea scallops
16 Croutons (page 274)
4 tablespoons olive oil

1. Melt the butter in a large soup pot and add the onion. Cook, stirring, until wilted. Add the garlic and potatoes and cook and stir for 2 minutes. Add the water, bay leaf, thyme, parsley, chives, and salt and pepper. Bring to a boil and simmer for 20 minutes. Add the cubed fish and cook for 5 minutes. Add the scallops and cook 2 minutes longer.

2. Arrange 2 Croutons in the bottom of each serving bowl and sprinkle ½ teaspoon of oil over each pair. Ladle the hot fish soup over the Croutons and serve immediately.

YIELD: 6 TO 8 SERVINGS.

Fish Soup Provençale

This recipe works with a variety of fish, including blackfish, tilefish, and red snapper.

4 tablespoons olive oil
2 tablespoons finely chopped garlic
2 cups finely chopped onion
1 cup finely chopped fennel leaves
½ cup finely chopped celery
2 teaspoons saffron threads, optional
1 tablespoon ground turmeric
4 sprigs fresh thyme, or 1 teaspoon dried thyme
1 bay leaf
¼ teaspoon hot red pepper flakes
1½ cups chopped ripe tomatoes (If out of season, use crushed
*   canned tomatoes.)*
2 tablespoons tomato paste
2⅓ pounds monkfish fillets, cut into ¾-inch cubes
8 cups Fish Broth (page 241) or bottled clam juice
1 cup dry white wine
18 cherrystone clams, cleaned and well washed
1 quart mussels, well scrubbed and with beards removed
2 tablespoons Pernod or Ricard
½ cup chopped fresh parsley leaves
Garlic Croutons (page 274)
Aïoli (page 253)

1. Heat the oil in a soup pot and add the garlic, onion, fennel, and celery. Cook, stirring, for about 5 minutes. Do not brown the garlic or onion. Add the saffron, turmeric, thyme, bay leaf, and hot pepper flakes. Stir. Add the tomatoes and tomato paste. Simmer for about 15 minutes. Remove from the heat and let cool to room temperature. Gently add the monkfish to the sauce and let it marinate for an hour or so (see Note).

2. Place the soup pot on top of the stove; add the fish broth, wine, clams, and mussels. Stir and bring to a boil; then lower

the heat and simmer for about 5 minutes. Add the Pernod and chopped parsley and cook for 2 minutes more. Serve with the Garlic Croutons and Aïoli.

YIELD: 8 TO 12 SERVINGS.

Note: Step 1 can be done ahead of time and the mixture refrigerated for several hours. Just before serving complete step 2.

French Codfish Chowder

This recipe also works well with monkfish, mako shark, tilefish, and swordfish.

4 tablespoons unsalted butter
1 tablespoon finely chopped garlic
2 cups finely chopped onion
½ cup finely chopped sweet green or sweet red pepper
¾ cup chopped well-washed leeks
4 tablespoons all-purpose flour
1 tablespoon ground turmeric
1 cup dry white wine
6 cups Fish Broth (page 241) or bottled clam juice
1½ pounds potatoes, peeled and cut into ½-inch cubes
  (reserved in water to prevent discoloration)
Salt and freshly ground black pepper to taste
2 pounds skinless cod fillets, cut into 1½-inch cubes
¾ cup heavy cream
2 tablespoons Ricard or Pernod
4 tablespoons finely chopped fresh parsley leaves

1. Melt the butter in a large frying pan and cook the garlic, onion, peppers, and leeks over medium heat for 5 minutes, stirring. Add the flour, stir, and cook for 2 minutes. Add the turmeric, white wine, and fish broth and stir to blend; bring to

a boil. Add the drained potatoes and salt and pepper. Simmer for 15 minutes.

2. Add the cubed fish and simmer for 5 minutes. Pour in the cream and bring to a boil; then stir in the Ricard. Serve hot garnished with chopped parsley.

YIELD: 6 SERVINGS.

Codfish and Potato Chowder

4 ounces salt pork, cut into small cubes
1½ cups finely chopped onion
1 tablespoon finely chopped garlic
1 bay leaf
1 teaspoon ground turmeric
2 cups peeled potatoes cut into small cubes
6 cups Fish Broth (page 241) or bottled clam juice
Salt and freshly ground black pepper to taste
⅛ teaspoon Tabasco sauce
2 pounds skinless and boneless fresh cod, cut into 1-inch cubes
2 cups milk
1 cup heavy or light cream

1. Put the cubes of salt pork in a small saucepan. Cover with water, bring to a boil, and simmer for 1 minute. Drain well.

2. Put the blanched salt pork in a large saucepan and cook briefly over medium heat. Then add the onion, garlic, bay leaf, and turmeric. Sauté, stirring, until the onion is wilted. Add the potatoes and cook, stirring, for 1 minute.

3. Add the fish broth, salt and pepper, and Tabasco sauce. Bring to a boil and simmer for 20 minutes.

4. Add the fish. Return to a boil and simmer for 1 minute. Stir in the milk and cream, bring to a boil, and serve very hot.

YIELD: 6 TO 8 SERVINGS.

Manhattan Clam Chowder

24 *chowder clams*
6 *cups cold water*
4 *strips bacon*
2 *cups finely diced carrots*
1½ *cups celery cut into small cubes*
2 *cups chopped onion*
1 *cup chopped sweet green pepper*
1 *tablespoon chopped garlic*
1 *teaspoon dried thyme*
1 *bay leaf*
⅛ *teaspoon cayenne pepper*
Salt and freshly ground black pepper to taste
2 *cups canned crushed tomatoes*
4 *cups peeled potatoes cut into small cubes*
1 *cup chopped fresh parsley leaves*

In 1607, Captain John Smith of Jamestown colony wrote in his journal that he found an "abundance of fish, lying so thicke with their heads above the water, as for want of nets . . . we attempted to catch them with a frying-pan."

1. Wash the clams well in cold water; then drain.

2. Put the clams in a kettle or large saucepan. Add the 6 cups of water and cover tightly. Simmer until the shells open, about 10 minutes. Drain well, reserving the liquid; let the clams cool.

3. Chop the bacon and put it in a soup kettle. Cook and stir until the bacon is rendered; then add the carrots, celery, onion, green pepper, garlic, thyme, bay leaf, cayenne pepper, and salt and black pepper. Cook about 5 minutes, stirring often.

4. Add 10 cups of the clam liquid to the bacon mixture. (If there are not 10 cups, add enough water to make that quantity.) Remove the meat from the clam shells and discard the shells. Chop the clams coarsely on a flat surface. Add the clams to the pot along with the tomatoes and potatoes. Simmer for 1 hour. Stir in the parsley and serve.

YIELD: 8 TO 10 SERVINGS.

New England Clam Chowder

24 chowder clams
3 cups cold water
2 ounces salt pork, chopped very fine
1½ cups finely chopped onion
2 cups peeled potatoes cut into ¼-inch cubes
Salt and freshly ground white pepper to taste
3 cups milk
1 cup heavy cream
3 tablespoons unsalted butter

1. Wash the clams well in cold water; then drain.

2. Put the clams in a kettle or a large saucepan and add the 3 cups of water. Cover tightly and simmer until the clams have opened, about 10 minutes.

3. When the clams are open, drain them and reserve the liquid. Remove the clam meat from the shells and chop it coarsely.

4. Put the chopped salt pork in another kettle and cook over medium-high heat for 1 minute; add the onion and cook, stirring, until it is wilted. Pour the reserved clam liquid into the kettle; then add the potatoes, clams, and salt and pepper. Bring to a boil and simmer for 1 hour. Add the milk, cream, butter, and salt and pepper to taste and bring to a boil. Serve very hot.

YIELD: ABOUT 10 SERVINGS.

Shrimp Bayou

2 tablespoons vegetable oil
2 tablespoons all-purpose flour
1 cup finely chopped onion
1½ cups finely chopped scallions
1 cup finely chopped celery
1 cup finely chopped sweet green pepper
1 tablespoon finely chopped garlic
1 cup cooked smoked ham, or southern-style tasso, cut into ½-inch cubes
2 cups canned crushed tomatoes
½ teaspoon dried thyme
1 teaspoon dried oregano
½ cup long-grain rice
¼ teaspoon hot red pepper flakes
6 cups Shrimp Broth (page 243)
2 pounds shrimp, shelled and deveined
Salt and freshly ground black pepper to taste

1. Heat the oil in a heavy bottomed soup pot over medium-high heat. Add the flour and cook, stirring constantly, until lightly browned.

2. Add the onion, scallions, celery, green pepper, and garlic and cook, stirring, until wilted. Stir in the ham, tomatoes, thyme, oregano, rice, hot pepper flakes, and shrimp broth. Bring to a boil, stir well, and cook for about 30 minutes. Add the shrimp and simmer for 5 minutes more. Adjust the seasoning with salt and pepper if necessary. Serve very hot in soup bowls.

YIELD: 6 SERVINGS.

Crab Meat and Shrimp Gumbo

3 tablespoons corn oil
1 pound Polish sausage (or andouille), cut into ¼-inch-thick
    slices
½ pound smoked ham, or southern-style tasso, cut into ¼-
    inch cubes
2 tablespoons finely chopped garlic
1½ cups finely chopped onion
1½ cups finely chopped scallions
1½ cups finely chopped sweet green pepper
1½ cups finely chopped celery
2 pounds fresh okra, thinly sliced, or 2 10-ounce packages
    frozen sliced okra
2 cups canned crushed tomatoes
2 bay leaves
5 cups Shrimp Broth (page 243) or bottled clam juice
1 teaspoon Tabasco sauce
2 teaspoons Worcestershire sauce
Salt and freshly ground black pepper to taste
4 tablespoons all-purpose flour
2 pounds raw shrimp, shelled and deveined
10 thin lemon slices, seeded
1½ pounds lump crab meat, shell and cartilage removed
Rice Creole (page 272)

1. Heat 1 tablespoon of the oil in a soup pot with a heavy bottom or a large frying pan. Add the sausage and cook over high heat, stirring often, until the sausage is lightly browned. Stir in the ham and cook for 1 minute. Transfer the meats to a bowl and set aside. Pour off the fat from the pot.

2. Add the garlic, onion, scallions, green pepper, and celery to the pot and cook, stirring, until the vegetables are wilted. Add the okra and cook until the vegetables become fairly dry, about 5 to 6 minutes.

3. Stir in the tomatoes, bay leaves, 4 cups of the shrimp broth, Tabasco and Worcestershire sauces, salt and pepper, and

the sausage and ham. Bring to a boil and simmer for about 30 minutes.

4. Heat the remaining 2 tablespoons of oil in a small frying pan. Add the flour and cook, stirring constantly with a wooden spatula, until the flour is browned but not burned. Stir in the remaining shrimp broth with a wire whisk. Bring to a boil and stir this mixture into the vegetable and meat broth. Cook for 15 minutes.

5. Add the shrimp and the lemon slices and cook for 5 minutes. Add the crab meat, stir gently to prevent breaking up the lumps, and cook for another 5 minutes. Serve with the Rice Creole.

YIELD: 10 TO 12 SERVINGS.

Codfish and Potatoes in Curried Cream Sauce

5 Idaho potatoes (about 1½ pounds total weight)
Salt to taste
2¼ pounds skinless fresh cod fillets
3 cups water, or more if needed
1½ cups milk
1 bay leaf
8 whole black peppercorns
4 parsley sprigs
2 tablespoons unsalted butter
1 tablespoon Oriental Curry Powder (page 266)
3 tablespoons all-purpose flour
1 cup chopped scallions, including the green part
¾ cup heavy cream

1. Put the unpeeled potatoes in a large saucepan and cover with cold salted water. Bring to a boil and simmer for about 20 minutes, or until tender. Drain and set aside.

2. Cut the cod into 6 serving portions of roughly equal size. Put the pieces in one layer in a frying pan and add the milk and enough water to cover. Add the bay leaf, peppercorns, salt, and parsley sprigs. Bring to a boil and simmer for 1 minute, no longer. Turn off the heat and let stand until ready to use. Keep warm.

3. In a saucepan, melt the butter over medium heat. Then stir in the curry powder and flour and blend well. Add the scallions and cook, stirring, for 1 minute.

4. Ladle out 1½ cups of the fish poaching liquid and add it to the curry mixture. Stir rapidly with a wire whisk until smooth; let simmer, stirring, for about 5 minutes. Add the cream and stir well. Cook briefly.

5. When the potatoes are cool enough to handle, peel them. Slice them into about ¼-inch-thick disks. You should have about 5 cups.

6. Transfer the fish to a warm serving platter; arrange the potatoes around the perimeter. Pour the curry sauce over the fisl and serve immediately.

YIELD: 6 SERVINGS.

Bouillabaisse Provençale

This is a festive dish for entertaining large groups.

¼ cup olive oil
2 cups finely chopped onion
2 cups finely chopped well-washed leeks
1 cup finely chopped fennel leaves
2 tablespoons finely chopped garlic

*Pour le vendredi
   maigre, un jour,
   certaine abbesse
D'un couvent
   marseillais cre'a la
   bouille-abaisse.*

*For a Friday
   abstinence meal, one
   day, a certain
   abbess
Of a Marseilles
   convent created the
   bouillabaisse.*

No seafood dish seems to create controversy like the famous fish stew of Southern France known as bouillabaisse. Dogmatists of Marseilles

1 *teaspoon crushed saffron threads*
3½ *cups canned crushed peeled Italian tomatoes*
1 *teaspoon dried thyme*
2 *bay leaves*
½ *teaspoon cayenne pepper*
Salt and freshly ground black pepper to taste
1½ *pounds skinless monkfish, cut into 1½-inch cubes*
1½ *pounds skinless tilefish, cut into 1½-inch cubes*
1½ *pounds red snapper fillets with skin, cut into 1½-inch cubes*
1 *eel (about 1 pound), cleaned and cut into 2-inch-lengths, optional*
10 *cups Fish Broth (page 241) or bottled clam juice*
6 *lobsters (about 1¼ pounds each), cut in half*
24 *mussels, well scrubbed and with beards removed*
24 *littleneck clams, well scrubbed*
3 *tablespoons Ricard or Pernod*
½ *cup finely chopped fresh parsley leaves*
Garlic Croutons (page 274)
Aïoli (page 253)

contend that nothing served beyond the region bordered by that port city and Toulon, to the southeast, is the real thing: The classic recipe calls for more than a dozen varieties of fish and shellfish.

In this country, the term has come to mean almost any kind of seafood stew based on an herbaceous red broth. The version offered here calls for four domestic fish that approximate those used in the original: monkfish, tilefish, red snapper, and eel (optional).

1. Heat the olive oil in a very large heavy skillet and add the onion, leeks, fennel, garlic, and saffron and simmer, stirring, for 5 minutes. Add the tomatoes, thyme, bay leaves, cayenne pepper, and salt and black pepper. Cook slowly for 20 minutes, stirring frequently. Let cool 1 hour.

2. Place the fish cubes and eel in the marinade, toss well to coat, and let stand in a single layer for about 30 minutes.

3. When ready to cook, add the fish stock to the marinating fish and stir well. Add the lobsters, mussels, littlenecks, Pernod, and parsley. Bring to a boil and simmer for about 7 minutes. Serve very hot with the Garlic Croutons and Aïoli.

YIELD: 10 TO 12 SERVINGS.

Oyster Stew Lyonnaise

This classic French-style oyster stew has been a popular dish at the world-famous restaurant of Paul Bocuse.

3 tablespoons unsalted butter
3 leeks (about 1½ pounds total weight), trimmed, washed well, and chopped coarsely (whites and a small amount of greens)
1½ pounds russet potatoes (about 4 potatoes), peeled and cut into 2-inch cubes
6 cups cold water
Salt and freshly ground black pepper to taste
¼ cup peanut, corn, or vegetable oil
3 cups crustless white bread cut into ¼-inch cubes
1 cup heavy cream
⅛ teaspoon freshly grated nutmeg
1 quart shucked oysters (liquid reserved)
¼ pound Gruyère cheese, grated
¼ cup finely chopped fresh chervil or parsley leaves

1. Melt 2 tablespoons of the butter in a large saucepan over medium heat. Add the leeks and cook, stirring often, for about 5 minutes. Add the potatoes, water, and salt and pepper. Bring to a boil and cook for 20 minutes.

2. Purée this mixture in a food mill, food processor, or blender.

3. Heat the oil and remaining butter in a heavy frying pan and sauté the bread cubes, tossing and stirring, until they are just golden brown. Drain them on paper towels.

4. Return the purée to a deep saucepan and bring to a boil. Add the cream and nutmeg and taste for seasonings. Add the oysters and their liquid and cook just until the oysters curl.

5. Pour the chowder into individual soup plates. Add croutons to each, some grated cheese, and garnish with chervil.

YIELD: 6 TO 8 SERVINGS.

Fish Stew with
Vegetables and Coriander

2½ pounds skinless and boneless monkfish, red snapper,
*   ocean bass, tilefish, or blackfish*
3 cups Fish Broth (page 241) or bottled clam juice
½ cup dry white wine
Salt and freshly ground black pepper to taste
1 pound carrots, scraped, trimmed, and cut into 1-inch
*   julienne strips*
1 teaspoon finely chopped garlic
¼ teaspoon hot red pepper flakes
½ cup finely chopped scallions
1 cup diced peeled and seeded tomatoes
1 pound cucumbers, preferably the seedless variety, cut into
*   ¾-inch cubes*
¼ cup chopped fresh coriander leaves
Aïoli (page 253)

1. Cut the fish into 1½-inch-square pieces. Set them aside.

2. Pour the fish broth and the wine into a soup pot. Bring to a boil and add the salt and pepper, carrots, garlic, and hot pepper flakes. Simmer for 5 minutes, or until the carrots are tender but still firm.

3. Add the scallions, tomatoes, cucumbers, fish, and coriander. Cover tightly and cook for 5 minutes. Serve immediately with the Aïoli.

YIELD: 6 SERVINGS.

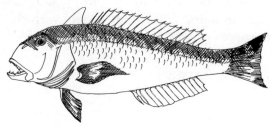

Old Stone Fish Stew

1¼ pounds skinless tilefish, monkfish, or cod fillets
1 pound halibut or red snapper fillets
¼ cup olive oil
1½ cups finely chopped onion
1 cup finely chopped celery
1 cup finely chopped sweet green pepper
1 teaspoon finely chopped garlic
1 cup dry white wine
1 bay leaf
1 teaspoon dried thyme, or 5 thyme sprigs
4 cups peeled and crushed canned tomatoes
¼ teaspoon hot red pepper flakes
Salt and freshly ground black pepper to taste
1 pound mussels, well scrubbed and with beards removed
½ pound shrimp, shelled and deveined
¼ cup chopped fresh parsley leaves
Herb-stuffed French Bread (page 272)

1. Cut all the fish into 1½-inch cubes. Set them aside.

2. Heat the oil in a large saucepan or kettle over medium heat and add the onion, celery, green pepper, and garlic. Cook, stirring, for 5 minutes. Add the wine, bay leaf, and thyme. Cook for 1 minute. Stir in the tomatoes, hot pepper flakes, and salt and pepper. Simmer for 10 minutes.

3. Add the fish and mussels, stir, and cook over high heat for about 3 minutes. Add the shrimp and parsley and simmer for 3 more minutes. Serve immediately with the Herb-stuffed French Bread.

YIELD: 6 SERVINGS.

Bourride

This garlic-flavored fish stew comes from Provence. Many species of whitefish can be used.

2 tablespoons olive oil
1 cup coarsely chopped onion
¾ cup coarsely chopped celery
¾ cup coarsely chopped well-washed leeks
1 tablespoon finely chopped garlic
½ teaspoon saffron threads
1 bay leaf
1 teaspoon dried thyme
1 cup dry white wine
6 cups Fish Broth (page 241) or bottled clam juice
1 pound small potatoes, peeled and sliced into thin rounds
Salt and freshly ground black pepper to taste
¼ teaspoon hot red pepper flakes
1½ pounds fish fillets, such as monkfish, red snapper, or
    tilefish, cut into ½-inch cubes
Garlic Croutons (page 274)
2 cups Aïoli (page 253)

1. Heat the oil in a large saucepan over medium-high heat and add the onion. Cook until wilted. Add the celery, leeks, garlic, saffron, bay leaf, and thyme. Cook over medium heat for about 2 minutes. Add the wine, fish broth, potatoes, salt and pepper, and hot pepper flakes. Bring to a boil and simmer for 30 minutes.

2. Force the ingredients in the saucepan through a food mill or purée them extremely well in a food processor.

3. Place the fish cubes in a large saucepan in one layer. Pour the soup mixture over the fish. Bring to a boil, lower the heat, and simmer for about 3 minutes.

4. Using a slotted spoon, transfer the fish pieces to warm serving bowls. Add 2 or 3 croutons to each bowl and then place a tablespoon of Aïoli over each crouton. Pour the hot broth over everything and serve.

YIELD: 8 SERVINGS.

CHAPTER 11

Pasta and Rice

Pasta with Shrimp and Vegetables

This recipe could be adapted to any kind of fresh or dried pasta.

2 yellow summer squash, cut into small cubes about 1/4 inch thick

18 medium-size asparagus spears with tough bottoms removed (about 1/2 pound total weight), peeled and cut on the diagonal into 1/2-inch-long pieces

4 tablespoons olive oil

6 tablespoons unsalted butter

1 tablespoon finely minced garlic

1 3/4 pounds ripe tomatoes, cored, peeled, and cut into 1/2-inch cubes

1/2 teaspoon hot red pepper flakes, or to taste

1/2 pound medium-size shrimp, shelled and deveined

1 cup heavy cream

Salt to taste

12 ounces fresh or dried fettuccine

Freshly ground black pepper to taste

4 tablespoons finely chopped fresh basil leaves

1. Bring enough salted water to a boil to cover the yellow squash and asparagus when they are added. Then add the vegetables and cook for 2 minutes. Pour the vegetables into a strainer set over a large pot.

2. Heat the oil and 3 tablespoons of the butter in a frying pan and add the garlic. Cook briefly, stirring, but do not brown. Add the tomatoes and the hot pepper flakes. Bring to a boil, stirring. Add the cooked vegetables and shrimp. Cook, stirring occasionally, for about 1½ minutes. Add the cream and salt and pepper to taste. Remove from the heat.

3. Add enough water to the reserved cooking liquid to make 10 cups. Season with salt to taste. Bring to a boil and add the pasta. If the pasta is fresh, cook it for about 5 minutes; if it is dried, cook about 4 minutes longer, or to the desired degree of doneness. Drain the pasta and return it to the pot.

4. Pour the vegetable mixture over the pasta. Add the remaining 3 tablespoons of butter and the basil. Toss well and serve.

YIELD: 6 SERVINGS.

Green Pasta with Shrimp and Clams

Salt
¼ cup olive oil
1 tablespoon finely chopped garlic
½ teaspoon hot red pepper flakes
1½ pounds medium-size shrimp, shelled and deveined
Freshly ground black pepper to taste
24 cherrystone clams, shucked (reserve liquid)
24 fresh basil leaves, or 2 tablespoons dried basil
4 tablespoons chopped fresh parsley leaves
1½ pounds fresh green noodles or fettuccine
4 tablespoons unsalted butter

1. Bring 4 quarts of lightly salted water to a boil in a large pot.

2. Heat the oil in a large pan over medium-high heat and add

the garlic. Cook briefly without browning. Add the hot pepper flakes, shrimp, and salt and pepper. Cook, stirring, for about 1 minute. Add the clams and cook for about 15 seconds. Add the basil leaves and parsley. Stir well and remove from the heat.

3. Meanwhile, drop the pasta into the boiling water. Return to a boil and cook until *al dente*. Reserve ¾ cup of the cooking water. Drain the pasta and return it to the dry pot. Add the reserved clam juice and the 4 tablespoons butter. Toss and heat thoroughly.

4. Scrape the clam and shrimp mixture into the pasta. Toss to blend. If the sauce needs some extra moisture, add some of the cooking liquid. Serve immediately.

YIELD: 6 SERVINGS.

Penne and Shrimp with Tomatoes

¾ pound string beans
Salt
4 tablespoons olive oil
2 tablespoons finely chopped garlic
4 cups canned crushed tomatoes
4 teaspoons tomato paste
1 teaspoon dried marjoram
1 teaspoon dried rosemary
Freshly ground black pepper to taste
¾ pound penne
1½ pounds medium-size shrimp, shelled and deveined
½ teaspoon hot red pepper flakes, or to taste
2 tablespoons unsalted butter

1. Trim and cut the string beans into about 1½-inch lengths. Drop them into lightly salted boiling water and cook for about 7 minutes, or until slightly crisp and tender. Immediately drain well.

2. Heat 2 tablespoons of the oil in a saucepan over medium

heat and add 1 tablespoon of the chopped garlic. Cook briefly without letting it brown; then add the crushed tomatoes and tomato paste. Add the marjoram, rosemary, and salt and pepper. Reduce the sauce to about 3 cups over medium-high heat, stirring well, about 15 minutes.

3. Bring 4 quarts of lightly salted water to a boil. Cook the penne for 12 to 14 minutes, or until *al dente*.

4. While the penne cooks, heat the remaining 2 tablespoons of oil in a saucepan over medium-high heat and add the shrimp, hot pepper flakes, and the remaining garlic. Cook, stirring, for about 1 minute. Add the string beans and the tomato sauce to the pan. Bring to a boil; then lower the heat to a simmer. Cook for 1 minute. Drain the penne and add it to the tomato mixture. Add the butter, heat thoroughly, stir, and serve.

YIELD: 6 TO 8 SERVINGS.

Scallops and Thyme Ravioli

This recipe comes from Christian Delouvrier, formerly of Maurice Restaurant in New York City. Mr. Delouvrier showed us how to make gossamer raviolis without going through all the fuss of rolling them. He uses Chinese wonton wrappers, the thinnest possible, which can be found at Oriental markets.

THE FILLING

About 24 sea scallops
Salt and freshly ground white pepper to taste
2 tablespoons olive oil
4 thyme sprigs

About 60 Chinese wonton wrappers (always have extra on hand in case any crack)
1 large egg, beaten
1 quart Fish Broth (page 241) or bottled clam juice
Beurre Blanc (page 243)

Wonton wrappers, which are available in most Oriental markets, make excellent ravioli dough. Lay one on a counter and fill with the filling of your choice and seasonings, leaving a rim all around for sealing. Brush egg wash (simply a beaten egg) around the perimeter and place the second skin on top. Seal well with your fingers. Trim the excess dough with a sharp knife. Cover the finished raviolis with a moist towel as you make them. Cook as you would any fresh pasta.

1. Cut the sea scallops into small cubes. Season generously with salt and pepper and add the oil and thyme sprigs. Stir well and let sit about 10 minutes.

2. Lay 1 wonton wrapper on a lightly floured dry surface. Brush it with some of the beaten egg. Top the wrapper with ¾ teaspoon of the scallops and some fresh thyme. Seal the ravioli with another skin, pressing the edges firmly with your fingers. Make sure it is completely sealed. Trim the wonton skin edges with a sharp knife or a pizza cutter to remove the excess dough. Repeat this procedure with the rest of the ingredients. Cover the finished uncooked raviolis with a moistened towel to keep them from drying out.

3. Poach the raviolis, 5 or 6 at a time, in the fish broth for about 1 minute, or until they rise to the surface. Drain and place 4 to 6 raviolis on each warm serving plate. Drizzle some Beurre Blanc over them and serve immediately.

YIELD: 4 TO 6 SERVINGS (ABOUT 24 RAVIOLIS).

Linguine with Clam Sauce

This recipe could be adapted to any kind of fresh or dried pasta.

*18 cherrystone clams, shucked and liquid reserved (you should
    have about 2 cups)*
¼ pound small zucchini
4 ripe tomatoes (about ¾ pound total weight), peeled
¼ cup olive oil
2 tablespoons finely minced garlic
¼ teaspoon hot red pepper flakes, or to taste
Salt to taste if needed
Freshly ground black pepper to taste
18 whole basil leaves, rinsed and patted dry
½ pound freshly made or dried linguine

1. Chop the clams coarsely. There should be about 1 cup chopped clams and 2 cups juice.

2. Trim off the ends of the zucchini. Cut the zucchini lengthwise into quarters; then cut each quarter into thin slices crosswise. There should be about 2 cups.

3. Cut the tomatoes into ½-inch cubes.

4. Bring 2½ quarts of lightly salted water to a rolling boil.

5. Heat the olive oil in a skillet over medium heat and add the garlic and hot pepper flakes. Cook briefly, stirring, and add the zucchini and tomatoes. Season with salt and pepper and stir. Add the reserved clam juice. Bring to a boil and add the basil leaves.

6. Drop the linguine into the boiling water. If the pasta is fresh, cook it for about 1 to 1½ minutes; if it is dried, cook for about 9 minutes, or until it reaches the desired degree of doneness. Drain quickly, and reserve about ½ cup of the cooking liquid.

7. Toss the linguine with the sauce and add the clams. If you find the dish a bit dry, add some of the pasta cooking liquid, which will moisten and bind it, and stir well.

YIELD: 4 SERVINGS.

Spaghetti with Fresh Mussels

3 pounds mussels, well scrubbed and with beards removed
1 bay leaf
6 whole black peppercorns
2 whole cloves
4 parsley sprigs
¼ cup dry white wine
1 pound spaghetti
3 quarts water
Salt to taste
4 tablespoons olive oil
1 tablespoon finely chopped garlic

3 cups Italian crushed canned tomatoes
½ teaspoon hot red pepper flakes, or to taste
Freshly ground black pepper to taste
1 cup chopped fresh basil or parsley leaves

1. Put the mussels, bay leaf, peppercorns, cloves, parsley sprigs, and white wine in a deep saucepan or pot. Cover, bring to a boil over high heat, and cook for about 4 to 6 minutes, or until the mussels open.

2. Remove the mussels with a slotted spoon and set them aside to cool. Pour any accumulated juices back into the pot. Strain the broth and set it aside. When the mussels are cool enough to handle, remove the meat and discard the shells.

3. Cook the spaghetti in a large pot of boiling salted water for about 6 minutes—it should still be short of *al dente*. Drain well.

4. While the spaghetti is cooking, combine the olive oil and garlic in a large pan. Sauté until golden but not brown. Add the tomatoes, mussel broth, and hot pepper flakes. Cook for 3 minutes. Add the partially cooked spaghetti to the pan and stir well. Cook until the spaghetti is *al dente;* then add the mussel meat. Stir and cook just to warm the mussels. Garnish with fresh basil and taste for seasonings. Toss and serve.

YIELD: 4 TO 6 SERVINGS.

Linguine with Squid in Tomato Sauce

3 pounds fresh squid, cleaned (see page 16)
⅓ cup olive oil
1 tablespoon finely chopped garlic
5 cups chopped whole canned Italian tomatoes
½ teaspoon dried oregano, crumbled
½ teaspoon dried rosemary leaves
¼ teaspoon hot red pepper flakes
Salt and freshly ground black pepper to taste
1 tablespoon Pernod or Ricard
1 pound linguine
4 tablespoons unsalted butter
½ cup chopped fresh basil or parsley leaves

1. Cut the squid tentacles and in half or in quarters, depending on size. Cut the squid bodies crosswise into rings about ½ inch wide. Set them aside. There should be about 4 cups of squid.

2. Heat the oil in a large saucepan or small kettle and add the garlic. Cook briefly but do not brown it. Add the tomatoes, oregano, rosemary, hot pepper flakes, and salt and pepper. Bring to a boil and add the squid. Simmer, stirring often, for 25 to 30 minutes. Stir in the Ricard.

3. Cook the linguine in boiling salted water to the desired degree of doneness. Drain the pasta and return it to the pot in which it was cooked. Pour in the squid sauce and add the butter and basil; then toss and serve immediately.

YIELD: 6 SERVINGS.

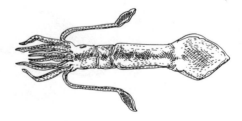

Pasta with Squid in Anchovy Sauce

3 pounds baby squid, cleaned and cut into 1½-inch squares
½ cup olive oil
1 cup minced onion
1 tablespoon minced garlic
Salt and freshly ground black pepper to taste
½ teaspoon hot red pepper flakes
2 tablespoons anchovy paste or chopped anchovy fillets
½ cup bottled clam juice
½ teaspoon dried oregano
⅓ cup chopped fresh parsley leaves
2 tablespoons fresh lemon juice
1 pound spaghetti or linguine or a pasta of your choice

1. Rinse and drain the squid.

2. Heat the oil in a saucepan over medium heat and add the onion. Cook, stirring, until the onion is translucent. Add the garlic, squid, salt and pepper, hot pepper flakes, and anchovy paste. Cook and stir over high heat for 3 minutes. Add the clam juice, oregano, and parsley and simmer for 30 minutes. When the sauce is done, add the lemon juice and taste for seasoning.

3. Bring a large pot of lightly salted water to a boil. Add the pasta and cook until it is *al dente.* Drain well and transfer to a serving platter. Pour the sauce over the pasta and toss well. Serve immediately on warm plates.

YIELD: 6 SERVINGS.

Linguine with Fresh Salmon

1½ pounds skinless salmon fillets
1 pound linguine
Salt and freshly ground black pepper
8 tablespoons unsalted butter
¼ cup finely chopped shallots
¼ cup dry white wine
½ teaspoon hot red pepper flakes, or to taste
1 cup heavy cream
¼ teaspoon freshly grated nutmeg
2 ounces imported lumpfish caviar
¼ cup finely chopped fresh basil leaves or fresh chives

1. Cut the salmon lengthwise on the diagonal into 2-inch-thick slices.

2. Cook the linguine in 4 quarts of lightly salted boiling water until it is *al dente.* Drain and return to the pot in which it was cooked.

3. While the pasta cooks, melt 4 tablespoons of the butter in a frying pan over medium-high heat. Add the shallots and cook briefly, stirring. Add the wine and cook for about 30 seconds. Add the salmon strips to the pan and season with salt and pepper and hot pepper flakes. Cook, stirring, for about 45 seconds.

4. Add the cream to the pan; then stir in the nutmeg. Return to a boil and cook over high heat, stirring, for 2 to 3 minutes.

5. Add the remaining 4 tablespoons of butter and toss well. Pour the salmon sauce over the pasta. Transfer to warm serving plates. Garnish with the caviar and basil and serve.

YIELD: 6 SERVINGS.

Linguine with Monkfish and Scallops

---

4 tablespoons olive oil
1 tablespoon finely chopped garlic
½ teaspoon hot red pepper flakes, or to taste
1 cup finely chopped onion
2 leeks, trimmed, rinsed, and finely chopped
   (about 2 cups)
½ cup finely chopped celery
1 teaspoon loosely packed saffron threads
2 cups canned crushed tomatoes
½ cup dry white wine
1 bay leaf
Salt and freshly ground black pepper to taste
4 tablespoons finely chopped fresh parsley leaves
¼ teaspoon fennel seeds
1½ pounds skinless and boneless monkfish, cut into
   ¾-inch cubes
1 pound sea scallops, cut into ¾-inch cubes
¾ pound fresh or dried linguine

1. Heat 2 tablespoons of the oil in a heavy skillet over medium heat and add the garlic. Sauté briefly, stirring; do not brown. Add the hot pepper flakes, onion, leeks, and celery. Stir, add the saffron, and stir again. Cook for 2 minutes, stirring often. Add the tomatoes, wine, bay leaf, and salt and pepper. Blend in the parsley and fennel seeds. Bring to a boil, cover, and simmer for 15 minutes, stirring often.

2. Add the monkfish and stir. Cover and cook for about 4 minutes; then add the scallops. Cover and cook for 2 minutes.

3. Meanwhile, cook the linguine in boiling salted water until it is *al dente.* Drain and transfer to a heated serving platter. Spoon the remaining 2 tablespoons of oil over it. Sprinkle with pepper and toss briefly. Spoon the seafood over it and toss.

YIELD: 6 SERVINGS.

Paella Valenciana

1 cup fresh or frozen peas
*1 pound chorizo sausage (If not available, substitute Italian
    hot sausages.)*
2 1¼-pound lobsters
½ cup olive oil
1 3½-pound chicken, cut into 10 pieces
Salt and freshly ground black pepper
18 medium-size shrimp, shelled and deveined
½ pound boneless lean pork loin, cut into ½-inch cubes
2 cups crushed canned Italian tomatoes
1½ cups coarsely chopped onion
1 tablespoon minced garlic
1 teaspoon saffron threads
2 cups converted rice
½ teaspoon hot red pepper flakes, or to taste
2 cups Fish Broth (page 241) or bottled clam juice
18 large mussels, well scrubbed and with beards removed
12 littleneck clams, rinsed
2 lemons, cut into wedges

1. Preheat the oven to 375 degrees.

2. Blanch the peas in lightly salted water, drain, and set them
aside. Prick the sausages in several places with a fork and blanch
the sausages in boiling water for 5 minutes; then drain. When
the sausages are cool, cut them into ½-inch-thick rounds.

3. Kill the lobsters instantly by plunging the tip of a large
chef's knife between the eyes (see page 17). Cut off the claws and
remove the tail. Using the large knife, cut the body and tail,
crosswise, into 1-inch-thick pieces and place them in a dish to
reserve any liquids. Remove and discard the small sac inside the
lobster near the eyes.

4. Heat ¼ cup of the oil in a paella pan. Sprinkle the chicken
pieces with salt and pepper and sauté them, moving the pieces
around the pan until thoroughly browned, for about 5 minutes.
Remove to a large platter.

5. Sprinkle the lobster pieces with salt and pepper and place them in the hot oil. Reserve the accumulated liquids in the dish for later. Sauté for 2 or 3 minutes, or until the shells turn deep red. Remove the lobster pieces to a platter.

6. Sprinkle the shrimp with salt and pepper and sauté in the paella pan very quickly, about 1 minute. Remove them to the platter with the lobster.

7. Sauté the sausage pieces in the same pan for 2 or 3 minutes. Remove to the platter with the chicken. Discard the oil in the paella pan.

8. Heat the remaining oil in the pan over medium-high heat. Sprinkle the pork with salt and pepper and sauté for 2 or 3 minutes, or until lightly browned all over.

9. Add the onions, garlic, and salt and pepper to taste to the pan. Cook and stir for 2 minutes. Add the tomatoes and saffron. Cook, stirring, for about 5 minutes, or until the moisture from the vegetables has evaporated.

10. Add the rice and mix thoroughly. Pour in the reserved lobster juices and the fish broth. Add the hot pepper flakes and bring everything to a boil. Add the chicken, lobsters, sausages, and shrimp. Add the clams and mussels and stir well. Bake for about 25 minutes, or until the rice and chicken are tender and all the liquid has been absorbed. Remove from the oven and toss lightly to distribute all ingredients throughout the dish.

YIELD: 6 TO 8 SERVINGS.

Risotto with Clams

24 large cherrystone clams (about 2 cups shucked, reserve the
   liquid)
⅓ cup olive oil
¾ cup finely chopped onion
1 tablespoon finely chopped garlic
½ pound mushrooms, thinly sliced (about 4 cups)
1 teaspoon loosely packed saffron threads
½ teaspoon dried oregano, crumbled
1¼ cups canned crushed tomatoes
½ teaspoon hot red pepper flakes
Salt and freshly ground black pepper to taste
1½ cups converted rice
½ cup finely chopped fresh parsley leaves
6 tablespoons unsalted butter

1. Add enough water to the clam liquid to make 6 cups.
Bring this mixture to a simmer in a pot. Chop the clam meat.

2. Heat the oil in a saucepan and add the onion. Cook, stirring, until the onion wilts; then add the garlic and mushrooms.
Cook, stirring, for about 2 minutes. Stir in the saffron and
oregano and then the tomatoes, hot pepper flakes, and salt and
pepper.

3. Bring the tomato mixture to a boil and add the rice. Stir
and pour in about ½ cup of the simmering clam juice mixture.
Cook, stirring frequently, until most of the liquid has been
absorbed, about 4 minutes. Continue cooking the rice, adding
about ½ cup of the clam juice in the same manner. Stir the
mixture frequently from the bottom.

4. Risotto should be moister than normal rice, but not soupy.
The total cooking time should be about 25 minutes, or until all
the clam juice has been absorbed and the rice is tender.

5. Add the clams, parsley, and butter to the rice and toss.
Cook briefly to heat everything. Check for seasonings and serve.

YIELD: 4 TO 6 SERVINGS.

CHAPTER 12

Sauces

There are no dogmatic rules about which of the following sauces go with which types of seafood. However, as a guideline, sauces high in acid, such as those made with tomatoes, are well-suited to fatty and oily fish. Vinaigrettes of all types foil fat well, too.

Lean fish marry particularly well with cream and butter sauces, while fried foods go well with any type of herb mayonnaise or other emulsion. So do cold seafood dishes.

Fish Broth

4 pounds fish bones from a non-oily fish, including heads with
gills removed
1½ cups coarsely chopped onion
1 cup chopped celery
6 parsley sprigs
1 bay leaf
1 teaspoon dried thyme, or 2 sprigs fresh thyme
10 whole black peppercorns
6 cups cold water
2 cups dry white wine

1. Chop the fish bones to fit into a saucepan.
2. Add the remaining ingredients to the saucepan and bring to a boil. Simmer for 20 minutes and strain. This can be tightly

covered and stored in the refrigerator for several days or frozen for a month or longer.

YIELD: ABOUT 6 CUPS.

Fish Broth with Red Wine

1 tablespoon vegetable oil
1 pound fish bones from a non-oily fish, including head with
    gills removed, chopped into pieces
½ cup coarsely chopped onion
½ cup coarsely chopped carrot
½ cup coarsely chopped celery
6 whole black peppercorns
4 cups dry red wine
3 cups cold water
1 bay leaf
2 thyme sprigs, or ½ teaspoon dried thyme
4 parsley sprigs

1. Heat the oil in a large saucepan over medium-high heat. Add the fish bones, onion, carrot, celery, and peppercorns. Lower the heat to medium and simmer for 2 minutes, stirring.

2. Add the wine, water, bay leaf, thyme, and parsley. Bring to a boil and then simmer, uncovered, for about 45 minutes. Strain the sauce through a fine sieve, forcing the solids against the bottom with a wooden spoon to extract as much liquid as possible. This can be tightly covered and stored in the refrigerator for several days or frozen for a month or longer.

YIELD: ABOUT 1¾ CUPS.

Shrimp Broth

Shells from 2 pounds raw shrimp
7 cups cold water
6 whole black peppercorns
1 cup coarsely chopped onion
2 celery stalks, coarsely chopped
1 bay leaf

Put all the ingredients in a saucepan and bring to a boil. Simmer for about 20 minutes. Strain. This can be tightly covered and stored in the refrigerator for several days or frozen for a month or longer.

YIELD: ABOUT 6 CUPS.

Beurre Blanc
WHITE BUTTER SAUCE

4 tablespoons finely chopped shallots
1 cup dry white wine
2 tablespoons white wine vinegar
2 tablespoons heavy cream
8 tablespoons cold unsalted butter, cut into small pieces
Salt and freshly ground white pepper to taste

1. Put the shallots, wine, and vinegar into a small heavy saucepan. Cook over medium heat until reduced to 4 tablespoons.

2. Add the cream. As soon as it reaches a boil, turn the heat

to low and whisk in the butter one piece at a time. Season with salt and pepper and keep warm.

YIELD: ABOUT 1 CUP.

Note: This sauce should be used as soon as possible. If you have to prepare the sauce in advance, it can be reconstituted by beating it very gently with a wire whisk in the top of a double boiler over simmering water.

Beurre Blanc with Herbs and Pernod
WHITE BUTTER SAUCE WITH HERBS AND PERNOD

¼ cup minced shallots
¾ cup dry white wine
¼ cup heavy cream
8 tablespoons unsalted butter
Salt and freshly ground white pepper to taste
2 tablespoons minced fresh parsley leaves
2 tablespoons minced fresh tarragon leaves, or 2 teaspoons
  dried tarragon
2 tablespoons minced fresh chervil leaves
2 tablespoons minced fresh chives
1 tablespoon Pernod or Ricard

1. Combine the shallots and wine in a heavy saucepan. Cook over medium-high heat until the wine has nearly evaporated.

2. Add the cream and reduce by half. Add the butter quickly, one tablespoon at a time, whisking constantly. Remove the saucepan from the heat and stir in the salt and pepper, herbs, and Pernod.

YIELD: ABOUT ¾ CUP.

White Wine Sauce

6 tablespoons unsalted butter
1½ cups sliced mushroom stems
½ cup thinly sliced shallots
1 cup dry white wine
2½ cups Fish Broth (page 241) or bottled clam juice
Freshly ground white pepper to taste
4 tablespoons all-purpose flour
2 cups heavy cream
Juice of ½ lemon
Salt to taste

1. Melt 1 tablespoon of the butter in a saucepan. Add the mushrooms and shallots and cook, stirring, for 1 minute. Add the wine, ½ cup of the fish stock, and some white pepper. Simmer until the liquid is reduced by half.

2. Melt 3 tablespoons of the remaining butter in another saucepan and add the flour while stirring with a wire whisk. When they are blended, add the remaining fish stock. Blend well, bring to a boil, and simmer for 10 minutes. Add the sauce to the mushroom mixture, stir well, and simmer for 10 minutes.

3. Add the cream and simmer for 15 minutes stirring frequently. Pour the sauce through a fine wire strainer. Return the strained sauce to a saucepan and add the lemon juice and salt. Swirl in the remaining butter. Serve very hot over a mousse or poached fish.

YIELD: 8 TO 12 SERVINGS, DEPENDING ON ITS USE.

Sauce Américaine

This classic seafood sauce, while admittedly time consuming, is well worth the effort, especially if you are entertaining a large group.

2 1-pound lobsters
2 tablespoons olive oil
5 tablespoons unsalted butter
Salt and freshly ground black pepper to taste
⅛ teaspoon cayenne pepper
¼ cup minced onion
¼ cup minced shallots
½ cup minced carrot
½ cup minced celery
1 teaspoon minced garlic
4 tablespoons Cognac
½ cup dry white wine
1 cup canned crushed tomatoes
2 tablespoons tomato paste
2 thyme sprigs, or ½ teaspoon dried thyme
1 tablespoon chopped fresh tarragon leaves, or 1 teaspoon
   dried tarragon
1 bay leaf
1 cup Fish Broth (page 241) or bottled clam juice
1 tablespoon all-purpose flour

Contrary to a widespread misconception, lobster à l'américaine did not originate in America. Actually, it is derived from an old Provençale recipe. It seems that the name change came about when a French chef who had spent time in Chicago started calling his version Américaine for no other than nostalgic reasons.

1. Cut the tails from the bodies of the lobsters. Using a cleaver or a heavy knife, cut off the claws. Split each body in half lengthwise and remove the sac near the eyes. Remove and refrigerate the liver and coral. Chop each body into small pieces.

2. In a heavy saucepan or kettle, heat the oil and 1 tablespoon of the butter. Add the lobster (except the liver and coral) and cook over high heat, stirring, for about 3 minutes. Add the salt and black pepper and cayenne pepper. Add the onion, shallots, carrot, celery, and garlic. Cook, stirring, for about 3 minutes. Add 2 tablespoons of the Cognac and ignite it with a long kitchen match. Add the wine, tomatoes, tomato paste, thyme,

tarragon, bay leaf, and fish broth. Stir, bring to a boil, and simmer for 10 minutes.

3. Remove the lobster claws and tails and set them aside to cool.

4. Pour the remaining mixture, solids and all, into a food mill or a wire strainer. Press to extract as much liquid as possible from the mixture. Pour the liquid into a saucepan and bring to a simmer.

5. Blend 2 tablespoons of the remaining butter and the flour with the coral and liver. Add this mixture to the saucepan. Stir and blend well; remove the pan from the heat.

6. Put the sauce through the finest possible strainer. It should be smooth and silky. Add salt and pepper if needed.

7. When the tail and claw are cool enough to handle, crack them and remove the meat. Cut it into small pieces and add them to the sauce.

8. Add the remaining 2 tablespoons of butter and 2 tablespoons of Cognac to the sauce, swirling them in. Serve piping hot.

YIELD: 6 TO 12 SERVINGS, DEPENDING ON ITS USE.

Mornay Sauce

2 tablespoons unsalted butter
3 tablespoons all-purpose flour
2 cups milk
½ cup heavy cream
1 cup freshly grated Swiss, Gruyère, or Cheddar cheese
1 large egg yolk
Salt and freshly ground white pepper to taste
⅛ teaspoon freshly grated nutmeg
⅛ teaspoon cayenne pepper

1. Melt the butter in a saucepan. Add the flour and stir with a wire whisk until it is blended.

2. Add the milk and cream all at once and stir rapidly with the whisk. Bring to a boil and add the cheese. Stir until the cheese has melted. Add the egg yolk while stirring rapidly with the whisk. Season with salt and pepper, nutmeg, and cayenne pepper.

YIELD: ABOUT 3 CUPS.

Monique Picot's Ginger Sauce

This unusual sauce is delicious with any type of grilled fish, especially fresh tuna, mako shark, halibut, and swordfish. It also enhances steamed fish.

4 tablespoons ground ginger
1 tablespoon minced fresh garlic
3 tablespoons light soy sauce
¾ cup water
4 tablespoons olive oil
2 tablespoons finely chopped fresh coriander leaves
1 teaspoon freshly ground black pepper

1. Put all ingredients, *except* the coriander and pepper, in a saucepan and bring to a boil over medium heat. Lower the heat, cover, and simmer for about 15 minutes. Remove from the heat.
2. Add the coriander and black pepper immediately before serving, either hot or at room temperature.

YIELD: ⅔ CUP; ENOUGH FOR 4 TO 6 SERVINGS OF GRILLED FISH.

Creole Sauce Base

*The Creole Sauce Base is zesty and delicious. It is extremely versatile
and can be used with all kinds of grilled, poached, steamed, and
sautéed fish.*

4 tablespoons unsalted butter
1 cup chopped onion
1 teaspoon finely minced garlic
1 cup celery cut into 1½-inch-long julienne strips
1 cup chopped sweet green pepper
1 cup canned crushed Italian tomatoes
3 tablespoons tomato paste
1½ cups Fish or Shrimp Broth (pages 241 and 243) or bottled
    clam juice
½ teaspoon cayenne pepper
½ teaspoon freshly ground white pepper
½ teaspoon paprika
3 or 4 thyme sprigs, or ½ teaspoon dried thyme
2 bay leaves
½ teaspoon dried oregano
1 tablespoon honey
½ teaspoon Tabasco sauce
Salt to taste

Melt the butter in a saucepan. Add the onion, garlic, celery,
and green pepper. Cook and stir for 5 minutes over medium
heat. Add the tomatoes, tomato paste, and broth. Stir well, and
add all the remaining ingredients. Bring to a boil, lower the
heat, and simmer for about 15 minutes, stirring occasionally.
Remove the thyme sprigs and bay leaves before serving. This
sauce can be stored in the refrigerator or freezer. Remove all fat
from the top before using or storing.

YIELD: ABOUT 3 CUPS.

Quick Tomato Sauce

2 tablespoons unsalted butter
1 cup minced onion
1 teaspoon minced garlic
1½ cups imported canned tomatoes with liquid
1½ tablespoons tomato paste
½ cup water
1 thyme sprig, or 1 teaspoon dried thyme
1 bay leaf
Salt and freshly ground black pepper to taste

1. Melt the butter in a saucepan over medium heat. Add the onion and garlic and cook, stirring, until wilted. Do not brown.
2. Stir in the tomatoes, tomato paste, water, thyme, and bay leaf. Cook, stirring occasionally, for about 15 minutes. Season with salt and pepper.
3. Purée the mixture in a food mill or a food processor. Return the sauce to the pan to warm. Serve hot.

YIELD: ABOUT 2¼ CUPS.

Tomato and Anchovy Sauce

¼ cup olive oil
1 tablespoon minced garlic
3 cups crushed canned tomatoes
1 teaspoon dried oregano
½ teaspoon hot red pepper flakes
½ cup chopped fresh parsley leaves
2 teaspoons anchovy paste
4 tablespoons drained capers
1 tablespoon Cognac

Heat the oil in a saucepan over medium-high heat and sauté the garlic briefly without browning it. Add the tomatoes, oregano, hot pepper flakes, parsley, anchovy paste, and capers. Bring to a boil and simmer for 20 minutes, stirring often from the bottom. Stir in the Cognac and serve.

YIELD: ABOUT 3 CUPS.

Tomato Sauce with Dill

1 tablespoon unsalted butter
4 tablespoons minced shallots
½ cup Fish or Shrimp Broth (pages 241 and 243) or bottled
  clam juice
1½ cups canned crushed tomatoes
¾ cup heavy cream
Salt and freshly ground white pepper to taste
2 tablespoons minced fresh dill leaves

1. Melt the butter in a saucepan over medium-high heat. Add the shallots and cook, stirring, until wilted. Add the broth and reduce until it has nearly evaporated. Stir in the tomatoes and cook for 5 minutes. Stir in the cream and cook for 5 minutes more.

2. Pour the sauce through a mesh strainer into a mixing bowl. Press the solids with the back of a wooden spoon or a rubber spatula to extract as much juice as possible.

3. Return the sauce to the heat and season with salt and pepper. Stir in the dill and serve immediately.

YIELD: 1½ CUPS.

Mushroom–Cream Sauce

½ pound small white mushrooms
2 tablespoons unsalted butter
3 tablespoons minced shallots
Salt and freshly ground white pepper to taste
¼ cup dry white wine
½ cup heavy cream

1. Rinse the mushrooms and pat them dry. Then cut them into thin slices.

2. Melt the butter in a small saucepan over medium-high heat. Add the shallots and cook until wilted. Add the mushrooms and salt and pepper and cook until the mushrooms are wilted, 3 to 4 minutes.

3. Pour the wine and heavy cream into the pan, bring to a boil, and simmer for 5 minutes.

4. Pour the mixture into a blender or food processor and purée thoroughly. Return the sauce to the saucepan and reheat it. Serve hot.

YIELD: ABOUT 1½ CUPS.

Fresh Ginger Sauce
with Tomatoes

6 tablespoons unsalted butter at room temperature
4 tablespoons minced shallots
2 tablespoons grated fresh gingerroot
¼ cup dry white wine
¼ cup white wine vinegar
⅓ cup heavy cream
Salt and freshly ground black pepper to taste
½ cup finely diced peeled and seeded tomatoes

1. Melt 1 tablespoon of the butter in a saucepan. Add the shallots and ginger and cook briefly. Do not let them brown.

2. Add the wine and vinegar and reduce over high heat until the liquid has almost evaporated. Add the cream and cook for 2 minutes.

3. Pour the sauce into a blender. With the machine running at high speed, add the remaining 5 tablespoons of butter 1 tablespoon at a time. Season with salt and pepper. Transfer the sauce to a small saucepan. Add the tomatoes and reheat gently. Serve hot.

YIELD: ABOUT 1 CUP.

Aïoli

1 tablespoon minced garlic
1 large egg yolk
1 tablespoon Dijon mustard
Salt and freshly ground black pepper to taste
1 cup olive oil

1. Crush the garlic using a mortar and pestle.
2. Put the garlic in a mixing bowl and add the egg yolk, mustard, and salt and pepper. Beat rapidly with a wire whisk while adding the oil gradually. Continue whisking until all the oil is incorporated and the Aïoli is smooth and thick.

YIELD: ABOUT 1 CUP.

Hollandaise–Mustard Sauce

¾ pound (3 sticks) unsalted butter
3 large egg yolks
2 tablespoons water
Salt and cayenne pepper to taste
1 tablespoon fresh lemon juice
2 tablespoons Dijon mustard

1. Put the butter in a 2-cup glass measuring cup. Place the cup in a shallow saucepan with enough boiling water to reach about 2 inches from the top. When the butter has melted, remove the cup from the water and leave the water simmering on the stove. Ladle the foam from the surface of the butter. Leave the whey at the bottom of the butter undisturbed. Let the butter cool to about 120 degrees.

2. Put the egg yolks and water into a small slant-sided saucepan. Mix well with a wire whisk. Place the saucepan in the simmering water. Stir rapidly in a controlled fashion so that all the mixture is moving. (A figure-8 motion is best, occasionally extending outward to get the edges.) Just before the yolk mixture is thoroughly thickened, remove the saucepan from the heat for the last seconds of whisking. The mixture is done when it is thickened to a paste-like consistency.

3. With the pan off the heat, slowly pour the clarified butter into the egg mixture in a very thin stream, beating continuously with the whisk to form an emulsion, as in mayonnaise.

4. Add the salt and cayenne pepper and lemon juice while stirring. Stir in the mustard and blend well.

YIELD: 1½ CUPS.

Fresh Ginger Vinaigrette

2 tablespoons Dijon mustard
4 tablespoons white wine vinegar
⅓ cup vegetable oil
⅓ cup olive oil
½ cup diced peeled and seeded ripe tomatoes
4 tablespoons finely chopped scallions
3 tablespoons grated fresh gingerroot
2 tablespoons finely chopped fresh coriander or parsley leaves
Salt and freshly ground black pepper to taste

Put the mustard and vinegar into a mixing bowl and whisk in the oil vigorously. Stir in the remaining ingredients. Serve at room temperature.

YIELD: ABOUT 2 CUPS.

Mignonnette Sauce

2 tablespoons whole black peppercorns
¾ cup red wine vinegar
6 tablespoons finely chopped shallots
Salt to taste

Crush the peppercorns coarsely using a mallet or the bottom of a heavy cast-iron pan. Combine with all the remaining ingredients, blend well, and serve.

YIELD: 1 CUP.

Mustard–Dill Sauce

½ cup Dijon mustard
2 teaspoons powdered mustard
5 tablespoons sugar
¼ cup white wine vinegar
⅓ cup vegetable oil
⅓ cup olive oil
½ cup chopped fresh dill leaves
Salt to taste

1. Combine the mustard, mustard powder, and sugar in a mixing bowl.
2. Using a wire whisk, stir in the vinegar. Gradually add the oils, stirring rapidly with the whisk. Add the dill and salt. Taste and correct the flavors by gradually adding more sugar, vinegar, or salt.

YIELD: ABOUT 1½ CUPS.

Sauce Ravigote

3 tablespoons finely chopped onion
3 tablespoons finely chopped shallots
1 teaspoon finely chopped garlic
3 tablespoons drained capers, chopped
¼ cup finely chopped fresh parsley leaves
2 tablespoons finely chopped tarragon leaves
2 tablespoons finely chopped fresh chives
2 tablespoons finely chopped fresh chervil leaves
¼ cup red wine vinegar
1 cup olive oil
Salt and freshly ground black pepper to taste

1. Combine all the ingredients, *except* the oil and salt and pepper, in a mixing bowl.

2. Gradually add the oil, stirring vigorously with a wire whisk. Season with salt and pepper.

YIELD: 1¼ CUPS.

Sauce Gribiche

---

1 cup vegetable oil
½ cup olive oil
1 tablespoon Dijon mustard
2 tablespoons minced shallots
3 tablespoons minced onion
1 large hard-boiled egg, minced
1 large egg yolk
Salt and freshly ground black pepper to taste
¼ cup white or red wine vinegar
1 tablespoon chopped fresh parsley leaves
1 tablespoon chopped fresh tarragon leaves, or ½ teaspoon
  dried tarragon
2 tablespoons chopped fresh chervil leaves or chives

1. In a bowl, combine the oils.

2. In another bowl, combine the mustard, shallots, onion, eggs, salt and pepper, and vinegar. Blend briefly with a wire whisk. Slowly pour the combined oils into the bowl, whisking to create an emulsion. Add the parsley, tarragon, and chervil. Blend well with a whisk.

YIELD: 6 TO 8 SERVINGS.

French-style Sauce Rémoulade

1 cup homemade Mayonnaise (page 259)
2 teaspoons anchovy paste
2 tablespoons minced pickles, preferably cornichons
2 tablespoons chopped fresh parsley leaves
1 tablespoon chopped fresh tarragon leaves
1 tablespoon chopped fresh chervil leaves
1 tablespoon chopped drained capers

Combine all the ingredients in a mixing bowl and blend well with a wire whisk.

YIELD: 1¼ CUPS.

Cajun-style Sauce Rémoulade

1 large egg yolk
4 tablespoons Dijon or Creole mustard
⅓ cup white wine vinegar
4 teaspoons paprika
1½ cups olive oil
3 tablespoons grated fresh horseradish or prepared horseradish
1 teaspoon finely chopped garlic
½ cup finely chopped scallions
½ cup finely chopped celery
3 tablespoons finely chopped fresh parsley leaves
3 tablespoons ketchup
Salt and freshly ground black pepper to taste

Put the egg yolk, mustard, vinegar, and paprika into a mixing bowl. Start blending with a wire whisk. Begin adding the oil gradually, beating briskly; then add all the remaining ingredients and blend well.

YIELD: 2½ CUPS.

Mayonnaise

1 large egg yolk
1 tablespoon Dijon mustard
1 tablespoon white wine vinegar
Salt and freshly ground white pepper to taste
1 cup vegetable oil
1 tablespoon fresh lemon juice

In a mixing bowl, combine the egg yolk, mustard, vinegar, and salt and pepper. Stir with a wire whisk. Add the oil in a thin stream, while beating briskly. When the oil is incorporated, add the lemon juice and blend well.

YIELD: 1 CUP.

Cucumber and Dill Mayonnaise

2 large egg yolks
2 tablespoons Dijon mustard
½ cup chopped scallions
2 tablespoons white wine vinegar
Salt and freshly ground white pepper to taste
1 cup olive or vegetable oil
½ cup peeled and seeded cucumber cut into ¼-inch cubes
2 tablespoons chopped fresh dill leaves

Combine the egg yolks, mustard, scallions, vinegar, and salt and pepper in a mixing bowl. Gradually pour in the olive oil in a thin stream, while whisking vigorously. When the mixture is smooth and thick, fold in the cucumber and dill and blend well.

YIELD: ABOUT 1¾ CUPS.

Mayonnaise with Fresh Herbs

A basic mayonnaise recipe can be enhanced with the fresh herbs of your choice.

1 large egg yolk
1 tablespoon Dijon mustard
1 tablespoon white wine vinegar
Salt and freshly ground white pepper to taste
1 cup vegetable or olive oil
2 tablespoons minced scallions
2 tablespoons minced fresh chives
2 tablespoons minced fresh parsley leaves
2 tablespoons minced fresh basil leaves
1 tablespoon minced fresh tarragon leaves or any fresh herb of your choice

In a mixing bowl, combine the egg yolk, mustard, vinegar, and salt and pepper. Add the oil in a thin stream, while beating vigorously with a wire whisk. When the mixture is thick and smooth, stir in the remaining ingredients and blend well. Cover and refrigerate until ready to serve.

YIELD: ABOUT 1 CUP.

Garlic Mayonnaise

2 garlic cloves
1 large egg yolk
1 teaspoon Dijon mustard
1/8 teaspoon cayenne pepper
3/4 cup olive oil
Salt to taste

In a mortar or small bowl, mash the garlic to a paste and add the egg yolk, mustard, and cayenne pepper. Slowly drizzle in the oil, while whisking vigorously. When all the oil is incorporated, season with salt.

YIELD: ½ CUP.

Red Pepper Mayonnaise

1 large sweet red pepper
1 cup Mayonnaise with Fresh Herbs (page 260)
1 large hard-boiled egg
4 tablespoons chopped shallots
Salt and freshly ground black pepper to taste

1. Preheat the broiler.
2. Broil the pepper on all sides until the entire skin is charred. Set it aside to cool slightly. When the pepper is cool enough to handle, peel off the skin, discard the seeds, and chop it coarsely.
3. Put the pepper through a food mill or purée in a food processor or blender.
4. Combine the mayonnaise with the pepper purée in a mixing bowl.
5. Put the egg through a fine sieve and stir it into the mayonnaise. Add the shallots and the salt and pepper and blend well.

YIELD: ABOUT 2 CUPS.

Warm Mayonnaise

1 *large egg, separated*
1 *tablespoon Dijon mustard*
1 *tablespoon white wine vinegar*
Salt and freshly ground white pepper to taste
1 *teaspoon minced garlic*
Dash of Tabasco sauce
1 *cup vegetable oil*

1. Pour 2 inches of water into a skillet large enough to hold a mixing bowl. Bring the water to a boil and remove from the heat.

2. Combine the egg yolk, mustard, vinegar, salt, pepper, garlic, and Tabasco sauce in a mixing bowl. Stir well with a wire whisk.

3. Place the mixing bowl in the water and gradually add the oil, beating briskly with a wire whisk. Continue beating until all the oil is used and the mixture is thick and smooth. As you beat, the mixture should become slightly hotter than lukewarm.

4. Beat the egg white to soft peaks and fold it into the mayonnaise. Let the bowl stand in the hot water as you stir gently until the mayonnaise is thoroughly hot but not cooked.

YIELD: ABOUT 2 CUPS.

Watercress Mayonnaise

1 *large egg yolk*
1 *tablespoon Dijon mustard*
1 *tablespoon white wine vinegar*
Salt and freshly ground black pepper to taste
1 *cup vegetable oil*
½ *bunch watercress, leaves cleaned and minced*

1. Put the egg yolk, mustard, vinegar, and salt and pepper in a mixing bowl. Beat the mixture with a wire whisk while slowly adding the oil, a few drops at a time at first and then in a slow drizzle.

2. When all the oil is incorporated, mix in the watercress and taste for seasoning.

YIELD: ¾ CUP.

Sauce Provençale

1 ripe tomato (about ½ pound)
2 tablespoons red wine vinegar
¼ cup olive oil
¼ cup finely chopped shallots
1 teaspoon finely minced garlic
¼ cup finely chopped fresh basil (parsley may be substituted)
½ teaspoon grated lemon rind
Salt to taste if desired
Freshly ground black pepper

1. Put the tomato in boiling water for about 9 seconds. Drain and pull away the skin; cut away and discard the core. Cut the tomato crosswise in half. Remove and discard the seeds. Cut into ¼-inch cubes; there should be about ½ cup.

2. Put the vinegar in a mixing bowl and add the oil, shallots, garlic, chopped herb, and tomato. Add the lemon rind, salt, and pepper. Blend well with a whisk.

YIELD: ABOUT 1 CUP.

Tartar Sauce

1 large egg yolk
1 tablespoon white wine vinegar
2 tablespoons Dijon mustard
Salt and freshly ground white pepper to taste
1 cup vegetable or peanut oil
2 tablespoons fresh lemon juice
4 tablespoons minced onion
2 tablespoons chopped drained capers
¼ cup chopped cornichons or sour pickles
¼ cup finely chopped fresh parsley leaves

1. Put the egg yolk in a mixing bowl and add the vinegar, mustard, and salt and pepper. Beat with a wire whisk for 5 seconds.

2. Add the oil gradually, beating vigorously with the whisk, until all the oil is used. Add the lemon juice.

3. Add the remaining ingredients and blend well. Cover and chill.

YIELD: 1½ CUPS

Melted Dill Butter

4 tablespoons unsalted butter
2 tablespoons chopped fresh dill leaves
Salt and freshly ground white pepper to taste

Melt the butter in a small saucepan over low heat. Add the dill and stir to combine. Season with salt and pepper.

Maître d'Hôtel Butter

½ cup unsalted butter at room temperature
4 tablespoons finely chopped fresh parsley leaves
3 tablespoons fresh lemon juice
Salt and freshly ground white pepper to taste

1. In a bowl, cream the butter with a spatula. Add all remaining ingredients and blend well.

2. Place the mixture on a sheet of wax paper or aluminum foil. Form the butter into a roll about 2 inches in diameter. Wrap with the paper and refrigerate. When you need the butter, slice it off in disks.

Anchovy Butter

8 tablespoons unsalted butter at room temperature
2 teaspoons minced anchovies or anchovy paste
3 tablespoons minced scallions
2 teaspoons fresh lemon juice

Combine all the ingredients in a small bowl and beat with a wire whisk until light and creamy. Scoop the butter into a mold and refrigerate until needed.

YIELD: ABOUT ½ CUP.

Oriental Curry Powder

Make a batch of this invigorating blend and store it in a small mason jar.

4 tablespoons ground turmeric
3 tablespoons ground coriander
2 tablespoons ground cumin
1 tablespoon white peppercorns
1 tablespoon whole cloves
2 tablespoons ground ginger
1 tablespoon ground cardamom
2 teaspoons cayenne pepper
1 tablespoon ground mace
1 tablespoon dried fine herbs (commercially packaged mixture
of thyme, oregano, sage, rosemary, marjoram, and basil)
1 tablespoon fenugreek seeds

Put all the ingredients in a spice grinder or blender and grind them to a fine powder. Store the powder in a cool place in a glass jar with a tight-fitting lid.

YIELD: 1 CUP.

CHAPTER 13

Side Dishes

Steamed Parsleyed Cucumbers

4 large firm cucumbers, washed to remove sand
2 tablespoons unsalted butter
4 tablespoons finely chopped fresh parsley leaves
Salt and freshly ground black pepper to taste
Juice of 1 lemon

1. Trim off the ends of the cucumbers and remove the skins. Cut the cucumbers into 2-inch-thick rounds. Quarter each slice lengthwise and remove the seeds.

2. Put the cucumbers into the rack of a steamer over boiling water and steam for 2 minutes.

3. Melt the butter in a frying pan and add the cucumber, parsley, salt and pepper, and lemon juice and toss for 30 seconds.

YIELD: 6 TO 8 SERVINGS.

Fried Parsley

2 medium-size bunches fresh parsley
Oil for deep-frying
Salt to taste

  1. Pick over the parsley to remove the long, tough stems. Place the parsley in a large basin of cold water and rinse it well to remove all sand. Dry it extremely well in a salad spinner. Pat the parsley dry with paper towels.
  2. Heat the oil to 360 degrees in a deep pot. Add the parsley, a handful at a time, using a slotted spoon to turn it while frying. Remove with a slotted spoon when it is dark green and crisp, about 45 seconds. Drain the parsley on paper towels and sprinkle with salt before serving.

YIELD: 4 TO 6 SERVINGS.

Green Sugar Snap Peas with Fresh Mint

½ pound sugar snap peas (about 1½ cups)
4 tablespoons unsalted butter
3 tablespoons finely chopped fresh mint leaves
Salt and freshly ground black pepper to taste

  1. Bring enough water to cover the peas to a boil in a saucepan. Add the peas and cook for 4 to 5 minutes, or until they are crisp-tender. Drain immediately.
  2. Return the peas to the saucepan and add the butter, mint, and salt and pepper. Stir until the peas are coated well. Serve immediately.

YIELD: 4 TO 6 SERVINGS.

Boiled Red Skin Potatoes
with Dill

12 small red skin potatoes (about 1½ pounds total weight)
8 dill sprigs
Salt to taste
3 tablespoons unsalted butter
3 tablespoons chopped fresh dill leaves
Freshly ground black pepper to taste

1. Using a sharp paring knife, cut the potatoes in half and peel some of the skin, leaving a band in the center for color.

2. Put the potatoes in a pot, cover with water, and add the salt and dill sprigs. Bring to a boil and simmer for 15 minutes, or until the potatoes are tender.

3. Drain the potatoes and discard the dill sprigs. Place the potatoes in a bowl and add the butter, chopped dill, and salt and pepper to taste. Stir gently to coat the potatoes. Serve immediately.

YIELD: 4 TO 6 SERVINGS.

Glazed Scallions

24 scallions
2 tablespoons unsalted butter
Salt and freshly ground black pepper to taste
1 cup water

Wash the scallions and trim both ends, leaving 5-inch-long stalks. Put the scallions in a saucepan large enough to hold them in one layer. Add the butter and salt and pepper. Pour the water over them and bring it to a boil. Cook, uncovered, over medium heat for 10 minutes, or until most of the water has evaporated. Serve immediately.

YIELD: 6 SERVINGS.

Pan-fried Tomatoes with Garlic

6 medium-size ripe tomatoes (about 1½ pounds total weight)
3 tablespoons olive oil
Salt and freshly ground black pepper
1 tablespoon finely chopped garlic
3 tablespoons finely chopped fresh parsley leaves

1. Core the tomatoes and cut them in half.

2. Heat the oil over medium-high heat in a nonstick frying pan large enough to hold the tomatoes in one layer. (If you do not have one, use two frying pans.) Put the tomatoes in the pan cut side down and cook for about 1 minute. Turn them and season with salt and pepper.

3. Cook the tomatoes for another 2 minutes. Sprinkle the garlic over the tomatoes, turn them over, and cook briefly, making sure the garlic doesn't burn. Sprinkle with the parsley and serve.

YIELD: 6 SERVINGS.

Rice Pilaf

3 tablespoons unsalted butter
¼ cup finely chopped onion
1 cup converted rice
3 parsley sprigs

4 thyme sprigs, or ¼ teaspoon dried thyme
2 dashes of Tabasco sauce
1 bay leaf
1½ cups water
Salt and freshly ground black pepper to taste

1. Melt 2 tablespoons of the butter in a saucepan and add the onion. Cook, stirring, until wilted. Add the rice, parsley, thyme, Tabasco sauce, bay leaf, water, and salt and pepper. Bring to a boil, stirring. Cover tightly and simmer for 17 minutes. Place the pan over a flame-tamer if you have one to assure the rice cooks very slowly.

2. Discard the parsley, thyme, and bay leaf. With a fork, distribute the remaining butter thoroughly through the rice. Keep the rice covered in a warm place until you are ready to serve it.

YIELD: 6 SERVINGS.

Curried Rice

2 tablespoons unsalted butter
1 cup converted rice
½ cup finely chopped onion
1 teaspoon finely chopped garlic
1 apple, peeled, cored, and cut into ¼-inch cubes
1 tablespoon Oriental Curry Powder (page 266)
Salt to taste
1½ cups Fish Broth (page 241) or water
1 bay leaf

1. Melt 1 tablespoon of the butter in a saucepan; then add the rice, onion, garlic, apple, curry powder, and salt. Cook briefly, stirring, but do not brown.

2. Add the fish broth to the pan and the bay leaf. Bring to a boil, stirring. Cover tightly and simmer for 17 minutes.

3. Add the remaining butter and fluff the rice with a fork. Discard the bay leaf and serve.

YIELD: 4 TO 6 SERVINGS.

Rice Creole

6 cups water
Salt
1½ cups converted rice
2 tablespoons unsalted butter
1 tablespoon fresh lemon juice
Freshly ground black pepper to taste

1. Bring the water to a boil in a saucepan. Add salt to taste and rice and return to a boil. Cook over high heat for 17 minutes.

2. Drain the rice in a colander, run hot water over it, and drain again.

3. Place the rice in a serving dish, and toss in the butter, pepper, salt (if necessary), and lemon juice. Stir gently until the grains are well coated.

YIELD: 6 TO 8 SERVINGS.

Herb-stuffed French Bread

1 French baguette
¼ cup olive oil
1 tablespoon chopped garlic

¾ cup finely chopped scallions
¾ cup finely chopped fresh parsley leaves
Salt and freshly ground black pepper to taste

1. Preheat the oven to 425 degrees.
2. Split the bread in half lengthwise.
3. Heat the oil in a saucepan over medium heat and add the garlic, scallions, parsley, and salt and pepper. Cook until the ingredients are just wilted. Spoon the mixture evenly on each baguette half and place the bread back together.
4. Wrap the bread in aluminum foil and bake for about 15 minutes. Serve hot.

YIELD: 4 TO 6 SERVINGS.

Parmesan Cheese Bread

2 medium-size loaves crusty French or Italian bread
4 tablespoons olive oil
1 tablespoon finely chopped garlic
6 tablespoons freshly grated Parmesan cheese

1. Preheat the oven to 425 degrees.
2. Split the loaves in half lengthwise and arrange them on a baking sheet cut side up.
3. Brush the top and interiors with the olive oil. In a mixing bowl, combine the garlic and Parmesan cheese and sprinkle the mixture evenly over the bread.
4. Bake for 10 minutes, or until golden brown.

YIELD: 6 TO 8 SERVINGS.

Croutons

8 ½-inch-thick slices French or Italian bread
8 tablespoons olive oil

1. Preheat the oven to 375 degrees.
2. Put the bread slices on a baking sheet and sprinkle a tablespoon of olive oil over each. Bake until golden.

YIELD: 4 SERVINGS.

Garlic Croutons

1 loaf French or Italian bread
2 garlic cloves, peeled
4 tablespoons olive oil
Freshly ground black pepper

1. Rub the crust of the bread all over with the garlic cloves. Cut the bread into ½-inch-thick slices and sprinkle one side with the olive oil; then grind some black pepper over it.
2. Place the bread slices on a baking sheet under a broiler until they are golden brown. Turn and broil on the other side.

YIELD: 8 SERVINGS.

CHAPTER 14

Wine and Seafood

Pairing food and wine, like matching ties and shirts, was a less intimidating task a generation ago. In the same way that striped ties called for solid shirts and solid shirts meant sporting striped ties, everyone knew, with a reassuring certainty, that red wines went with meat and white wines went with fish. It was, admittedly, an oversimplification, but sticking to these rules meant not being embarrassed in polite company.

By contrast, look at the muddled wine and food situation today. Repeating the incantation "white wine with fish" is little help when the dish is spicy blackened redfish with a Cajun hollandaise sauce. Or how about fusilli with radicchio and smoked trout in a pink tomato-cream sauce? What kind of white wine stands up to those assertive flavors? Is a rosé perhaps more appropriate, or maybe even a light-bodied red?

Not only has cooking become more herbaceous and complex, but also the selection of wines available to the consumer has expanded tremendously in recent years. In addition to French, Italian, and American labels, we now have a flood of appealing wines from Australia, Chile, Hungary, Spain, Rumania, and Argentina, to name just a few. Then, too, there are new blends of old grapes, such as white zinfandels and blush wines.

But don't panic. Now that we have illustrated how befuddling the fish and wine equation can be, we will explain how you can cut through the vinous thicket and easily make the right choices that will enhance any seafood dish. Don't get obsessed trying to memorize hundreds of wine names and regions; instead, step back and look at the puzzle from a distance. Seeing the broad outlines will give you a better idea how to fill in the individual pieces.

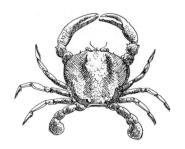

There are three simple questions to ask yourself when choosing a wine to serve with a seafood dish: (1) Is the fish lean and mild or fatty and strong flavored? (2) Is the sauce light and delicate or heavy and spicy? (3) Which is the dominant flavor, the fish or the sauce? Once you have answered these you are three fourths of the way there.

Now we can apply what might be called the "like with like" rule. For example, consider poached sole with a beurre blanc sauce.

1. Is the fish lean or fatty? Go to the chart on page 280, which groups seafood by its flavor and texture characteristics. You see that sole is a light and delicate-tasting fish. So it marries well with most dry, light-bodied wines.

2. Are the seasonings and sauce delicate or spicy and full flavored? The light beurre blanc is delicate. Therefore, we want a light, dry white. A heavy-hitting, wood-aged California Chardonnay would overpower it.

3. Does the fish or the sauce dominate? Neither, really. Both are light and mild. To find a list of dry, light-bodied white wines go to the chart on page 278.

The appropriate choices include French Muscadets, Chablis and Mâcon-Villages as well as Italian Pinot Grigios, Verdicchios and Trebbianos, to name a few. If you are not familiar with some of the wines on the list, ask your local wine merchant to recommend one from a reputable shipper. (A handy pocketbook wine guide can also help you determine the better labels. One that is highly recommended is Hugh Johnson's *Pocket Encyclopedia of Wine,* Simon and Schuster; updated annually.) Also, remember that when it comes to white wines, the general rule is, the younger the better.

Now let's use the "like with like" rule on a more intensely flavored dish, aforementioned blackened redfish.

1. Is the fish lean or fatty? Redfish, and most of the species substituted for it in this recipe (snapper, bass), have mildly flavored, lean and meaty flesh. Your first thought, of course, is a mild, crisp, and reserved white wine.

2. Are the seasonings and the sauce delicate or spicy and full flavored? The fillet is coated with a mixture of various peppery

spices, then flash sautéed in a red-hot pan, and accompanied by a flavorful hollandaise sauce. The puzzle now has a new twist. When we think of peppery foods, we think of zesty and spicy wines, such as Alsatian Gewürztraminers and Sancerre or California Sauvignon Blanc.

3. *Does the fish or the sauce dominate?* In this case, the seasonings and sauce. Hence they will be the paramount factors in choosing a wine. Such a peppery dish would no doubt blow a fragile Chablis into orbit. We now want a zesty and spicy wine.

Look at the wine chart. What varietals are described as vigorous and spicy? Among whites there are the Gewürztraminers, Rieslings, and Tokays from Alsace, Sancerre from the Loire and Tocais from northeastern Italy; a lively rosé, such as those made in California with Cabernet and Zinfandel, perhaps would do the trick. Because the dish is so aggressively seasoned, we might even put aside the "white with fish" rule and go with a lively young red wine that can be served cool. A young Beaujolais would have sufficient spirit to keep pace, so would many of those acidic and perky nouveau-style wines from Italy, California, and the eastern United States that are trying to ride the grape wagon of Beaujolais nouveau.

Probably the best foil to a really spicy dish is sparkling wine. Whether real Champagne or one of the better "méthode champenoise" sparklers (the term refers to a sparkling wine produced according to the traditional Champagne method that involves bottle fermentation to produce effervescence), they have plenty of spunk to match highly seasoned foods.

One of the few exceptions to the "like with like" rule is fatty fish, such as bluefish, mackerel, and certain types of salmon, including smoked salmon. A wine with high acid is needed to cut through the fat and cleanse the palate. This also applies to rich cream-based sauces.

Let's look next at a summertime favorite on the East Coast, barbecued bluefish basted with olive oil and some fresh herbs.

1. *Is the fish lean or fatty?* Fatty. This calls for a wine high in acid.

2. *Are the seasonings and the sauce delicate or full flavored?* The light herb seasoning is delicate and there is no sauce.

3. Does the fish or the sauce dominate? Clearly, the fish. Therefore, we look for a high-acid white wine; if it has an herbal accent, all the better. Look at the chart. Our options include lively Alsacian Gewürztraminer and Rieslings, California Sauvignon Blancs (sometimes called Fumé Blancs and Chenin blancs, and some northern Italian Tocais and Müller-Thurgaus. This one-two-three method will pull you through most situations. Above all, though, remember that wine is only a beverage, and these are only guidelines. There is no accounting for individual tastes. If you like certain wines with particular foods, don't be intimidated by so-called experts.

Finally, a word about cooking seafood with wine. It has been said before but is worth repeating. If you take the time and effort to buy the best quality seafood and follow a recipe diligently, don't shortchange yourself by cooking with inferior wine. The wine you choose to cook with does make a difference. To prove the point, make two identical sauces some day, one with cheap jug wine, the other with a quality white. Hold a blind tasting with friends and you will be amazed at the difference. This is not to say you should use $50 Pavillon Blanc of Château Margaux in a shellfish sauce. There are plenty of perfectly good wines on the market in the $3 to $5 range that make pleasant sipping and cooking wines.

WHITE WINES

To Have with Mild- and Delicate-Flavored Dishes

(FRANCE)   Mâcon-Villages, Aligoté, Beaujolais Blanc, Chablis, dry
   Vouvray, Muscadet, certain white Bordeaux, Alsace Pinot Blanc.
(ITALY)   Cortese di Gavi, Frascati, Chardonnay and Pinot Bianco, Pinot
   Grigio, Soave from Trentino-Alto-Adige, Trebbiano, Verdicchio.
(U.S.)   light California Sauvignon Blancs and drier Chenin Blancs.
(OTHER)   certain dry German Riesling Kabinetts, whites from Penedés in
   Spain, Vinhos Verdes from Portugal.

To Have with Fatty Fish or Rich Sauces

(FRANCE)   Champagne, Alsace Gewürztraminer and Riesling, Pouilly-Fumé and Sancerre, some White Graves, dry Vouvray, Mersault, Chassagne-Montrachet.

(ITALY)   Müller-Thurgau wines and Tocai from Friuli.

(U.S.)   California Chenin Blanc, lighter-style Chardonnays and drier Rieslings and certain Sauvignon Blancs (also called Fumé Blancs); dry sparkling wines from California and New York State.

(Other)   Seyval Blanc from Eastern U.S., medium-dry German Riesling, Portuguese Dâos, Spanish sparkling wines and white Riojas.

To Have with Spicy or Highly Seasoned Dishes

(FRANCE)   Champagne, Alsace Gewürztraminer and Riesling.

(ITALY)   Sparkling wines, Gewürztraminer.

(U.S.)   Some California Gerwürztraminers and Rieslings, California sparkling wines, some New York State Rieslings.

(OTHER)   Spanish sparkling wines, medium-sweet German Rieslings.

In addition, some light-bodied reds and most dry rosé wines can enhance a spicy seafood dish. Among reds consider those that can be served cool, such as French Beaujolais, Côtes de Beaune-Villages, Côtes du Ventoux, all nouveau-style reds, some Côtes-du-Rhône; Italian Bardolino, Valpolicella, lighter-style Chianti, and Cabernet del Friuli; California Gamays and light Zinfandels; and Italian Merlot and Cabernets Dolcetto d'Alba.

FISH PROFILE CHART

FIN FISH

White Meat, Lean
Very Light, Delicate Flavor   Cod, Dover Sole, Haddock, Lake Whitefish,
Pacific Halibut, Sole, Southern Flounder, Witch Flounder, Yellowtail
Flounder, Yellowtail Snapper

White Meat, Lean
Light to Moderate Flavor   American Dab, Butterfish, Catfish, Dover Sole,
Cod, Mahi Mahi, Pacific Whiting, Red Snapper, Rock Sole, Snook,
Spotted Sea Trout, White King Salmon, White Sea Trout, Whiting,
Winter Flounder, Wolffish

Light Meat, Moderately Lean
Very Light, Delicate Flavor   Alaska Pollock, Brook Trout, Grouper, Pacific
Ocean Perch, Rainbow Trout, Sea Bass, Smelt, Tautog (also known as
Blackfish), White Sea Bass

Light Meat, Moderately Lean
Light to Moderate Flavor   Atlantic Perch, Atlantic Salmon, Buffalofish,
Carp, Chum Salmon, Coho Salmon, Croaker, Eel, Lake Chub, Lake
Herring, Lake Sturgeon, Lake Trout, Monkfish, Mullet, Northern Pike,
Pink Salmon, Pollock, Pompano, Rockfish, Sablefish, Scup (Porgie),
Striped Bass, Swordfish, Turbot

Light Meat, Fatty
More Pronounced Flavor   Atlantic Mackerel, King Mackerel, Spanish
Mackerel

Darker Meat, Fatty
Light to Moderate Flavor   Black Sea Bass, Bluefish, Ocean Pout, Red Salmon
(Sockeye)

SHELLFISH TYPES

CRABS   Alaska King Crab, Blue Crab, Dungeness Crab, Jonah Crab, Red
Crab, Snow Crab, Soft-Shell Crab

SHRIMP   Blue Shrimp, Brown Shrimp, California Bay Shrimp, Northern
Shrimp, Pink Shrimp, Rock Shrimp, White Shrimp

LOBSTERS   American Lobster, Rock Lobster, Slippery Lobster, Spiny
Lobster

BIVALVES   Butter Clam, Geoduck Clam, Hard or Quahog Clam, Littleneck
Clam, Pismo Clam, Razor Clam, Soft-shell Clam (steamer), Surf or
Skimmer Clam

OYSTERS   Eastern/Atlantic Oyster, Gulf Oyster, Pacific Oyster, South
American Oyster

SCALLOPS   Bay Scallop, Calico Scallop, Sea Scallop

CEPHALOPODS   Octopus, Squid

Source: National Marine Fisheries Service.

Index